Teacher Leadership for Social Change in Bilingual and Bicultural Education

I0127647

BILINGUAL EDUCATION & BILINGUALISM
Series Editors: Nancy H. Hornberger *(University of Pennsylvania, USA)* and Wayne E. Wright *(Purdue University, USA)*

Bilingual Education and Bilingualism is an international, multidisciplinary series publishing research on the philosophy, politics, policy, provision and practice of language planning, Indigenous and minority language education, multilingualism, multiculturalism, biliteracy, bilingualism and bilingual education. The series aims to mirror current debates and discussions. New proposals for single-authored, multiple-authored, or edited books in the series are warmly welcomed, in any of the following categories or others authors may propose: overview or introductory texts; course readers or general reference texts; focus books on particular multilingual education program types; school-based case studies; national case studies; collected cases with a clear programmatic or conceptual theme; and professional education manuals.

All books in this series are externally peer-reviewed.

Full details of all the books in this series and of all our other publications can be found on http://www.multilingual-matters.com, or by writing to Multilingual Matters, St Nicholas House, 31-34 High Street, Bristol BS1 2AW, UK.

BILINGUAL EDUCATION & BILINGUALISM: 113

Teacher Leadership for Social Change in Bilingual and Bicultural Education

Deborah K. Palmer

MULTILINGUAL MATTERS
Bristol • Blue Ridge Summit

DOI https://doi.org/10.21832/PALMER1435
Library of Congress Cataloging in Publication Data
A catalog record for this book is available from the Library of Congress.
Names: Palmer, Deborah K.- author.
Title: Teacher Leadership for Social Change in Bilingual and Bicultural
    Education/Deborah K. Palmer.
Description: Bristol, UK; Blue Ridge Summit, PA: Multilingual Matters,
    [2018] | Series: Bilingual Education & Bilingualism: 113 | Includes
    bibliographical references and index.
Identifiers: LCCN 2018012620| ISBN 9781788921435 (hbk : alk. paper) |
    ISBN 9781788921428 (pbk : alk. paper) | ISBN 9781788921466 (kindle) |
    ISBN 9781788921442 (pdf) | ISBN 9781788921442 (epub)
Subjects: LCSH: Educational leadership--Texas. | Multicultural
    education--Texas. | Education, Bilingual--Texas. | Social change--Texas.
Classification: LCC LB2805 .P295 2018 | DDC 371.209764--dc23 LC record available
at https://lccn.loc.gov/2018012620

British Library Cataloguing in Publication Data
A catalogue entry for this book is available from the British Library.

ISBN-13: 978-1-78892-143-5 (hbk)
ISBN-13: 978-1-78892-142-8 (pbk)

Multilingual Matters
UK: St Nicholas House, 31-34 High Street, Bristol BS1 2AW, UK.
USA: NBN, Blue Ridge Summit, PA, USA.

Website: www.multilingual-matters.com
Twitter: Multi_Ling_Mat
Facebook: https://www.facebook.com/multilingualmatters
Blog: www.channelviewpublications.wordpress.com

The policy of Multilingual Matters/Channel View Publications is to use papers
that are natural, renewable and recyclable products, made from wood grown in
sustainable forests. In the manufacturing process of our books, and to further
support our policy, preference is given to printers that have FSC and PEFC Chain of
Custody certification. The FSC and/or PEFC logos will appear on those books where
full certification has been granted to the printer concerned.

Typeset by Deanta Global Publishing Services Limited.
Printed and bound in the UK by the CPI Books Group Ltd.
Printed and bound in the US by Thomson-Shore, Inc.

XXXII

Hope is the thing with feathers -
That perches in the soul -
And sings the tune without the words -
And never stops - at all -

And sweetest - in the Gale - is heard -
And sore must be the storm -
That could abash the little Bird
That kept so many warm -

I've heard it in the chillest land -
And on the strangest Sea -
Yet - never - in Extremity,
It asked a crumb - of me.

— Emily Dickinson (1924)

Contents

Acknowledgments

This work emerged from the Proyecto Maestría Collaborative for Leadership in Bilingual/ESL Education at UT Austin, a National Professional Development project supported by a grant from the US Department of Education (Palmer & Ortiz, 2007–2013) whose goals were to *increase the quantity* and *improve the quality* of bilingual education and English as a second language educators in the Austin metro area. The grant project was supported by the Department of Curriculum and Instruction at the UT College of Education, and by the Department of ELLs, now called Multilingual Education, in the Austin Independent School District; both institutions contributed resources. The project was a platform for the research I will report on here – although to be clear, the grant did not fund the research. It is impossible to acknowledge everyone involved in making this project successful; however, I do want to take a little space to try.

All of us who were on the faculty in the Bilingual/Bicultural Education Program during these years contributed tremendous effort: my co-director Alba Ortíz, Haydée Rodriguez, María Fránquiz, Rebecca Callahan and Carmen Martínez-Roldán each participated in admissions meetings, responded to candidates' needs and planned for classes, collaborations and advising to enrich the students' experiences with their own expertise.

Project staff members over the seven years of the project included administrative assistants Sandy Salinas, Yolanda Muñoz and the Office of Bilingual Education administrative support Marsha Tapley; and clinical coordinators Laura McFarland, Elisa Paredes, Elizabeth Villarreal, Patricia Nuñez, Monica Valadez, Blanca Caldas and Brenda Rubio. These women also made the program thrive on so many levels: they built our web page, reached out to surrounding school districts, created materials to explain and share our project, scheduled meetings, reached out individually to potential participants, supported teachers' applications to graduate school and ultimate matriculation and orientation into the program, and supported our maintenance of a strong professional network post-graduation. As part of their efforts, each of these project staff members contributed her own strengths and ideas making the project unique and better for her participation.

Special acknowledgment to Monica and Blanca who, along with all your regular job responsibilities, collected many of the interviews from which I drew in this analysis. Also special thanks to Elizabeth for creating the special partnership with *¡Ahora Sí!* and for your dedication to the critical core that made Proyecto powerful; and to Sandy for lending your talents to help us create a 15-minute promotional video that reflected the program's strengths. Thanks also to our final co-coordinators, Blanca and Brenda, for helping participants and graduates bridge from Proyecto to the ¡Adelante! Conference (http://www.aaabe.org/conference.html) and to Academia Cuauhtli (Valenzuela *et al.*, 2015); you knew it was the future, and you saw the possibilities.

And of course, the teachers who participated, all 65 of them (including the pilot cohort) contributed to the project, each supporting its ongoing dialogue of incompletion: contributing their own words to transform the world of Proyecto and the worlds of schooling in the region. This book is lovingly dedicated to you and the work you do every day: the hard, hope-filled and joyous work of teaching and leading, coaching and mentoring, loving and struggling, in bilingual communities, schools and districts. Con mucho cariño por sus pedagogías de esperanza tras comunidades, culturas, lenguas, e ideas, gracias a todxs – me siguen inspirando cada día.

I also must thank the patient and caring editors who supported this work at Multilingual Matters, and the colleagues who looked at it and talked me through important revisions that have strengthened the ideas herein. Thank you to Kim Strong, my CU Boulder doctoral student, who helped me research and write Chapter 2 and designed the graphics in Chapters 3 and 8; thank you to Ruth Friede, a generous friend with a camera and photography skills in the right place at the right time. A huge thank you to my family: David, Ellie and Jacob (who was born around the same time as the grant). You put up with this grant project for seven years, and then the book project for several more, as an ongoing seemingly endless item on my to-do list. As with any major project, this one required all hands on deck; I was far from alone in this endeavor.

That said, the findings reported here do not necessarily reflect the position of the US Department of Education, the National Professional Development project funders, nor the viewpoints of others mentioned or acknowledged; they are the sole responsibility of this author. And while I have used pseudonyms and deliberately changed some details to protect the privacy of the Proyecto teachers, all errors are mine.

¡Adelante!

1 Why Bilingual Teacher Leadership?

'Are you sitting down?' asked Alba. 'Are *you*?' I replied. When I picked up the phone in July 2007 to learn from my colleague Dr Alba Ortiz that the US Department of Education had funded our grant proposal for the *Proyecto Maestría Collaborative for Teacher Leadership in Bilingual/ ESL Education* (Palmer & Ortiz, 2007), I was in fact sitting down: in a friend's living room. I had just shared my own exciting news, that I was expecting my second child the following January. To be honest, at that moment, I had very little conception of all that might be involved in running a 1.4 million dollar federal service grant. I knew only that I would have the opportunity to recruit and bring to the University of Texas (UT) more cohorts of fantastic bilingual teachers like the group I had had the privilege of teaching during my first year as a professor. Proyecto Maestría had started as a pilot program funded by the Austin Independent School District (AISD), and I had filled my classes in 2005–2006 with 12 experienced bilingual education teachers seeking master's degrees, fully funded by their employer. Dr George Blanco, associate professor emeritus, had recruited and admitted them just before he retired in 2005 in order to pursue a collaborative opportunity with AISD.

When I sat down to write a proposal for a US Department of Education Title III National Professional Development Project in March 2007, I was already missing that cohort of students. I had in my mind's eye the astounding growth I'd watched them experience – men and women with established careers as bilingual educators in elementary schools throughout the district, many of whom also had families and busy lives outside their jobs. They had spoken up in class to express their amazement at the way in which Gloria Anzaldúa or Gramscii or Paolo Freire was putting words to their own experiences as teachers, as bilingual individuals and for most of them as Latinx[1] in America. These 12 teachers in Austin, Texas, some of whom had been alternatively certified and had therefore never experienced a college course treating the subject of their profession, taught me – a native of Massachusetts having spent 12 years as a teacher and graduate student in California – what Spanish and Spanglish and bilingualism meant to Tejanos, what most concerned bilingual education teachers in Central Texas and how resilient and powerful full-time professional teachers could be when inspired by an opportunity to come together to learn and to transform their workplaces. I also had a fully articulated draft of the grant proposal, written by the experienced Dr Blanco, which had almost been funded three years previously.

I did modify George's draft, specifically adding ideas to respond to the experiences of the teachers in the pilot-year cohort and including my own aspirations for teacher-research and transformation, but for the most part, I let Dr Blanco's words guide my proposal. The executive director of the Department of English Language Learners (ELLs) in AISD contributed a letter of support, as did the Texas Education Agency, both attesting to the increasing numbers of students carrying the label 'English Language Learner' and the high need in the region for professional development to support 'Increased quantity and improved quality' for bilingual and English as a second language (ESL) educators.

Institutionally, I had the crucial support of a long-established partnership with our local school district, a well-respected master's degree program in Bilingual Education, Dr Alba Ortiz and her staff in UT's Office of Bilingual Education and several key senior colleagues in my department to support the project.

This book is partially about the program we ran; I will describe Proyecto Maestría and share details about the kinds of experiences teachers had during their time at UT. However, primarily the program provided a context, a laboratory, a productive platform, from which to explore what it meant for bilingual education teachers to become leaders. I have come to understand bilingual teacher leadership as intricately tied to cultural and linguistic identities and praxis, and building broad networks of professional allies. Teacher leadership in general terms is teachers embracing roles beyond the confines of their classrooms, but for bilingual teachers this necessarily implies embracing identities as advocates on behalf of their bilingual students and families within the frequently marginalizing structures of public schooling. Bilingual teachers need particular kinds of support to embrace leadership, and they experience leadership in particular kinds of ways. With the ongoing insights of the Proyecto Maestría teachers, I have developed a more complex, nuanced and layered understanding of leadership identities as bilingual teachers take them up. The primary purpose of this book is to explore definitions of bilingual teacher leadership as manifested in this space, with these teachers, in the hopes that it might serve others to better understand what is necessary, and what is possible.

Sociohistorical and Demographic Context: Language Ecology of Central Texas

Our project attempted to directly address what was and continues to be a tremendous need in our local community in Central Texas: professional development to prepare experienced bilingual teachers with leadership skills, and to support a broader base of general education teachers to develop the skills and dispositions necessary to work effectively with the large and increasing population of bilingual and emergent bilingual (EB) students. The stated primary goal of the grant was twofold: to improve the quality and to increase the quantity of qualified bilingual and ESL teachers in the Austin, Texas region, where there is a large and growing number of students entering public schools as speakers of languages other than English – primarily Spanish.

Texas, with over 980,000 students in public schools who are identified as 'English Language Learners' (ELLs)[2] – approximately 18.5% of the total student population – and many more who speak an additional language beyond English, is one of the most linguistically and culturally diverse states in the United States (Division of Research and Analysis, Office of Academics, 2016). It has long been a border-crossing state; Texans are proud to assert that 'six flags' have hung over the region during the time since the first arrival of European colonists from Spain in the 1500s, including a 10-year period from 1836 to 1845 when Texas stood as its own young nation, flying the flag of the Texas Republic. Texas joined the United States in 1845. Then in 1848 the Treaty of Guadalupe Hidalgo moved the US/Mexico border south to the Rio Grande, known in Mexico as the Rio Bravo, ceding all of Texas plus all or parts of what is now Arizona, California, Nevada, New Mexico, Utah, Wyoming and Colorado.

Bilingualism and bilingual education have had a 'strange career' in Texas (Blanton, 2005). The territory that is now known as Texas has always been a linguistically diverse space – first with Native American languages, then with the violent colonizing dominance of Spanish, followed by multiple waves of European and Asian immigrant languages, including German, French, Polish, Czech, English, Vietnamese, Arabic and Chinese (Kloss, 1998). As political control shifted back and forth across the state, so did loyalties to various languages, and schooling options along with them. For an extended period of time prior to the early 1900s (when nativist hysteria related to World War I led to a push for English-only), schooling was available in different regions of Texas in German, Spanish, Polish, Dutch and Czech – sometimes bilingually with English, sometimes not (Blanton, 2005). Spanish-medium schools in particular were widespread and popular. Called 'escuelitas' [little schools], many were private, non-sectarian schools created by Mexican Americans unhappy with exclusionary and racist practices in public schools (Blanton, 2005; San Miguel & Donato, 2010). It is also interesting to note that public schools prior to World War I supported bilingual education in Spanish; as historian Carlos Kevin Blanton (2005: 29) noted: 'Those schools choosing to educate Spanish speakers in an English-Only manner paid the price of losing Tejano patronage'.

As the Progressive Movement gained traction in Texas, merging and centralizing school districts and developing larger-scale education projects that would reach all children, and simultaneously during US participation in two World Wars, xenophobic anti-bilingual, English-only ideologies prevailed (Blanton, 2005; Delgado Bernal, 2000; Schmid, 2000). For nearly 50 years, from 1918 until the late 1960s, state law in Texas mandated a rigid and violent English-only policy of instruction for all children, particularly for young Spanish-speaking children. The results were devastating in terms of educational outcomes; for example, 81% of children in Laredo in the late 1920s were classified as 'overage' (i.e. having been retained at least one year), with other districts along the US/Mexico border reporting similar high rates of educational failure (Blanton, 2005). Many older adults, some of them still practicing bilingual educators or their parents, remember attending school in the English-only era; they remember paying money, or suffering humiliating punishments, for the crime of speaking their language in a classroom or on the playground. Many associate their language and culture with shame, as something that should be hidden in the home. Because of their own experiences in school, many Tejanx parents chose to raise their children monolingually in English.

Bilingual education returned to Texas alongside the Chicano Civil Rights Movement in the 1960s. The laws that eventually mandated bilingual programming, however, drew on deficit discourses of remediation and compensatory education, the result of a political compromise in order to move the legislation through (Flores, 2016; Grinberg & Saavedra, 2000; Wiese & Garcia, 1998). The most prominent of these laws was the 1968 Bilingual Education Act (BEA) – Title VII of the federal Elementary and Secondary Education Act, negotiated into President Lyndon B. Johnson's signature education bill by Texas Senator Ralph Yarborough (Blanton, 2005; Crawford, 2004). The BEA provided grant-based funding for innovative programs to support bilingual education for 'limited English proficient' children. Around the same time, a combination of court cases and legislation established that children with limited English had a right to 'accommodation' to ensure they understood the education they were being offered. This led Texas, in 1981, to mandate transitional bilingual education programs in districts and at elementary-grade levels with 20 or more students from the same language group requiring it (Blanton, 2005; Texas Education Code, 1995).

Yet, with the powerful negative history around Spanish in the region, even today many current and aspiring bilingual teachers lack academic confidence in the language, as most have never had the opportunity for formal study beyond second grade (Ek *et al.*, 2013; Guerrero & Guerrero, 2017). Many parents lack the desire or understanding to support their children to develop bilingualism, and many school systems maintain early-exit transitional bilingual programming with the primary goal (albeit less directly stated in this day and age) to support 'linguistically disadvantaged' children to acquire English quickly without losing ground in their academic subjects. This legacy of subtractive schooling and transitional ideologies toward Latinx and Spanish-speaking students has been difficult to overcome (Palmer, 2011; Valenzuela, 1999).

In very recent years, there has been some movement toward additive dual language programming for Texas schoolchildren. Dual language programs are bilingual programs that have the stated goal of developing children's 'bilingualism, biliteracy and biculturalism', and maintain substantial instruction in the non-English language for at least the duration of elementary school, preferably longer (Gomez *et al.*, 2005; Palmer *et al.*, 2015b). A rapidly increasing number of schools and districts in Texas are adopting dual language programs to replace their transitional bilingual education programs (Wilson, 2011). These dual language programs are most certainly not without their issues (Cervantes-Soon *et al.*, 2017). In particular, ideological resistance has been strong, given the troubled history of bilingualism in the state (Fitzsimmons-Doolan *et al.*, 2015; Palmer, 2011), and accountability systems that ultimately emphasize English achievement have impeded the implementation of strong, additive bilingual programs (Palmer *et al.*, 2015a; Palmer & Snodgrass-Rangel, 2011). However, discourses do appear to be shifting, and additive bilingualism is becoming attractive to many in the state.

This is a pivotal moment in the history of bilingual education in Texas, and bilingual teachers are key players in these shifting policy contexts. It is a timely opportunity to invest in educator leadership in the area of bilingual/ESL education.

Getting (Re)Started

In the fall of 2007, I reached out to our cohort of pilot-year graduates to help me run some recruitment meetings for our new grant program. I listened as one graduate from the pilot cohort, a man on his way to becoming a principal, described to prospective participants the feeling of having 'new words' in his mouth like 'hegemony' and 'heteroglossia'. I heard two women from the cohort talk about being inspired to return to graduate school for a PhD, when they had 'never imagined' they would be able to actually enter a graduate program at an institution like UT Austin.

In late February and throughout March, with my infant son in tow, I hired a program coordinator and administrative assistant and coordinated our admissions process. By April 1, we had selected our first grant-supported cohort of nine teachers, all of whom happened to be Latina women. When I had the privilege of calling them on the telephone to inform them of their admission to Proyecto Maestría, I remember smiling broadly at their whoops of joy.

In all, the Proyecto Maestría grant provided full scholarships to 53 participants in five cohorts, who entered UT Austin in June for five consecutive years from 2008 to 2012. Each cohort spent approximately 15 months earning their master's degrees. While they attended UT and in the months and years that followed, most of the participants found ways to express a sense of transformation. Graduate school seemed to offer them an opportunity to explore empowering new identities.

Partway through the first cohort's tenure, I decided to explore participants' routes to embracing professional leadership identities (Palmer *et al.*, 2014b). I began to collect data about their experiences. I also began archiving students' reflections during their participation in my fall and spring semester master's degree classes: 'Teaching in the Elementary Classroom: Bilingual Education' and 'Teacher Leadership for Bilingual/ESL'. I held onto their final projects and written class work. I began recording interviews with participants after they completed the program, and holding voluntary reunion 'study group' meetings for participants about a range of topics. A few program graduates became involved in research projects with me, my colleagues or one of the doctoral students in our program. I particularly sought to learn about what 'teacher leadership' can mean in a bilingual education context, and what becoming a leader can mean for bilingual teachers as they claim new identities through the potentially empowering space of a university cohort-based degree program. This book will present the findings from an analysis of these data, allowing the teachers' voices to tell the story as often as possible.

Throughout this analysis, I rely on Bakhtin's (1998) assertion that identities are co-constructed within *dialogue*, that individuals are constantly engaged in *authoring* – carrying out agentic work co-constructing their and others' identities within social contexts, and that we often move from 'authoritative' to 'internally persuasive discourses' as we firm up our identities through ongoing, never closing dialogue within community. Bakhtin's theory supports my analysis of the kinds of work that teachers did together and the kinds of identities that became possible for them in our community. Originally, Bakhtin's ideas were an adequate theoretical frame for my analysis; however, when I sat down to write in November 2016, I found that Bakhtin alone was not enough. I found I needed to bring Paolo Freire's (2000) ideas into the analysis.

Writing This Book: Bringing in Freire

The moment that I sat down to put together the elements of this book became a watershed moment for our understanding of structure and agency in the United States: it was the month that reality television star and businessman Donald Trump won the presidency. All of a sudden, we had a government and seemingly all the structures related to it dominated and headed up by an individual who willingly appealed to racist, misogynistic, anti-immigrant, anti-Latinx and anti-Muslim rhetoric. We had an opening for white supremacy to reassert itself more overtly in our society, and a widespread fear among bilingual Latinx educators that the families and communities they served were at risk: of violence, deportation, further marginalization. We had a moment in which agency, heteroglossia and the pluralistic ideals that were embedded in the best bilingual education programs suddenly seemed to have lost, while a monoglossic structure seemed to have won. It became a personal imperative for me to write this book, to bury myself in the intrinsic hope that shone through in the work of Proyecto's teachers. I turned to Paolo Freire (2000) to express this imperative for hope:

> Nor yet can dialogue exist without hope. Hope is rooted in men's incompletion, from which they move out in constant search – a search which can be carried out only in communion with others. Hopelessness is a form of silence, of denying the world and fleeing from it. The dehumanization resulting from an unjust order is not a cause for despair but for hope, leading to the incessant pursuit of the humanity denied by injustice. Hope, however, does not consist in crossing one's arms and waiting. As long as I fight, I am moved by hope; and if I fight with hope, then I can wait. (Freire, 2000: 92)

At that point, Freire's conception of dialogue and of pedagogy as praxis became another organizing theory for this book. His inspiring words intermingle in my mind and my heart with the words and actions of so many of the Proyecto teachers.

The Argument... and Overview of Chapters

Mi meta, mi deseo siempre ha sido el trabajar con maestros y contribuir al crecimiento profesional de los expertos en educación bilingüe que muchas veces son ignorados. Yo he visto como tantos maestros altamente calificados son tratados como ignorantes porque trabajan con estudiantes bilingües e igual que ellos son minospreciados por la población que se siente superior en todos los aspectos de la educación. La mayoría de las veces son estas personas las que deciden el tipo de programa que se implementa en nuestras escuelas y que afectan a nuestros niños. También son estas personas las que determinan el tipo de entrenamiento profesional que reciben los maestros bilingües sin tomar en cuenta las diferencias culturales que debemos considerar cuando planeamos lecciones para nuestros ninos. [My goal, *my desire has always been to work with teachers and contribute to the professional growth of the experts in bilingual education who many times are ignored. I have seen how so many highly qualified teachers are treated as if they are ignorant because they work with bilingual students and like them [their students], they are depreciated by the population that feels superior in all aspects of education. Most of the time it is those people who decide the type of program that is implemented in our schools and that affect our children. It is also those people who determine the type of professional training that bilingual teachers receive without taking into account the cultural differences that we need to consider when we plan lessons for our children.] (Patricia, Cohort 4, online reflection)*

Leadership takes on a tone of urgency when we are struggling for justice. At the same time, the right to lead – the agency to embrace a leadership identity – can also feel more distant when we are marginalized by the dominant society. For bilingual education teachers, the development of critical consciousness, pride in the cultural and linguistic resources of the bilingual community, the vocabulary to name and directly face the marginalization that Patricia describes above and a strong professional network to give them strength, are fundamental to their development of professional identities as leaders and advocates. Regardless of teachers' own cultural and linguistic backgrounds, having a strong sense of this personal cultural/linguistic identity and a deep awareness of the richness of the culture and language backgrounds of their students supports teachers' empathy for their students and the families they serve. Love, as a central element to teaching as praxis (Valenzuela, 1999; Wall, 2016), pushes teachers toward the development of strong and empowered professional identities as bilingual teacher leaders. For many – I would venture to say most – of the teachers who participated in Proyecto Maestría, accessing the courage to embrace leadership identities seems driven by the need to advocate for students and families within a sometimes hostile and oppressive system of education. Freire (2000: 88) defines dialogue as 'the encounter between [people], mediated by the world, in order to name the world'. It was through the co-construction of the professional and cultural/linguistic community of the cohort that teachers found a path to embrace critical dialogue in the various worlds of which they were a part: their homes and families, schools and districts, churches and communities; and to support one another's construction of selves as advocates, critical thinkers and leaders.

The next chapter will provide a thorough review of the literature on teacher leadership, pedagogy for bilingual students and critical pedagogies in bilingual education. Research in the field of educational leadership has begun to define and explore the potential of teacher leadership. A range of definitions have emerged in an effort to draw on new structures for leadership to improve instructional outcomes at the school or district level (Ackerman & Mackenzie, 2007; Hilty, 2011; Katzenmeyer & Moller, 2009; Krovetz & Arriaza, 2006; Mangin & Stoelinga, 2008; York-Barr & Duke, 2004). Research on teaching in bilingual/ELL education, a subfield within the broader field of teaching and teacher education, has developed constructs related to the nuances and particular demands of teaching in diverse, multilingual contexts (Echevarria *et al.*, 2008; Fillmore & Snow, 2000). Some have pushed this field to frame teachers as actors upon their structural worlds of schooling: as language and education policymakers in their classrooms, as advocates and as agents (Ladson-Billings, 1995b; Menken & García, 2010; Palmer & Martínez, 2013; Urrieta, 2009). To my knowledge, however, the fields of teacher leadership and bilingual/ELL teacher preparation have yet to come into meaningful contact. Through synthesizing these literatures, I begin to specifically define *bilingual teacher leadership* and explore the ramifications for bilingual instruction of equipping teachers with tools for empowerment and agency and to own the title of leader.

Chapter 3 will present Bakhtin's 'dialogue' and 'authoring' as central conceptions to guide my construction of identity, and Freire's different yet related conception of 'dialogue' within praxis. I will lay out the theoretical grounding for the connections I see in my data between these identity constructions that have generally been treated separately: sociocultural/linguistic, advocate and professional. I will explore the ties between culture, agency and identity that might be specific to the particular positioning of bilingual education teachers who work with minoritized language communities in schools. Theory provides some tools to make sense of the powerful experiences of a coming together of higher education, the K-5 bilingual classroom and engaged, thoughtful, creative professional teachers. I hope, then, to further theorize these concepts for this context drawing on the teachers' own words in subsequent chapters.

Chapter 4 will present an explanation of the context, methods, procedures, participants and data for the study that emerged from this project. I will describe the Proyecto Maestría cohort master's degree program, including the overall structure, the courses and the recruitment, admissions and matriculation procedures we developed. I will share some of the challenges and hurdles we faced, in the hopes that sharing this information might support others as they work to design or improve graduate school programming for bilingual and ESL teachers in their own contexts. This chapter will also introduce the participants: a demographic overview of the 53 teachers who passed through our program in the five cohorts that received grant support, with more biographic details of the focal teachers and cohort whose voices will be most prominent in my analysis.

Chapters 5 through 7 will present findings of this analysis of the experiences of 53 bilingual education teachers: bilingual teacher leaders are critical reflexive practitioners, they are cultural/linguistic brokers and they are collaborators who work within communities. Chapter 5 will describe the ways in which the teachers took up different course assignments throughout the program in order to deeply reflect on their practice and to build connections between theory, practice and personal selves that were central to their authoring as critically conscious leaders. Using the teachers' own responses to assignments, I will explore the ways in which teachers used graduate school and other experiences to present and construct themselves as agents, advocates, professionals and leaders. Chapter 6 will make the case that it is essential for bilingual teacher leaders to cultivate well-developed cultural/linguistic identities and deep empathy for their students' contexts, lived experiences, cultures and languages; essentially, critical multicultural consciousness. Chapter 7 will outline the central role of the community of the cohort in supporting participants' identity construction as professional leaders and their engagement in praxis and dialogue. This community experience was powerful and key, and led to transformation for many participants; several cohorts remain close, and participants have maintained ties both professional and personal. What's more, the practice of seeking out and building professional networks and collaborations has become integral to many teachers' work. I will argue, drawing from the teachers' own words, that this makes sense both theoretically and practically; that, as Freire and Bakhtin would assert, such community and the strength engendered by it is essential to the larger transformation project.

In Chapter 8, I will pull these conceptions together to develop a definition of bilingual teacher leadership that places advocacy and critical consciousness at the core, reiterating the central role that participants' reflexive praxis, understandings of cultural/linguistic identity and professional communities had in pushing them to embrace advocacy and transformative pedagogies, and ultimately to take on leadership in a range of forms in their schools and districts. Having developed a theoretically and empirically grounded set of defining principles for the process of co-construction of bilingual teacher leadership, I will conclude with recommendations for teachers, teacher educators, researchers and policymakers in order to apply these ideas.

I write this book as a space for the voices of the teachers who I worked with in Proyecto Maestría to ring out clearly – and they are calling not merely for improvement to our current systems, but for *transformation*. The barely contained energy of hope with which so many Proyecto teachers talk about and go about their work in schools and classrooms is contagious, and I wish to share that with the world, in order to expand possibilities for transformational educational experiences for bilingual and EB children, their parents and their teachers in our public schools.

Notes

(1) In most cases, I have chosen to use the term 'Latinx' to refer to people of Mexican or Latin American descent, in order to transcend the gender dichotomies of the traditional Spanish terms 'Latina' or 'Latino' (Salinas & Lozano, 2017).

(2) I use the terms 'ELL' and 'EB' interchangeably in this book, although their origins and emphases do differ. In line with García (2010), I prefer EB for its emphasis on bilingualism rather than merely English acquisition. But ELL is still prevalent in the literature, and was the predominant term when the grant period began.

2 Literature Review: Defining Bilingual Teacher Leadership

(with Kimberly Strong)

The Proyecto Maestría Collaborative was an effort that brought together two key fields: bilingual education instruction and program implementation, and teacher leadership/professional development for teacher excellence. The result was an appropriate context within which to define *bilingual* teacher leadership in terms of the particular leadership identities and practices that best serve bilingual education teachers as they work to support excellence for bilingual and emergent bilingual students in their schools and districts.

Currently, although approximately 25% of school-age children (ages 5–17) speak a language other than English (US Census Bureau, 2015), the literature addressing teacher leadership and educational excellence rarely mentions these students, let alone the unique assets, needs and challenges of bilingual education. Instead, much of the traditional teacher leadership literature, which for our purposes is defined as work that *promotes teachers assuming broader/more responsibility for school functions* (Katzenmeyer & Moller, 2009), describes teacher roles as if all students were members of a homogeneous group with homogeneous needs. A branch of teacher leadership literature emerging from the field of teacher preparation/curriculum and instruction, rather than the leadership field, which we will refer to as social justice teaching, addresses the need for teachers to develop 'ideological clarity' (Bartolomé & Balderrama, 2001), or critical awareness about the positioning of marginalized students in schools and to draw on specific educational practices through lenses like critical pedagogy (Darder *et al.*, 2003; Freire, 2000) or culturally responsive/relevant/sustaining pedagogies (Gay, 2010; Ladson-Billings, 1995b; Paris, 2012). There is also a branch of the leadership field that deals primarily with critical social justice leadership (Santamaría, 2014), drawing on critical frameworks to explore the role of school leaders in focusing schools around work that centers social justice and equity for minoritized communities (Rodríguez *et al.*, 2016; Tillman & Scheurich, 2013). This work, however, rarely mentions teachers. It is primarily concerned with school and district leadership from the principal on up, whose roles in schools and institutional constraints differ significantly from teachers. As such, this work is mostly beyond the scope of this review.

While there are some overlaps between the teacher leadership literature, the teacher advocacy literature and the critical social justice leadership literature, there is little work that unites these fields while specifically addressing the unique needs of bilingual teachers and students. In order to ensure I was capturing the field of current research in the nexus of teacher leadership, advocacy and bilingual education, I enlisted the help of my colleague and doctoral student, Kimberly Strong, who is therefore my co-author for this chapter. We worked together to develop the strategy for the search, and consulted throughout the process of review, analysis and writing.

In the following literature review, we will outline the current state of bilingual education research, detailing what pedagogies and practices have been confirmed to produce improved learning outcomes and a more positive, equitable experience for bilingual students. These imperatives will then be contrasted with key research on teacher advocacy and teacher leadership. It will become clear that the needs of bilingual students are alluded to but not explicitly addressed in teacher leadership/advocacy research.

The social justice teaching or advocacy/activist teaching framework outlines the importance of pedagogical practices that specifically address the needs of marginalized students, yet largely omits the specific needs of bilingual students and teachers. Likewise, teacher leadership literature purports to improve learning outcomes for all students but fails to address the unique circumstances and needs of bilingual students – and does not address the leadership preparation of bilingual teachers. We contend that there is a need for the literature on teacher advocacy and teacher leadership to take up specificity toward bilingual education; until it does so, our educational system will continue to fall short in meeting the needs of the nearly 25% of students in US schools who are members of culturally and linguistically minoritized communities. The remainder of this book is meant to contribute to efforts to begin to address this gap.

Methods

We began our search with the base of research in the field of teacher leadership and advocacy that I had uncovered over the years teaching and directing Proyecto Maestría, particularly the work that had guided my construction of the syllabus for the capstone course taken by all participants: 'Teacher Leadership in Bilingual/ESL Education'. This included readings from scholars and practitioners in the field of teacher leadership, with special attention to any work that addressed cultural or linguistic diversity or equity. On the reading list were Katzenmeyer and Moller (2009), Krovetz and Arriaza (2006), Lieberman and Miller (2008) and Lindsey *et al.* (2007), along with chapters and articles selected from a range of work in the field including Barthes (2007) and York-Barr and Duke (2004) among others. It also included specific readings in the fields of bilingual education and critical social justice education that addressed teachers as potential or actual leaders and advocates, even if they did not use these terms (Delgado Bernal, 2001; Fitts & Weisman, 2010; Freeman, 2004; McCarty, 2005; Nieto, 2003, 2013) and short pieces by critical feminist theorists Gloria Anzaldúa (1987) and bell hooks (2003) (see Appendix B for the 2013 course syllabus). The principal goals of the course were to stimulate participants' thinking about themselves as potential leaders, to empower them as professionals and to broaden their perspectives about the possibilities and mechanisms for positive change in their professional contexts; there was never an intention to provide students with a thorough overview of the field.

Realizing, therefore, that this was really the barest of beginnings, we conducted literature searches in the leading educational online databases: SAGE, Educational Resources Information Center (ERIC), ERIC Proquest and EBSCO. We searched for peer-reviewed scholarly articles that combined teacher leadership *and* teacher advocacy *and* bilingual education since the purpose of this literature review was to discover what work, if any, had already been conducted to develop this hybrid field. Finally, in order to augment the exploration of bilingual student needs and the pedagogical approaches currently employed to meet them, a secondary search was conducted in EPIC Proquest and EBSCO using the terms 'bilingual' *and* 'culturally relevant'.

Due to the breadth of each of these three areas and their lack of definitive shared vocabulary, during the search we used the following synonymous terms in order to capture all relevant articles that dealt with the topics:

- For 'teacher leadership', we included the search terms 'leadership', 'leadership effectiveness', 'educational leadership', 'teacher leadership' or 'transformative leadership'.
- For 'social justice teaching', we included the search terms 'critical leadership', 'social justice', 'educational reform', 'teacher advocacy', 'advocacy', 'activist teacher leadership', 'teacher activism', 'culturally responsive pedagogy', 'critical race theory', 'critical consciousness' or 'critical pedagogy'.
- For 'bilingual education', we included the search terms 'English as a second language', 'ESL', 'bilingual education', 'bilingual schools', 'bilingualism', 'bilingual students', 'bilingual teachers', 'dual language',

'immersion programs', 'English language learners', 'ELL' or 'second language learning'.
- For 'culturally relevant', we included the search term 'culturally sustaining'.

We restricted our search to works that included each of the three elements. Additional filters proved helpful to limit the results to issues relevant to programs within the United States, across K-12 public education teaching practice and across content areas. As such, we excluded the term 'international'; terms referring to subjects outside of K-12 public education such as 'private', 'federal legislation' and 'higher education'; and terms referring to specific content and ages such as 'language arts', 'language instruction', 'reading', 'social studies', 'mathematics', 'humanities', 'elementary', 'middle school' and 'secondary'. At first, we excluded works that dealt exclusively with principals' leadership activities, development and qualities as we were focused on *teacher* leadership. In the end, however, since so much of the leadership literature is dominated by issues relating to principals, we chose to include articles that addressed principals as long as they also addressed teachers to a significant degree. These limitations were used because this literature review seeks to understand bilingual teacher leadership in the United States K-12 public schools, so specificity regarding content focus and grade level would have been inapplicably narrow while a focus on foreign education, private education, higher education and legal educational issues would have been too broad.

Finally, our searches were complimented by citation chaining, i.e. looking at the reference lists of articles relevant to our topic to lead us to other articles (Phelps *et al.*, 2007). This actually helped significantly broaden the works discovered, because even with expanded search terms the field of bilingual teacher leadership is still nascent and combines such widely defined areas that relevant literature as found in citation chaining was often absent in the database searches – and extremely useful. By combining all three search avenues, we were able to accumulate a robust body of literature that built on the current state of bilingual education in order to examine how the seminal works in teacher leadership and teacher advocacy inform and expand the parameters of the fledging field of *bilingual teacher leadership*. In fact, we believe that this literature review lends significant heft to one of the primary claims of this book: that in order for teacher leadership and teacher advocacy work to fully meet their goals of providing quality education for *all* students, we must develop this new field of bilingual teacher leadership to address the unique needs and challenges specific to the growing bilingual student population.

Analysis of search results

The literature review is organized into four sections: (a) an overview of bilingual education that will explore its current state, why it is a field deserving of particular attention and its unique needs and challenges; (b) an overview of important works that define and explore teacher advocacy; (c) an overview of the seminal works in teacher leadership, with a brief look at the separate field of leadership for social justice; and (d) a closer look at the few articles we found that fit into the precise nexus I will be discussing in the remainder of the book: research that incorporated teacher advocacy into the teacher leadership framework specifically for bilingual education.

Bilingual Education: Teachers' Beliefs and Knowledge Matter for Emergent Bilingual Students

According to the US Census, approximately one in four school-age children in the United States speaks a language other than English (US Census Bureau, 2015). While Spanish is the most common home language of bilingual students, the students themselves represent a variety of economic classes, nationalities and legal statuses, with the majority being US-born citizens (Murakami *et al.*, 2013; Scanlan & López, 2013). Despite the complexity and diversity of this group, a common feature of bilingual students is that as a student population they experience segregation, with only 57% of schools enrolling essentially the entire bilingual student population (Scanlan & López, 2013).

This segregation has resulted in inferior access to quality educational experiences for these students (Orfield & Lee, 2005). Academically, Spanish-speaking bilingual students are more likely to repeat a grade, to not graduate high school and to be tracked into less rigorous classes and special education while struggling against a decreased likelihood of pursuing higher education (Scanlan & López, 2013). The classes that are available to many emergent bilingual students, like English as a second language (ESL) and transitional bilingual classes, are often limited to curriculum that focuses on English acquisition at the expense of academic content like reading, writing, history, social studies and math. Consequently, when students emerge from these classes they are so unprepared for the general academic content that higher education ceases to be a plausible option (Callahan, 2005; Valenzuela, 1999). Inequities in access to high-quality education for emergent bilingual youth in public schools are well documented (Cervantes-Soon *et al.*, 2017; Noguera, 2003; Olsen, 1997; Valdés, 2011; Valenzuela, 1999) and participants in the Proyecto Maestría master's program read about and discussed these issues in their courses.

Proyecto Maestría participants also read Ruiz' (1984) work articulating common orientations toward language as a *problem*, language as a *resource* and language as a *right*, and the distinction between additive and subtractive bilingualism (Lambert, 1975) and educational experiences (Valenzuela, 1999). How children feel about themselves, and how educators view them, their families and their language(s) and culture(s), affects how well they do in school. Policies and practices that teach students that they or their languages/cultures are not welcomed or valued while depriving them of content knowledge, connections to their families and communities and proficiency in their home languages are termed 'subtractive' (Valenzuela, 1999) or 'weak' (Téllez & Varghese, 2013) for the high cost they impose on students. By contrast, culturally relevant (Ladson-Billings, 1995b) or sustaining (Paris, 2012) pedagogies and additive/enrichment bilingual education programs (Cloud *et al.*, 2000; Lindholm-Leary, 2001) see bilingualism and biculturalism as assets to embrace. Programs with this orientation work to maintain home languages, value home cultures and communities and support bilingual students with caring educators (Cloud *et al.*, 2000; Scanlan & López, 2013). There is empirical support for culturally sustaining, additive educational programming for emergent bilingual students. There is considerable consensus in the research literature that subtractive schooling widens achievement gaps, while additive enrichment-oriented and culturally/linguistically sustaining programs show long-term success with emergent bilingual students, in terms of both their academic success and their acquisition of English (Collier & Thomas, 2004; Rolstad *et al.*, 2005; Slavin & Cheung, 2005; Umansky & Reardon, 2014).

Although described in a range of ways in the literature (Crawford, 2004; de Jong, 2011; Scanlan & López, 2013), additive/enrichment/resource-oriented bilingual education programs share these characteristics: they value students' ongoing development of bilingualism/biliteracy; they engage in a pedagogy of caring toward students and their families/ communities that supports positive identity development; and they ensure teachers are critically aware and well-informed about bi(multi)-lingual language and literacy acquisition, and the languages and cultures of their students. Schools that are committed to these principles have the potential to promote improved student learning outcomes and to redress the current and historical disenfranchisement of linguistically and culturally minoritized communities. At the heart of strong educational programs for emergent bilingual students are the beliefs and actions of the professionals involved: educators' centering of bilingualism as a positive skill to be valued rather than a negative obstacle to be overcome can make the difference for a child between success and disengagement in school (den Hartog King & Peralta Nash, 2011). It also becomes imperative, given widespread subtractive schooling (Valenzuela, 1999) experiences in the United States, for educators to be critically aware of the impact of marginalization on the students and families they serve, and to actively *counter* students' prior negative experiences through authentic caring and proactively sustaining pedagogies (Ek *et al.*, 2013; Noddings, 1984; Prieto & Villenas, 2012).

Yet, as important as it is, valuing students' cultures and languages and caring for them alone is insufficient to ensure school success. Caring must be complemented by teacher competence in linguistics and language acquisition (Bunch, 2013; Faltis & Valdés, 2016; Fillmore & Snow, 2000; Valdés, 2004). Language acquisition is not a discrete or linear process but occurs dynamically throughout the day and throughout content instruction. As such, teachers of all content areas must understand how to support both content and language development simultaneously (de Jong, 2011; Faltis & Valdés, 2016; Levine & McCloskey, 2012; Scanlan & López, 2013). Unfortunately, few teachers know enough about their bilingual students' cultural and linguistic backgrounds or the challenges of being a non-native speaker to best serve them (Bunch, 2013; Fillmore & Snow, 2000; Palmer & Martínez, 2013). Without the requisite understanding of language acquisition and the dynamics of language and power in schools, even the best-intended and most caring teachers will fall short of meeting their bilingual students' needs.

Providing teachers with the training and professional development in language acquisition is just one example of the important role that schools, administrators and policies play in supporting the success of bilingual teachers and students. Many bilingual educators actually report feeling unsupported and misunderstood by their peers and administrators (Carranza, 2010). This lack of support compounds the already-challenging work of bilingual education. In addition, overall the bilingual teaching force is more likely to be novice and alternatively certified, and lingering in the early 'survival stage' of development, reflecting a likelihood of high teacher turnover in this field (Ovando & Casey, 2010). Ideally, to best support bilingual teachers and students, school administrators and all school staff would receive training in bilingual education and language development to reflect the belief that the success of all students is the responsibility of all school personnel, although in reality this proves challenging given the range of paradigms and expectations for those who work in schools (Carranza, 2010; Scanlan & López, 2013; Valdés, 2004).

Cahnmann and Varghese (2005) remind educators that bilingual education should not be divorced from the racialized and economically disadvantaged contexts within which most bilingual teachers and students live and work. Inequitable educational opportunities can be addressed through a critical, additive/enrichment, culturally sustaining bilingual program. Instead of framing bilingualism as a problem to be solved, teachers must seek to develop students' home language(s), partner positively with students' families and communities and support students to acquire new language practices for success in school. Teaching emergent bilingual students is a unique and rewarding experience that absolutely requires special preparation along several dimensions.

Social Justice Teaching

The need to support culturally and linguistically minoritized bilingual students is reflected in the literature on teaching for social justice. Grounded in critical perspectives, including critical pedagogy (Duncan-Andrade & Morrell, 2008; Freire, 2000), the field of social justice teaching, which is also referred to as advocacy or activist teaching, is concerned with developing pedagogies to directly counter inequity and marginalization in schools. Social justice teachers acknowledge the many ways that schools act as political institutions serving the interests of some groups at the expense of others, often allocating educational opportunities and resources along lines of race, class, culture and language, which result in reproducing systems of power and inequality (Dantley & Tillman, 2006; Evans, 2013; Lerma et al., 2013). Recognizing that schools are serving more minoritized students than ever before and that this trend is projected to continue, social justice teaching envisions advocacy and political engagement as central to the work of teaching. The field asserts that teaching is by its nature political, and teachers should engage a social justice framework to advocate on behalf of the students and communities they serve to confront and reform marginalizing educational policies and practices (Lerma et al., 2013; Villegas & Lucas, 2007).

While by definition all work in this arena deals with issues of power and social justice within schools, it has been taken up in various ways. For example, Burke and Adler (2013) examined how urban teachers enacted social justice reform, concluding that teaching itself can be an act of political resistance, while López (2008) used participant observation of bilingual teachers who fought against the racial stigmatization of their students to contend that an antiracist pedagogy was the key to creating welcoming and empowering educational opportunities for minoritized students and their families. Urrieta (2009) collected narrative life histories from self-proclaimed activist Latinx teachers, analyzing strategies these activist teachers drew upon to sustain and grow their efforts for equity for Latinx students in urban classrooms. Nieto (2003, 2013) began working with a group of social justice teachers in an informal study group; as she engaged with the teachers around issues of importance to all of them, she explored their motivations and identities in order to understand what drives teachers to become activists and advocates. Athanases and

Martin (2006) talk with groups of program graduates to explore how well their teacher preparation program prepares teachers to advocate for equity and teach to diversity; their program holds these goals at the center, and articulates them richly across coursework and fieldwork. Wong *et al.* (2017) track one beginning bilingual teacher's development of agency and critical awareness through self-reflection and inquiry over the course of three years as she completes a teacher education program and moves into the field. Basing their work on a wide range of research in the field, Villegas and Lucas (2002, 2007) developed a framework outlining the attitudes and practices that they contend are essential for meeting culturally and linguistically diverse students' needs. Their framework centers on a call for 'sociocultural consciousness'. However, Jacobs *et al.* (2014) contend that a supportive school environment is fundamental to social justice teaching, as teacher attitude alone is often unable to surmount administrative and social barriers. These researchers were all centered around enacting reforms that improve access to quality education for students who are members of historically marginalized communities.

Various practices fall under the larger umbrella of social justice teaching or advocacy/activist teaching. Social reconstructionist schooling is a tool wherein a class community critically examines school norms in order to then reconstruct them in more equitable ways (Marshall & Oliva, 2006). Literature also serves as a tool to promote critical encounters for students of a variety of ages (Lara & Leija, 2014; Lewis *et al.*, 2009; Simon & Campano, 2013). There is also a movement of activist teachers and social justice curriculum development, represented by several practitioner-oriented journals, websites and conferences including Radical Teacher (https://radicalteacher.library.pitt.edu), Rethinking Schools (https://www.rethinkingschools.org/), Teaching for Change (http://www.teachingforchange.org/), Teaching For Social Justice (T4SJ) (http://www.teachersforjustice.org/), Badass Teachers (http://www.badassteacher.org/) and others that share the goal of supporting teachers' work as engaged advocates for social justice in their communities.

Rethinking Schools in particular has recently paid close attention to bilingual education and bi(multi)lingual schooling contexts, with occasional Spanish language articles and a Facebook page dedicated to bilingual education issues; they recently published an edited volume of essays and critical social justice curriculum dedicated to bilingual teaching for advocacy and social justice (Barbian *et al.*, 2017). All these manifestations of social justice teaching encourage educators to draw upon the lived experiences of students to talk about issues of power and oppression, leading students to new awareness while validating their experiences and identities as valuable sources of knowledge (Hafner, 2006).

Culturally relevant pedagogies and *funds of knowledge for teaching*

A well-known form of social justice teaching that has direct relevance to bilingual students and contexts is found in the framework of 'culturally relevant pedagogy' (CRP), developed as a response to cultural deficit models that blamed minoritized students' communities and cultures for low academic achievement (Ladson-Billings, 1995b, 2009). CRP asserts that 'students are more likely to learn and achieve when communication, curricula, and instruction are shaped in ways that acknowledge, honor, and reflect their language, heritage, prior knowledge, and learning styles' (Johnson & Willis, 2013: 443). As such, it seeks to promote quality teaching for all students in order to explicitly confront the exclusionary schooling practices that marginalized students face (Khalifa *et al.*, 2016). Specifically, Ladson-Billings (1995a: 160) called for educators of minoritized students to follow three tenets for best practice: striving toward high academic success, 'developing and/or maintain[ing] cultural competence' and fostering a critical awareness in students.

Bilingual contexts are particularly appropriate spaces where such pedagogy could reshape students' experiences, and there is a growing body of work that takes up a CRP approach in these spaces. Research drawing on CRP in bilingual educational contexts spans a range of content areas including arts education (Garcia, 2012; Palkki, 2015; Schroeder-Arce, 2014), science (Martínez-Álvarez & Bannan, 2014), literacy/reading (Feger, 2006; Huerta & Riojas-Cortez, 2011; Lohfink & Loya, 2010; Puzio *et al.*, 2013; Rosado *et al.*, 2015), dual language/ELL/ESL (Ernst-Slavit & Wenger, 2006; Freire & Valdez, 2017; Jiménez, 1997; Lucero, 2010; Wortham & Contreras, 2002) and general education classrooms (Adair *et al.*, 2012; Craviotto *et al.*, 1999; Souto-Manning, 2010).

The majority of these studies focused on either students (eight articles) or teachers (six articles); a few focused on parents of school-age children (Huerta & Riojas-Cortez, 2011; Rosado *et al.*, 2015) and preservice bilingual teachers (Ernst-Slavit & Wenger, 2006; Estrada, 1999). Across all studies, the most commonly cited benefit of CRP for bilingual students was the improved engagement with academic content that students experienced when allowed to draw upon their full linguistic and cultural resources (Craviotto *et al.*, 1999; Feger, 2006; Huerta & Riojas-Cortez, 2011; Jiménez, 1997; Martínez-Álvarez & Bannan, 2014; Puzio *et al.*, 2013; Rosado *et al.*, 2015). Less frequently discussed was students' development of their home language, both as a skill in itself and as a means of improving English language and academic content learning (Jiménez, 1997; Lohfink & Loya, 2010). Finally, some work addressed the benefit of increased pride in home cultures and the ability to formulate sociocultural critiques (Garcia, 2012) in addition to improved school experience socially (Wortham & Contreras, 2002).

Recently, Paris (2012) expanded Ladson-Billings' original notion, introducing the idea of 'culturally *sustaining* pedagogies'. Paris (2015) argued that we should not merely seek *relevance* to marginalized students' languages and cultures in the classroom, but in fact we should actively work to maintain, enhance and develop them. Embracing the term 'sustaining' rather than merely 'relevant' is an effort to explicitly embrace the strongest, most critically oriented work in the resource pedagogy tradition, in order to clarify and reinforce the goals of the movement. As Paris (2012: 93) explains, 'In the face of current policies and practices that have the explicit goal of creating a monocultural and monolingual society, research and practice need equally explicit resistances that embrace cultural pluralism and cultural equality'.

Among pedagogical practices that support CRP for bilingual students, the most commonly referenced was a *fund of knowledge* (Gonzalez *et al.*, 1995) approach in which students' and their families' home cultures, languages and practices are framed as a resource to be drawn upon in the creation of academic content and learning methods. Within this category, Craviotto *et al.* (1999), Jiménez (1997) and Lohfink and Loya (2010) called for incorporating multicultural, culturally relevant literature as a *fund of knowledge*, while Martínez-Álvarez and Bannan (2014), Palkki (2015) and Souto-Manning (2010) detailed the process of eliciting and incorporating students' and their families' home cultural and linguistic practices into classroom learning. Some work used multicultural literature as a way to activate families' recognition of their own *funds of knowledge* (Huerta & Riojas-Cortez, 2011) or conversely used families' *funds of knowledge* in the creation of multicultural literature (Rosado *et al.*, 2015).

Other work addressed the socio-emotional element of CRP when they called for teachers to strive to create a community between students or personally care about those they teach (Craviotto *et al.*, 1999; Garcia, 2012; Palkki, 2015; Wortham & Contreras, 2002). Many articles referenced the importance of school support in implementing CRP, both at an administrative/institutional level (Freire & Valdez, 2017; Wortham & Contreras, 2002) and also at a professional level in that the *funds of knowledge* framework be extended to bilingual or immigrant teachers by other peers so that they can fully draw upon the unique understanding of and connections to their bilingual students (Adair *et al.*, 2012; Ernst-Slavit & Wenger, 2006; Lucero, 2010).

Other avenues for implementing CRP in bilingual schools or communities were through increased teacher sociocultural self-awareness of bias and cultural practices (Freire & Valdez, 2017; Souto-Manning, 2010; Valenzuela, 2016), participatory action research (Garcia, 2012) and engaging students and families directly in curriculum decisions (Palkki, 2015). Meanwhile, some researchers described the barriers to implementing CRP for bilingual students (Adair *et al.*, 2012; Estrada, 1999; Freire &

Valdez, 2017; Jiménez, 1997; Wortham & Contreras, 2002) while Jesse *et al.* (2004) found that CRP was not an apparent factor in determining the success of schools with large bilingual populations as measured by a state standardized test.

While social justice/advocacy teaching is described and practiced in a range of ways, teacher advocates must confront common challenges like the belief structures that perpetuate deficit school models. Not only are students subject to the limitations of majoritarian norms but teachers of color are too, as Alemán (2006) found in his qualitative study of educators and educational stakeholders advocating for Latinx students. These majoritarian norms can be so hostile to teachers of color that they contribute to teachers leaving the profession entirely (Montaño & Burnstein, 2006). Teacher advocates are fighting against not only inequitable educational practices but also mainstream normed beliefs that minimize the importance of socioeconomic and historical systems of inequality and oppression that shape marginalized students' learning opportunities. Often, normative beliefs in education designate advocacy work and social justice teaching as superfluous to the essential work of teaching and best relegated to a few school specialists (Marshall & Oliva, 2006) or extracurricular times and places. Such pervasive beliefs can make teachers – especially teachers of color – reluctant to push back against systems of oppression with transformative pedagogy; they can feel isolated or intimidated, questioning their own perceptions in the midst of these hegemonic normed beliefs (Ekiaka Nzai *et al.*, 2012).

Social justice teaching as a field remains somewhat broadly defined, but activist/advocacy teaching models regardless of origin or framing appear to share a theoretical foundation in critical pedagogy; a commitment to social justice and critical consciousness; and a dedication to fighting for equitable access to education for marginalized students. This fight orients teacher advocates/activists around issues of power and oppression as they relate to race, class, culture and gender and how these intersecting identities, which historically have been used to marginalize students, can be transformed into tools for more positive student outcomes and experiences. Some of this literature is attentive to the specific issues of language and culture that are at the center of equitable education for bilingual students, especially work that draws on a CRP framework or takes a *fund of knowledge* approach. Dubetz and de Jong's (2011) review of the literature affirms that others in the field have framed bilingual teachers in particular as advocates, and thought about advocacy as an element of the work of bilingual teachers, due to the marginalized positioning of emergent bilingual students and bilingual programs, especially in the current political context. The field has a small but strong foundation and is demonstrating powerful potential; however, there is certainly a need for more work that unpacks the characteristics and possibilities of advocacy/activist teaching for social justice in bilingual contexts. We hope to support this work by tying advocacy/activism directly to bilingual teacher leadership identities; in the process of constructing identities as leaders, teachers in this study became advocates and activists for social justice.

Teacher Leadership

As this review seeks to understand the elements of bilingual teacher leadership, an overview of the field of teacher leadership can help to define the parameters of the work that has been done in order to point to the work that remains to be addressed. A growing body of literature is beginning to document the potential of empowering teacher leaders for positive school change (Ackerman & Mackenzie, 2007; Hilty, 2011; Johnson & Hynes, 1997; Katzenmeyer & Moller, 2009; Krovetz & Arriaza, 2006; Lieberman & Miller, 2008; Mangin & Stoelinga, 2008).

Often, the leadership field defines positive school change as improving student outcomes (Crowther *et al.*, 2007; Forster, 1997; Katzenmeyer & Moller, 2011; O'Hair & Reitzug, 1997). This common goal of improved outcomes is accomplished, researchers argue, by teachers assuming more responsibility for school operations (Barthes, 2007), initiating professional development and professional learning communities (PLCs) (Katzenmeyer & Moller, 2009; Lieberman & Miller, 2008) and being positive role models for their students and peers (Crowther *et al.*, 2007).

While some researchers appear to define teacher leadership primarily as fulfilling official roles in a distributed leadership model, such as instructional coaches, department heads or committee chairs (Mangin & Stoelinga, 2008), definitions of teacher leadership are expanding to include a wide range of informal leadership tasks and performed identities. Predicated on the belief that authentic school reform must originate with teachers as they are the ones best positioned to positively impact students by positively transforming themselves (Katzenmeyer & Moller, 2011), teacher leadership models are beginning to envision teachers enacting system-wide change through grassroots transformations of typical job duties whereby teachers assume more ownership of school functions (Boylan, 2016). Teacher leadership has been defined variously as (among other things): an inherent part of one's role as a teacher (Forster, 1997); a set of dispositions including inquiry, discourse, equity, authenticity, shared leadership and service (O'Hair & Reitzug, 1997); membership in a community of practice that supports inquiry-based instruction (Lieberman & Miller, 2008); and in the words of one teacher, 'initiatives by teachers which improve schools and learning' (Barthes, 2007: 11). A definition that offers space for empowering all teachers as learners and agents of change is that put forth by Katzenmeyer and Moller (2009):

Teacher leaders lead within and beyond the classroom; identify with and contribute to a community of teacher learners and leaders; influence others toward improved educational practice and accept responsibility for achieving the outcomes of their leadership. (Katzenmeyer & Moller, 2009: 6)

Katzenmeyer and Moller's definition was among those presented to Proyecto Maestría teacher participants during their master's coursework.

Not surprisingly, given the diversity of definitions for teacher leadership, the field has not come to a consensus on the specific areas of knowledge and skills teacher leaders should develop; there is a need for more empirical work that specifically addresses teacher leadership preparation (York-Barr & Duke, 2004). Sherrill (1999, 2011) offers a 'set of expectations' for teacher leaders that includes specific skills to effectively manage the three 'phases of the career continuum': preparation, induction and ongoing professional development. Zimpher (1988) similarly proposes a model for teacher leadership preparation that involves preparing teachers to engage in instructional leadership with knowledge and skills in five areas: needs assessment, interpersonal and adult development, classroom processes and school effectiveness, instructional supervision and inquiry. Drago-Severson (2007), grounding her idea in a developmental perspective toward adult (i.e. teacher) learning in order to ensure ongoing support for teachers at all stages of career, proposes a four-pillar approach to supporting teachers to become active leaders: teaming, providing leadership roles, collegial inquiry and mentoring. Katzenmeyer and Moller (2009) propose a model for preparing teacher leaders that involves posing a series of questions: 'Who am I?' asks teachers to begin with a personal assessment of their own skills, dispositions and identities; 'Where am I?' urges them toward a deepening understanding of local school and policy context and the process of school change; 'How do I lead?' offers them practice and experiences developing the skills necessary for effective instructional leadership, including coaching/mentoring, curricular knowledge, effective presentation, etc.; and finally, 'What can I do?' guides them to create an action plan to move their school/community in positive directions.

To a certain extent, Katzenmeyer and Moller's questions were reflected in the sequence of courses in the Proyecto Maestría Master's Program; students' very first assignment in their first cohort course was to create and share a literacy journey box and written narrative of their own journey to biliteracy (Fránquiz et al., 2011; Labbo & Field, 1999). Their major assignment in the second cohort course in the fall was to investigate and elaborate a description of their own school campus' services to emergent bilingual students, and to develop an action plan for addressing campus needs in this area. The focus of their third cohort course, 'Teacher

Leadership for Bilingual/ESL', was to develop practical leadership skills. This included hands-on projects in mentoring, writing op-ed pieces for a local Spanish language newspaper, developing a conference-ready professional presentation and creating and presenting professional development sessions that supported meeting their campus goals as identified in the fall semester. Thus, we encouraged teachers to look at themselves, their schools and contexts, and their potential role in change and growth beyond their own classrooms.

There is debate in the field as to why and how teachers assume leadership. Bernhardt (2012) maintains that teachers are motivated by moral commitments to their students, while Forster (1997: 82) contends that leadership is 'a function inherent in their role as teachers and professionals'. Both views conflict with those of Dunlap and Hansen-Thomas (2011) who propose that leadership can be fostered through professional development, a proposition at odds with the view of Barthes (2007) that, since all teachers can lead just as all students can learn, whether or not a teacher assumes a leadership role depends on teacher self-identification and personality. Whether the means to becoming a leader are moral, professional, bureaucratic or interpersonal, these authors agree – and it seems to be a consensus in this field – that teachers taking on leadership is a requisite to improving school and student success.

Teachers of emergent bilingual students becoming leaders

Some work drawing on the teacher leadership preparation literature pays attention to the preparation of teachers who serve emergent bilingual students. Much of this work does not overlap with the advocacy literature. For example, Baecher (2012) conducted a qualitative study about the leadership needs of novice K-12 teachers of English to speakers of other languages (TESOL), concluding that leadership should be taught during certification programs and fostered through professional development. Hoffman *et al.* (2009) conducted a similar study of ELL professional learning teams, while Capitelli (2015) sought to understand ELL teacher leadership needs by investigating an ELL teacher inquiry group. All these qualitative studies adopted a traditional leadership model, and concluded that PLCs and teacher inquiry groups were complex yet useful tools for teacher empowerment and improvement. Perhaps because they did not directly take up the struggle for equity, even though these studies were specific to bilingual contexts, they largely overlooked the specific needs of marginalized bilingual students. For the most part, they seemed to treat leadership development as an end isolated from the social, economic and historic contexts of their students and schools.

Concerns for equity in diverse communities drive some work exploring the potential of teacher leadership (Krovetz & Arriaza, 2006;

Lindsey *et al.*, 2007) although, as Proyecto teachers noted during class discussions about this literature, much of this work seems to be written from the perspective of mainstream, white teachers serving minoritized communities of students, whereas the teachers in Proyecto Maestría were bilingual educators, often marginalized in their schools due to their assignments, and very often members of marginalized communities themselves. There were several exceptions. Chestnut (2015), for example, explored the identity construction of dual language teachers as they navigated grade-level PLCs in a strand dual language program in the Midwest. She noted that these teachers voiced feelings of exclusion, difference and powerlessness in part because they served a largely ELL student population in a school and policy context dominated by the mainstream. With this exception, the mainstream teacher leadership literature often omits bilingual contexts and bilingual educators, and tiptoes around issues of advocacy.

In fact, it could be argued that literature in the leadership field in general falls into these same traps (Rodríguez *et al.*, 2016). There is, however, a small body of work developing advocacy leadership models, including transformative leadership (Shields, 2004, 2010); social justice or advocacy leadership (Khalil & Brown, 2015; Marshall & Oliva, 2006); collective leadership or leadership for community development (Guajardo, 2009); and a call for radical re-centering of equity in leadership standards (Galloway & Ishimaru, 2015).

Shields (2010: 564) distinguishes *transformative leadership* from transactional and transformational leadership. Unlike transactional leadership, whose end is 'a reciprocal transaction', and transformational leadership, which focuses on 'improving organizational qualities, dimensions, and effectiveness', transformative leadership is premised upon a critical analysis of systems of power – both within education and the broader society – and how those systems promote privilege that leads to inequitable school practices. Drawing upon a Freirean model, Shields (2010: 572) frames transformative leadership as a means to challenge these inequities and ultimately 'move through enlightened understanding to action—action to redress wrongs and to ensure that all members of the organization are provided with as level a playing field as possible—not only with respect to access but also with regard to academic, social, and civic outcomes'.

Khalil and Brown (2015) outline 'the Cs' of *advocacy leadership*: cultural competence, communication and a commitment to serving both students and the larger community, factors that emerged as essential in their case studies of educational leaders. They contend that this framework is needed to reorient teaching goals that have been consumed with professionalism metrics and test scores, measures that fail to pursue the end of just and equitable education or even recognize the diversity of needs of urban students. Along similar lines, Marshall and Oliva (2006: 4) propose a *social justice leadership* framework that promotes 'the strategies, *revolutionary* ones in some contexts, for rethinking school practices to better meet diverse students' needs and the language to translate intellectual concepts into practice and experiential understanding'. They aim to create caring communities based on democratic ideals and antiracist curricula as a means to challenging dominant structures that are oppressive.

Moving even closer toward centering (or re-centering) standards for leadership around social justice concerns, Galloway and Ishimaru (2015) argue that a radical shift in national leadership standards has the potential to change leader preparation and professional development, leadership policy and practice, and ultimately the persistent disparities in schools. They have created 10 practices for equitable leadership guided by three ideological drivers that they contend should structure and measure leadership preparation programs, thereby refocusing social justice work from the practice of individuals to the practice of institutions as schools can be checked against these measures. The leadership practices span the range from individualistic to community oriented, involving both reflective exercises such as recognizing one's ideological and practical biases and actionable steps that involve resource allocation, collaboration with families, hiring decisions and influencing local social contexts. These practices represent a shift in thinking about school issues, such as how disparities are understood, the structure of leadership and data-driven decision-making, both in terms of the focus and measures of data collected and the grounding principles upon which data are brought into decisions. Galloway and Ishimaru (2015) offer these tools as a way to advance the conversation about what equity-centered leadership practice looks like and how it might be achieved.

Guajardo and Garcia (2016), in contrast, move away from any conversation about standards or frameworks. Instead, they connect the health of a school to the health of its surrounding community, claiming that the values, culture, practice and well-being of one necessarily reflect that of the other. As such, they propose a *community development framework* that integrates the community context into school leadership development. Drawing upon Yosso's (2005) community cultural wealth model and Freire's (2000) call for leadership work to begin with a 'radical shift in consciousness' (Guajardo & Garcia, 2016: 72), Guajardo and Garcia's (2016: 73) community development framework questions the assumptions that have previously guided educational decisions. They opt for a grassroots approach that is centered around knowing and interacting with the local community wherein leadership becomes 'an act of caring, guided by a spirit of love and a deep commitment to human dignity, equity, and respect'.

This framework emerges from Guajardo's (2009) earlier work in which he argues that leaders are both a reflection of their social contexts and actors who work to change and shape those contexts. He envisions leaders as those who 'foster pedagogical conditions that create change. The change process is a necessary outcome in this transaction. This change is guided by actors who are committed to the common good and are working to improve the human condition' (Guajardo, 2009: 71). Accordingly, this model for leadership is not oriented around the individual but rather includes groups and communities as actors who work together in an ongoing process of transforming power relations into more equitable and just forms.

While these different scholars are proposing a wide range of models, all would agree that approaches to leadership that fail to explicitly acknowledge the structures of power or directly address issues of equity ultimately fail to address quality in education (Galloway & Ishimaru, 2015). For educational leaders to truly strive toward academic success for all students, issues of marginalization, social justice, inclusivity, equity and transformative practices must be incorporated into all educational approaches (Shields, 2004). In fact, Lerma *et al.* (2013) argue that 'traditional' (mainstream) leadership models are merely a means to protect the privileges and status of dominant-culture students; whereas advocacy leadership models, while still less developed, have as their essential purpose to advocate for more opportunities for marginalized students and to challenge systems of oppression. Advocacy leadership, like advocacy/activist teaching, is based on critical frameworks and directly addresses issues of marginalization in schooling – but, as in most of the research in the leadership field, advocacy leadership models primarily focus on principals and administrators as leaders, paying far less attention to teachers.

Schoolwide Leadership for Emergent Bilingual Learners

A few studies focused on the qualities of school leadership that best serve emergent bilingual students in schools (Ascenzi-Moreno *et al.*, 2016; Brooks *et al.*, 2010; Menken & Solorza, 2015). Similar to the advocacy leadership models highlighted above, these studies primarily focused on principals and administrators as leaders, mentioning teachers only as participants in schoolwide leadership's distributed networks or PLCs. However, given that they did address the roles of teachers within schoolwide leadership structures, and given their specific focus on bilingual learners, their findings were relevant to this review of research on bilingual teacher leadership.

Brooks *et al.* (2010), for example, explored the work of principals who shifted focus from superficial aspects of a school's supports for emergent bilinguals such as translated signage, to deeper discourses about relations of power though social justice-focused PLCs. Given the greater success of emergent bilingual students in schools with an explicit focus on social justice among faculty, the authors shared insights on supporting school leadership to make this transformation to deeper discourses.

Along these same lines, one of the key findings in Ascenzi-Moreno *et al.*'s (2016) research was that strong leadership for emergent bilingual students becomes less hierarchical and more collaborative, in which principals share responsibility with unofficial leaders at a school, including teachers with particular expertise in bilingual or ESL education. These authors also found that as principals gained more knowledge about language acquisition and bilingualism, they shifted their schools' policies and their own ideologies in ways that favored emergent bilingual learners' success. Menken and Solorza (2015) also found that principals with a strong foundation in language acquisition and bilingualism ran more successful programs for emergent bilingual students. They found that these principals were more consistent about preserving and expanding bilingual services at their schools and less susceptible to the pressures of monolingual and monoglossic high-stakes standardized testing, than were principals who were not as well-grounded in foundations of language education.

Bilingual Teacher Leadership

Our goal in this review has been to uncover and describe scholarship that – like the Proyecto Maestría Teacher Leadership Collaborative – lies at the nexus of *teacher* leadership, advocacy/activism and bilingual education. While there is little work to date that intersects all three of these areas, some recent work does exist.

Bilingual teachers as language policymakers

First, there is a growing field that explores the agency of bilingual (and ESL) teachers in the face of policy mandates. Faced with complex and sometimes contradictory policy mandates, individual teachers, along with educators at all levels, have the potential to serve as buffers or conduits by supporting or undermining the implementation of policies in education (Hornberger & Johnson, 2007; Menken & García, 2010; Palmer, 2011; Valdiviezo, 2009; Varghese & Stritikus, 2005).

Teachers' own complex sets of beliefs, as embodied in their decision-making about curriculum and pedagogy, and questions such as language of instruction, can drive the ultimate outcomes of policy implementation efforts and can greatly influence the opportunities for learning of students in their classrooms (Henderson & Palmer, 2015; Menken & García, 2010; Palmer *et al.*, 2015b). Dubetz and de Jong's (2011) literature review of bilingual teacher advocacy articulates several ways in which bilingual teachers, in the current political context, find themselves advocating for their emergent bilingual students. Their definition of bilingual teacher advocacy encompasses work that bilingual teachers carry out *within* their classrooms, in terms of their choices of curriculum, pedagogy and language; and *beyond* their classrooms, as they support other teachers' learning or open spaces for bilingual parent voices. Although researchers in this area do not usually refer to teachers' agentic actions as *leadership per se*, they are essentially naming actions that fulfill the definition, involving teachers in work that moves – and often has repercussions – beyond their classrooms.

Models of bilingual teacher leadership

Wiemelt and Welton (2015), who conducted a qualitative study of a successful schoolwide implementation of bilingual teacher leadership, or what they termed *Liderazgo* ('leadership' in Spanish), outline three values central to *Liderazgo*: (a) valuing bilingualism and biculturalism; (b) centering the experiential knowledge of students and families; and (c) caring for students' whole person. These central values are framed from a critical perspective; they all challenge and replace deficit models, Euro-centric curriculum and marginalizing identities. The larger purpose of *Liderazgo* as they describe it is to address the specific needs of bilingual students through teacher advocacy.

Some teacher education and professional development programs have sought to promote just these qualities with the end of creating bilingual teacher leaders. One example, documented by Holmes and Herrera (2009), was a teacher education program that sought to foster culturally responsive pedagogy and leadership skills for its predominantly bilingual, Latinx preservice teachers. This was achieved through critical reflection on social, political and economic themes coupled with students incorporating their personal cultural, linguistic and ethnic backgrounds into the classroom. Such foci were intended to create an open community space wherein students could critically analyze their own histories and biases as well as the systems of injustice and oppression around them.

Another program that fostered bilingual teacher leadership, Programa CRIAR, was documented by Palmer *et al.* (2014b) in a case study that investigated how a graduate-level master's degree program for practicing bilingual education teachers could promote critical consciousness and identification as teacher advocates. Using a model of transformative leadership, this master's program sought to develop a sense of morally oriented responsibility in teachers for the well-being of their marginalized students, a characteristic that would lead these teachers to then take ownership for advocating for change and equitable access to education. By creating 'cultural spaces' (Palmer *et al.*, 2014b), the program encouraged teachers to embrace leadership roles and develop critical consciousness as a means not only of becoming increasingly aware of systems of power and oppression but also of wanting to take action to challenge them.

Both of these programs appeared to demonstrate success in developing bilingual teacher leadership; another program with similar intentions (Dantas-Whitney & Dugan Waldschmidt, 2009) was less successful in achieving these outcomes despite having similar theoretical orientations and goals. Unfortunately, even at the end of the program, the study found that the preservice teachers who participated failed to move beyond reductionist views of bilingual education and students. Teacher participants evidently retained a view of teaching and language as apolitical and neutral, only superficially acknowledged cultural issues and maintained contradictory attitudes about ESOL/bilingual education such as a professed respect for multiculturalism, while simultaneously harboring deficit views about their students. Not surprisingly, the authors acknowledged that structural problems with the program did not allow students the necessary opportunities to connect and reflect in a cohesive community, which ultimately led to students' inability to fully embrace or understand social justice pedagogy or issues of culturally relevant teaching.

Thus, in the instances we located of programs or projects already working to develop a conception of bilingual teacher leadership from a critical framework, there was success when the programs were able to build safe communities, break down barriers to engagement for all participants and support teachers to engage in authentic caring with the families and communities they serve.

There is still precious little research, however, that directly explores questions of leadership for bilingual educators working in culturally and linguistically diverse schooling contexts. Combining what we know about strong bilingual instruction, about strong leadership and its importance for successful bilingual programs and about the ways in which critically aware teachers and leaders can support advocacy for bilingual students and families, what are the key characteristics and requirements of successful bilingual teacher leaders and what do they contribute to schools and students' lives? What, essentially, makes for powerful and empowering bilingual teacher leadership?

In the following chapters, I will draw on data from the 53 participants in Proyecto Maestría's master's level professional development project to further develop this framework. Based on these teacher-leaders' experiences, what does it mean to be a bilingual teacher leader? What are the key elements in a program that can successfully support the development of leadership identities for empowerment for bilingual teachers? and what are the characteristics of successful and critically engaged bilingual teacher leaders?

3 Developing Teacher Agency and Identity in Bilingual/Bicultural Educational Contexts: Critical Pedagogies for Hope and Transformation

Intuitivamente la mayor parte de nosotros lo sabemos y lo hemos sabido por mucho tiempo, nos lo decía nuestro instinto, pero muchas veces carecíamos de la palabra, del discurso, del contexto histórico para definirlo. *[Intuitively the majority of us know it, and we have known it for a long time, our instincts have told us, but many times we lacked the word, the discourse, the historical context to define it.]* (Daniel, Cohort 4, on Leadership)

'Agency' has been consistently framed as in tension with 'structure' (Bourdieu, 1991; Foucault, 1995; Holland *et al.*, 1998). Some theorists have appeared to favor a structural – and thus somewhat more deterministic – understanding of the ways in which humans shape their social worlds, leaving little room for individuals or groups of people to assert themselves against the realities of bureaucratic, governmental or economic forces (Bowles & Gintis, 2002; Foucault, 1995). In our present moment, this has profound significance given the ways that a range of neoliberal top-down reforms in education – e.g. widespread high-stakes standardized testing for school and teacher 'accountability', privatization through vouchers or charters of public schooling – have asserted structural forces in new and impactful ways into classrooms, schools and districts. Likewise, structural forces of inequality have asserted themselves into immigrant and bi(multi) lingual communities in unprecedented ways. Teachers feel the pressures of these structural influences, and often assert that in their view these pressures, both those within educational systems and those in the communities that surround their schools, run counter to the best educational interests of marginalized or bilingual students and communities.

On the other hand, Holland *et al.* (1998) and others (Nieto, 2013; Palmer & Martínez, 2013; Urrieta, 2009) assert the prominence of agency in the equation, in a 'tension-filled' (Bakhtin, 1998: 279) but potentially more balanced dialogue with structure. The Proyecto Maestría Master's Degree Program was grounded in the hope-filled assumption that within educational spaces, there is *always* agency. This is a theory of hope (Freire, 2000; Freire & Freire, 1994): hope in the individual and in communities, operating to counter structural inequalities and oppression. As Freire (2000: 85) explains, 'the point of departure must always be with men and women in the "here and now," which constitutes the situation within which they are submerged, from which they emerge, and in which they intervene'. For Freire (2000: 88), it is essential to the definition of humanity to act upon our structural world and to transform it: 'To exist, humanly, is to *name* the world, to change it'. Because this is a story of hope and of the power of teachers to act upon the world, Bakhtin's and Freire's conceptions of agency and praxis undergird this analysis.

Using the experiences of the Proyecto teachers as windows, I have tried to better understand the kinds of power that teachers in bilingual spaces can gather and assert, and the processes/mechanisms by which they do so, in the face of structural (institutional, political, interpersonal, socioeconomic, etc.) barriers. I variously refer to this as 'teacher agency', to align myself with critical conceptions of teachers' efforts within the structural organizations of schooling and to support the work of teachers as empowered actors and changers (Palmer & Martínez, 2013; Urrieta, 2009), and 'teacher leadership', to call to mind the under-theorized but definitely powerful potential of teachers to be and become leaders in their spaces (Ackerman & Mackenzie, 2007; Barthes, 2007; Katzenmeyer & Moller, 2009; York-Barr & Duke, 2004).

Bakhtinian Dialogue and Identity Development

At a recruitment meeting for our first grant-supported cohort in fall 2007, a pilot-year participant described to an audience of bilingual education teachers the feeling of learning a new word: 'hegemony'. He talked about having that new word roll around in his mouth and begin to roll off his tongue, and the way in which that word provided him with a label for the experience of marginalization he'd lived with all his life. The teacher described the power of naming, and of being pulled into a community of shared language and negotiated meanings for powerful ideas; he described what I think is best understood as Mikhail Bakhtin's 'dialogue'. This teacher's experience with Bakhtinian dialogue was typical of participants during the program.

Another pilot-year participant, a kindergarten teacher with an 'integrated' transitional bilingual class in which half of her students came from English-speaking homes, while the other half spoke Spanish at home, expressed marvel after having read Crawford's (2004) textbook chapter on dual language education, explaining to me in office hours, 'This is exactly what I've been doing! It has a name! My grade level colleagues are telling me I'm wrong [to teach my English and Spanish speaking students together in both languages] ... but the book says this is a good practice, just like I've always known!' (Palmer *et al.*, 2006).

One participant from Central America explained the power that the funds of knowledge work of Luis Moll *et al.* (1992) had in transforming her perspectives of her young Tejanx students, due to the synergy of the readings, learning tasks, discussions and ongoing dialogue she'd had with cohort classmates about their own lives and life histories. Now, she felt she had the language, and the respect, to better understand and support her students' home and community cultural wealth (Yosso, 2005; more on this example in Chapter 6).

Bakhtin (1998) might have argued that these teachers were appropriating 'alien' words, transforming those words, forcefully shaping those words to serve their own individual and collective needs:

> The word does not exist in a neutral and impersonal language...but rather it exists in other people's intentions: it is from there that one must take the word, and make it one's own. (Bakhtin, 1998: 294)

As they did so, they were reshaping their own individuality, their own place in the various worlds they inhabited, and they were asserting a powerful agency because:

> Not all words for just anyone submit equally easily to this appropriation, to this seizure and transformation into private property: many words stubbornly resist, others remain alien, sound foreign in the mouth of the one who appropriated them and who now speaks them... (Bakhtin, 1998: 294)

Bakhtin developed a philosophy that related language to life and words to the objects to which they 'point', grounded entirely in dialogue. Interaction through language(s) in society, according to Bakhtin, shapes who we are and how we perceive both ourselves and the worlds in which we live. Dialogue shapes and has the potential to transform our identities. We can imagine individuals swimming in a sea of language, grabbing at the water all around them and changing it with their touch as they go – as much a part of the water as separate from it.

Bakhtin's definition of language, the water in which we swim, is broad enough to include all engagements of human communication. According to Bakhtin, we have many different discourses, or different languages that we use in different ways and for different purposes, throughout our days and lives; we may use them separately, or we may merge them in 'hybrid' utterances. These different discourses come together in a tension-filled 'heteroglossia', the multilingual, multidialectal expressions of human experience. Heteroglossia is 'tension-filled' (Bakhtin, 1998: 279) because of the constant tension between the different discourses – they do not sit comfortably together. Bakhtin describes the constant push/pull between centrifugal and centripetal forces. On the one hand are the disunifying centrifugal forces that tend toward diversity – the heteroglossic, 'creative, style-shaping' constant evolution of the word (Bakhtin, 1998: 271). Heteroglossia are the forces of ongoing language variation, a natural part of living languages. Different language varieties are of course valued differently within and between societies, as 'language is not a neutral medium' (Bakhtin, 1998: 294) and inequity is inevitable, but dialogue in written and oral language inherently tends toward this messy overlapping multivocal chaos; this tendency appears to be what most interests Bakhtin about language. It is also what most interests me about education and the kinds of dialogue we can begin in classrooms, and it is what seems to have resulted from the bringing together of many bilingual teachers in Proyecto Maestría classes.

At the same time, there are also 'centripetal forces' pushing toward uniformity, monoglossia, domination and standardization in our language and semiotic practices. We see these forces so clearly in Texas education systems, wrought with standardized curriculum and high-stakes multiple-choice standardized examinations for every student at every grade level. It is particularly fierce for bilingual students, who are so often classified as 'at risk' and whose inherent heteroglossia tends to instill fear in administrators that their scores on monoglossic tests might be too low (Palmer & Snodgrass-Rangel, 2011; Valenzuela, 2005). Thus, bilingual teachers are very often faced with even more rigid curricular and instructional mandates, restrictions on language use and practices, and monitoring practices than their monolingual counterparts (Palmer & Snodgrass-Rangel, 2011).

The struggle against monoglossic ideologies came up repeatedly in Proyecto teacher conversations, both in class and online. It seemed at times as though every topic eventually led back to the question, 'but how can we accomplish this when we're mandated to…?' The teachers were struggling in what Bakhtin termed the 'zone of contact' between the *authoritative discourses* of curriculum and accountability in their districts, and the *internally persuasive discourses* they were developing an ear and a heart for in their courses: humanizing pedagogies, funds of knowledge, direct engagement with the languages and cultures of the children who formed their classroom communities. The struggle for the authority to use what are often marginalized language practices – the struggle to be heard and listened to when one uses these in official spaces – is illuminated in this distinction between *authoritative* and *internally persuasive* discourses. Bakhtin defines the 'authoritative word' as:

> ... the word of the fathers. Its authority was already acknowledged in the past. It is a prior discourse. It is therefore not a question of choosing it among other possible discourses that are its equal. It is given [its sounds] in lofty spheres, not those of familiar contact... (Bakhtin, 1998: 342–343)

The *authoritative discourses* most relevant to this situation are the 'official' and 'standard' registers, dialects or languages: English, the all-important 'academic language' that remains poorly defined but highly touted in English as a second language (ESL) and bilingual education schooling spaces (Valdés, 2004), and standard registers of Spanish that systematically undervalue Texas regional language practices (Martínez *et al.*, 2015; McCollum, 1999). Authoritative discourses in Texas schools also include the accountability conversations that define success as high standardized test scores, that define bilingual parents as lacking the resources to support their children in school and that define teachers' work as pushing underperforming kids into categories of higher test-score performance. Authoritative discourses dominate in many teacher planning meetings, staff meetings and official schooling spaces. Meanwhile, as teachers struggle to develop their own ideologies about teaching and learning, language and culture, leadership and advocacy, they come into contact with *internally persuasive* discourses: the heteroglossic voices of their own local communities, the wide range of voices in the readings for their classes, the words of their cohort classmates, which are compelling – internally – for their ring of truth and the match with their own experiences.

Thankfully, the push toward monoglossia according to Bakhtin, though powerful and inexorable, will never fully succeed. This is due to both individual *agency* as we appropriate words from all kinds of sources and shape them for our own ends, and the inherent heteroglossic nature of language. Change and variation will happen in living languages regardless of society's efforts to curb them:

> The centripetal forces of the life of language, embodied in a 'unitary language,' operate in the midst of heteroglossia... stratification and heteroglossia widen and deepen as long as language is alive and developing. Alongside the centripetal forces, the centrifugal forces of language carry on their uninterrupted work; alongside verbal-ideological centralization and unification, the uninterrupted processes of decentralization and disunification go forward. (Bakhtin, 1998: 271–272)

Bakhtin's description therefore makes an explicit space for emergent bilingual students and their teachers engaging in the process of becoming bi(multi)lingual in school, and drawing on everyday language practices in the official space of the classroom even as they carry out standardized tasks within rigid public school structures (Figure 3.1).

These theoretical constructs serve as useful tools for my analysis of the ongoing work of bilingual teachers to understand the tensions inherent in their own daily practices and make sense out of their own attempts at leadership. As they carry out their daily life and work within the borderlands, the 'contact zones' (Pratt, 1999) both real and metaphoric of Texas public school classrooms, bilingual teachers must take a stand in that tension-ridden space. These *internally persuasive* discourses are

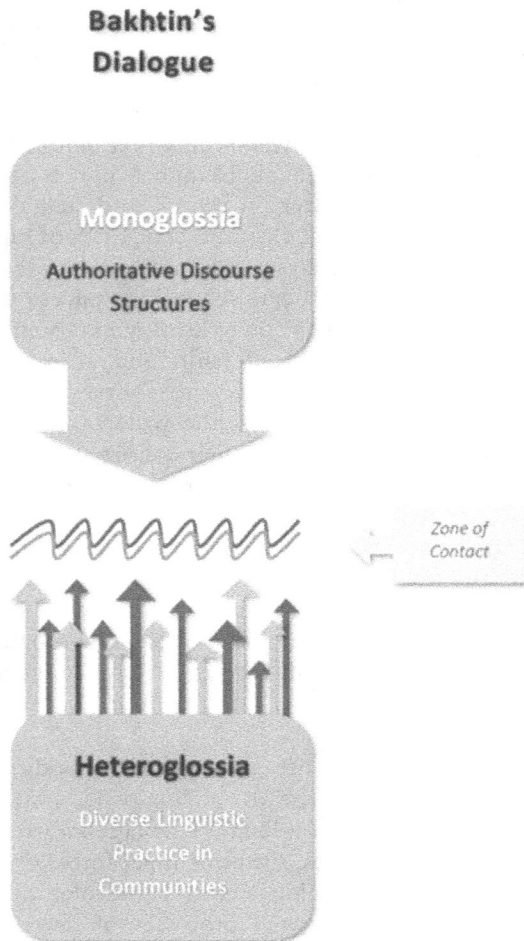

Figure 3.1 Monoglossia vs. heteroglossia in Bakhtin's Dialogue

not something they can ignore; neither can they ignore authority. They must account for the linguistic and cultural heteroglossia of their and their students' meaning-making processes, at the same time and in the same spaces where they must teach rigid mandated curriculum and ensure students master standard registers of language. In taking a stand, they both shape their own identities and become advocates for their students – in a hope-filled, ongoing *lucha*, or struggle.

Bakhtin's theory helps me deepen my understanding of these dynamics. Other researchers in education, looking at teacher identities and teacher communities, have turned to Bakhtin for theoretical tools for analysis. I have selected a sampling in order to further illustrate the applicability of these ideas to my exploration of bilingual teacher leadership/agency.

Menard-Warwick (2014) draws on Bakhtinian theory to explore the identities of English teachers in two very different Pacific coastal contexts: a small city in northern Chile and a city in California, USA. Menard-Warwick (2014: 33) explains Bakhtin's theory of identity construction through language in this way: 'there is a communism to language that has nothing to do with Stalinism, and it is through this communism that we construct our identities within the historical moment we inhabit'. Menard-Warwick's teachers, both Chilean and Californian, construct identities within their specific contexts that are constantly in dialogue with the ideologies about language within which they live.

Ball and Freedman (2004) illustrate Bakhtinian dialogue and Bakhtin's conception of *ideological becoming* among educators and education researchers across several contexts. They propose that *ideological becoming* implies three things for educators: that we must 'take diversity seriously and see how it can be a resource'; that we must 'seek to understand the [ongoing] mechanisms of growth and change'; and that we must 'seek to understand peoples' struggles to creatively manage those tensions and conflicts that are critical to learning' (Ball & Freedman, 2004: 9). In other words, Bakhtin encourages us to take an assets-based approach to diversity, and to understand learning as change that emerges from tension – of which there is plenty in diverse classrooms.

Going beyond teachers to immigrant adults, Vitanova (2010) also draws on Bakhtin's theories around identity construction as she examines the work of immigrant couples in the United States as they narratively construct themselves and one another in their second language (English) during life-history interviews with her. Arguing that narratives are inherently dialogic, Vitanova begins with Sarup's (1996 as discussed in Vitanova, 2010: 10) definition of identity as 'whatever story we tell about ourselves and the story others tell about us'. Bakhtin, she argues, offers more space for agency than many other theorists, in that Bakhtin's conception of dialogism consistently places the self and the other/society in contact – and in tension – with one another.

According to Bakhtin, discourse is a social event. The self is constantly defined within conflict-ridden dialogue as we each grapple with the 'struggle against various kinds and degrees of authority' (Bakhtin, 1998: 345). Bakhtin (1998: 345) refers to this as the 'zone of contact' between different words, 'half-ours, half someone else's'. This theoretical framework is echoed in Borderlands theories (Anzaldúa, 1987), pushing for not just a negotiation of linguistic or cultural practices that historically emerged from 'separate' communities but for the erasure of boundaries as individuals' authoring strives to define and engage the heteroglossia of voices in their actual contexts.

The university, the public school, the cohort, the family, the community, their own students and their families – these are all discourses in dialogue surrounding the Proyecto Maestría teachers. As they author themselves as leaders, drawing on these voices that surround them, their tendency is to consistently engage multiple discourses – to erase boundaries and leverage the authority or *persuasiveness* of one set of discourses within another. In so doing, they demonstrate that individuals operating as they are within such rich *heteroglossia* have and can assert tremendous agency. It is through asserting agency that they come into their power as leaders, teachers and members of their various communities. In coming into an awareness of their agency, teachers come to embrace their various selves: cultural/linguistic, professional, advocate, leader. It is, of course, an ongoing and conflict-ridden process.

Freire, Praxis and Proyecto Maestría as Problem-Posing Education

While Bakhtin's robust theory of the interrelation of language and identity offers tools to explore the teachers' experiences and the co-construction of their various identities in and beyond graduate school, I must turn to a Freirean lens to further develop an understanding of the relationship of this educational experience to the teachers' development of critical consciousness and the drive to activate for change in society – essentially, to what was consistently the teachers' central perception of their purpose in embracing leadership.

Freire, and the tradition of critical pedagogy that emerged from his and others' (e.g. Darder *et al.*, 2003; Giroux, 2003; Greene, 1995) transnational work in critical literacy education, informed this project in very direct ways. The teachers read Freire in my class; they read other critical educational theorists throughout their program beginning on the first day, and they experienced what Freire would term a 'problem-posing education' (to the best of our ability, of course). In many cases, the teachers directly carried Freire's ideas with them into their schools, communities and classrooms.

The magic of Paolo Freire's work is that it is very intuitive; it has a powerful ring of truth to anyone who has experienced the transformation of which he speaks, anyone who has opened their eyes to their own oppression and/or their own role in oppressing, and been forever changed by the experience. His seminal book, *Pedagogy of the Oppressed* (Freire, 2000), originally published in Portuguese in 1968, has sold over 750,000 copies worldwide. People around the world have read Freire, sometimes at great personal risk (Macedo, 2000). The impacts of Freire's particular call to action are immeasurable. Yet, in the United States, his work is still surprisingly unknown, even by educators in marginalized communities. Introducing the teachers to Freire's ideas quickly led into profound conversations about oppression and liberation, about the ultimate purposes of public education and about the links between past, present and future.

In Chapter 5 'Bilingual Teacher Leaders are Reflexive Practitioners', I will elaborate further on the teachers' direct application/appropriation of Freire and other theorists presented to them during their master's coursework for their own work as teachers of Latinx bilingual children and advocates for change in their school communities. In what follows here, I will explore my own understandings of Freire's most essential theoretical constructs as they apply to my analysis of the teachers' development of bilingual teacher leadership and advocate identities through and beyond their master's program.

In terms of his role in the development of a theoretical and practical grounding for critical pedagogy, Freire is in good company alongside several other radical scholars, theorists and educators of the 20th century. These include John Dewey (1938) the founder of the progressive educational movement in the United States; Myles Horton *et al.* (1990b) who founded the Highlander Folk School – often described as the spark that ignited the US Civil Rights Movement; Herbert Kohl (1994, 2003) whose Open Schools Movement sought to transform US public schooling; Maxine Greene (1995) the 'mother of aesthetic education'; and radical educator Ivan Illich (1971, 1992), among others. Giroux (2003) asserts that the Frankfurt School with its early 20th-century critique of instrumental reason served to begin educational theorists on the path toward theoretical grounding for the critical perspectives required for a radical liberatory mission for education. Even as Freire developed his ideas independently in Brazil in the middle of the 20th century, similar movements were emerging throughout the world with tremendous alignment (Darder *et al.*, 2003). The field of critical pedagogy continues to develop and evolve; at its core are the fundamental assertions that oppression pervades in society, and education can serve as a tool for liberation (Darder *et al.*, 2003; Duncan-Andrade & Morrell, 2008). Although I have been inspired by all of these educators and often turn to them for needed inspiration, for my purposes here, Freire's own unique fusion of ideas offers adequate theoretical tools to support a deepened understanding of bilingual teacher leadership for hope and change.

Humanizing pedagogies

Freire juxtaposes 'humanization' and 'dehumanization' on the very first page of his foundational text *Pedagogy of the Oppressed*, immediately offering an extremely hope-filled vision:

> While both humanization and dehumanization are real alternatives, only the first is the people's vocation. This vocation is constantly negated, yet it is affirmed by that very negation. It is thwarted by injustice, exploitation, oppression, and the violence of the oppressors; it is affirmed by the yearning of the oppressed for freedom and justice, and by their struggle to recover their lost humanity. (Freire, 2000: 43)

Freire (2000: 44) asserts that dehumanization, although 'a concrete historical fact', is a 'distortion' of the human endeavor. Because of this, he argues, 'sooner or later being less human leads the oppressed to struggle against those who made them so'. He lays the power, and the responsibility, of liberation in the hands of the oppressed: 'only power that springs from the weakness of the oppressed will be sufficiently strong to free both' (Freire, 2000: 44). He further defines freedom as the 'quest for human completion', which although challenging and frightening especially at first, when the oppressed are accustomed to following the structures and rules of the oppressor, is deeply satisfying once embraced. Freedom, however, is never fully attained, but rather 'must be pursued constantly and responsibly' (Freire, 2000: 47). Thus, in a few pages of inspiring prose, Freire (2000: 44) places the power of the liberation of society in the hands of the oppressed and asserts that this struggle for freedom and the 'completion' of their whole human selves is no less than the 'great humanistic and historical task of the oppressed: to liberate themselves and their oppressors as well'. What does this conception of the process of liberation and humanization mean for bilingual teachers, working with marginalized students, within often obviously oppressive public education structures?

Finally, one of the 'gravest obstacles to the achievement of liberation' is the oppressed losing hope in its possibility: since 'humankind produce social reality', Freire (2000: 51) argues that we are charged with 'transforming that reality', and quite simply, losing hope is not an option. Hope is, as Freire explained, an 'ontological need'. It is 'an existential, concrete imperative' (Freire & Freire, 1994: 8). This has profound implications for the work – and the outlook – of teachers (and parents and students) in underfunded, under-resourced public schools serving largely minoritized emergent bilingual children, where hope can sometimes seem scarce.

Dialogue

Freire's understanding of the relationship between self and society is embedded within this struggle: he describes a 'dialectical relationship between the subjective and the objective', the self and the other, the oppressed and the oppressor, which actually makes possible a critical confrontation with reality, the tension between reflection and action that he terms *praxis*. This reflection–action is not possible for a person alone, but depends upon a collective larger than the self. The oppressed must engage in dialogue with the oppressor in order to achieve liberation. The violence of oppression, of silencing and dehumanizing the oppressed, must be ended in order to reach this goal. Dialogue is, quite literally and quite practically, expressing one's humanity directly to one's oppressor. It is the merging of verbal reflection and ongoing collective action. Violence, for Freire, cannot lead to liberation; violent 'overthrow' would only lead the oppressed to turn into oppressors themselves, and the cycle would continue.

Thus, for Freire, the fusion of reflection and action into *praxis*, which the oppressed must come together to engage in through *dialogue* with the oppressor, is ultimately humanizing for themselves and their oppressors... and preparing the oppressed for this enormous responsibility is the purpose of education.

Moraes (1996: 122), who similar to this project pulled together Bakhtin with Freire to propose a 'dialogic-critical pedagogy' for bilingual education, proposed moving bilingual education 'from a monologic into a dialogic existence'. She pushed educators to consider the implications of Freire's dialogism for creating learning spaces that actually engage bilingual students in learning grounded in their own experiences of language and culture: learning spaces that push students and teachers to consider the tensions between oppressor and oppressed in all their manifestations, and to use the space of the bilingual classroom to work toward liberation. She argued that a dialogic bilingual education would necessarily fuse language and culture, and would insist upon teachers not only respecting but actually 'understanding their students in light of the community in which they live' (Moraes, 1996: 123). At the same time, Moraes drew on critical pedagogy, posing important questions about current (alienating) regimes of curriculum and assessment for bilingual children. What would a *humanizing* bilingual education look like, she wonders? Like Moraes, I will fuse Bakhtin's dialogue with Freire's praxis, drawing on each theorist to craft something new.

Problem-posing education

Establishing the central importance of dialogue, Freire goes on to describe the 'narration sickness' that has plagued formal education spaces, such that they have in fact endeavored to exactly the opposite purpose: to deaden learners to the reality of their oppression, to turn them into submissive workers, to dehumanize. Although he is of course not directly referring to Texas public education systems, it almost seems as if he is when he describes what happens in a typical oppressive classroom:

> The teacher talks about reality as if it were motionless, static, compartmentalized, and predictable. Or else he expounds on a topic completely alien to the existential experience of the students. His task is to 'fill' the students with the contents of his narration... words are emptied of their concreteness and become a hollow, alienated and alienating verbosity. (Freire, 2000: 71)

He calls this depositing of information into students the 'banking' concept of education (Freire, 2000: 72). Teachers in Texas public schools recognize this as the 'delivery' of the mandated state curriculum, often through use of a school district's mandated materials, to prepare students for mandated high-stakes standardized tests. Lessons in this curriculum are pre-written, sometimes scripted, purportedly to support teachers in their work, and certainly to 'obviate thinking' (Freire, 2000: 76). Miguel, a member of the fifth cohort, explained this link himself in his posted reflection to his classmates after having read three chapters of Freire's *Pedagogy of the Oppressed* early in the fall semester of his program year:

> Banking education is a practice that still exists in many classrooms. According to this approach, students are merely empty vessels in which teachers just have to deposit knowledge. Teachers are the subjects (experts) of education and students are the objects (do not know anything) of such education. Such practice deprives students from innovation, creativity, and transformation for they are only docile listeners and not critical thinkers...I see this practice every year in many students coming to my classroom. Such students are used to be[ing] told what to do in reading and what to read, math is just memorization of facts, and students are always prompted what to write about. They do not feel responsible for their education, they do not take ownership of their learning, they are not independent, and they have not become critical thinkers yet. As mentioned in chapter three, banking education exists where there is absence of dialogue and just narration. This practice is obvious where students do not participate in conversations with the teacher and classmates in whole, and small group conversations and inquiry. If we want for our students to take

ownership of their education, they need to be in a constant conversation and reflection about their learning. Freire mentions in chapter three that the difference between animals and ourselves is that we are able to re-present and reflect about the world around us. This is going to be the challenge of my classroom this school year.

As Miguel explained, Freire (2000: 79) contrasts 'banking' education with what he calls 'problem-posing' education, offering a beautiful and concise expression of the human imperative to learn:

> For apart from inquiry, apart from the praxis, individuals cannot be truly human. Knowledge emerges only through invention and re-invention, through the restless, impatient, continuing, hopeful inquiry human beings pursue in the world, with the world, and with each other. (Freire, 2000: 72)

As teachers begin to see through the system that they have served, to label it 'banking' education, to understand it as governed by *authoritative discourses* and to envision alternatives, they re-author their understanding of their own task, both as learners in their graduate courses and as educators in their own classrooms. They become 'critical co-investigators in dialogue' (Freire, 2000: 81). They begin to see their own work as going far beyond helping their students to 'read the word'. Rather, they learn to 'name the world, to change it', and they move to help their students do the same. In Bakhtin's terms, they begin to pay closer attention to *internally persuasive* discourses, to engage more fully with the heteroglossia of their classroom community.

For Freire, *dialogue* that transforms the world cannot exist without four key ingredients: love, humility, faith in humankind and hope. Like Bakhtin, Freire argues that our world is exceedingly complicated, that any attempt to reduce reality to comprehensible bites of information is inevitably false and misleading and that endeavoring to understand the true complexity of reality requires an acknowledgment of the eternal 'incompleteness' of humankind. Education is the process of continuously endeavoring to understand the world, through continuously developing our understanding of the words that we use to characterize and to transform it. As we grow to understand the world, at the same time we endeavor to transform it, to liberate the oppressed – through a combination of love, humility, faith and hope. The process never ends.

The process for teachers of shifting their understanding of their own roles in the classroom from transmitter of information to problem-poser and co-investigator, and embracing the liberatory power of education and the oppressive nature of both society and the structures of schooling, Freire refers to as *conscientizão* (in the original Portuguese), or conscientization.

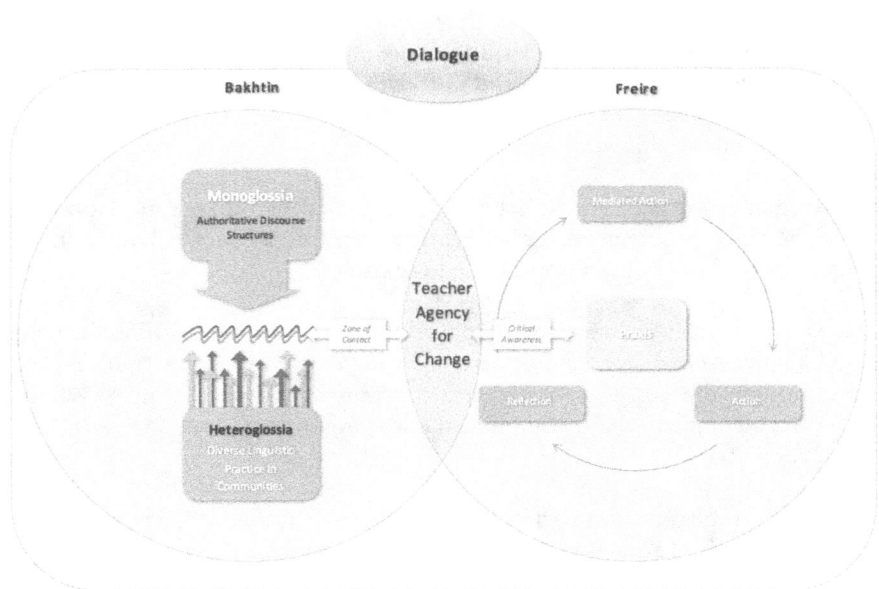

Figure 3.2 Bringing Together Bakhtinian and Freirean Dialogue

This experience is precisely the character of transformation that the teachers repeatedly referenced in reflections, interviews, group conversations, etc. This awakening to political clarity was key to their urgency to develop leadership skills: they wanted to embrace empowerment for themselves and their students/parents/communities in order to help transform their students' (and the larger) world.

I would assert that through their day-to-day praxis, the teachers are in fact accomplishing this, giving us reason to hope that schools can be sites for pedagogies of hope and change. In the coming chapters, I will use the teachers' own words and practices to explore several dimensions of this praxis/dialogue: critical reflection as action in the classroom; co-construction of cultural/linguistic identities as they endeavor to build rapport and solidarity with their students and families; engaging in collective professional work and building a professional community of practice; and explicitly authoring themselves as activists, advocates and agents of change (Figure 3.2).

This is what I (and they) will define as bilingual teacher leadership.

4 The Proyecto Maestría Program and the Teachers

Who are the Proyecto Maestría teachers? In this chapter, I will describe the five cohorts, sharing basic information about the 53 grant-funded Proyecto Maestría teachers and more details about those who ended up as focal participants, and details about the data collection and analysis process. I will begin with a description of the program they went through, as it evolved over time through our own reflections as faculty working with practicing master bilingual education teachers.

The Proyecto Maestría Cohort Master's Program

University of Texas College of Education website

Proyecto Maestría Special Master's Program provides a pathway for current, bilingual-certified teachers with classroom teaching experience from the Austin area to pursue a Master's degree in Curriculum and Instruction: Bilingual/Bicultural Education with a special emphasis on the specific concerns of teacher leadership. Our aim is to continually build upon the pool of qualified master teachers in the region in order to support our teacher education and professional development efforts. The cohort design provides participants in-depth opportunities for building professional learning communities through positive and collaborative relationships with teacher peers from across local and surrounding school districts. Each year a cohort is assembled representing area schools. Students participate in specially designed coursework centered in their own elementary schools and classrooms to guide them in developing mentorship and leadership skills. Students develop a strong grounding in theory, policy, and practice of critical bilingual/bicultural education, as well as have the opportunity to explore their own particular and theoretical interests through coursework in the department of Curriculum and Instruction and beyond. If they so choose, they also have the opportunity to participate in classroom-based research in collaboration with UT professors. Graduates of Proyecto Maestría have remained involved in our program in the capacity of cooperating teachers, hosts, guest speakers and instructors in our teacher education program. They have engaged with our professors in conference presentations and publications, and have worked in their districts as mentor teachers, resource teachers, and professional development presenters. The strength of this program is our ongoing commitment to maintaining a strong connection to the practice and realities of teaching in the elementary bilingual classroom.

Funded as a federal Department of Education National Professional Development Project (Palmer & Ortiz, 2007–2013; https://ed.gov/ programs/nfdp/index.html), Proyecto Maestría wore two hats: it was an intensive, 15-month long professional development experience, targeted at practicing bilingual teachers and carried out as they continued teaching; and it was a graduate program, taught by research faculty, with all the rigor and intensity of any master's degree program at a research-focused institution.

This can be an uncomfortable marriage; as faculty, we were not necessarily accustomed to considering our teaching to be 'professional development', which has the unfortunate reputation of superficiality in its approach to teacher learning in part because in-service teachers are assumed to be far too busy for thoughtful, reflective engagements. Meanwhile, the teachers sometimes balked at our reading, writing and analysis-heavy approach to courses, wondering out loud and among themselves whether they really needed all this theory and how these particular research findings applied to the students they would face the next morning.

Yet, as I think the literature review in Chapter 2 makes clear, this uncomfortable marriage was also definitely generative in that it allowed all of us, including faculty and teacher participants, to engage with the process of teacher-learning in productive ways. As a faculty member, I found my own university and graduate studies classrooms, both during the program and since, influenced by the visceral presence of my students' teaching contexts – real children and their families, real policy consequences, real curricula and lack of resources. Once, a colleague in the social studies education program in my department, teaching just a few of the students in our 'pilot cohort' in 2005 who were taking her course to fulfill one of their elective slots, saw me walking on campus. She pulled over in her vehicle, rolled down her window and called out to me, 'Send me more of your students; they are pushing me. They are wonderful!'. Inviting a sizeable cohort of practicing bilingual teachers into our department had the impact of shifting our master's degree program in healthy ways toward more attention to the local context, to the realities in schools and to practice in general.

Likewise, as will be evident in the teachers' own words in the next chapter, overall they very much valued the theory, reflection and research findings in their own journeys to self-inform, to find and develop their voices, to advocate and to build better programs and more equitable structures in their contexts. Each cohort that graduated committed to maintaining a connection to research as they continued their practice.

Rarely do professional development opportunities for teachers carry the level of rigor and intensity that Proyecto Maestría did; professional development experiences do not usually expect participating teachers to engage in deep dialogue with the many challenging voices of theory, research and one another. As Greenleaf and Katz (2004: 175) explain, '... professional development settings are most often characterized by monologic forms of discourse, participation structures that deny learners roles and valid voices in these settings'. Our purpose was precisely to equip the teachers with the professional tools and knowledge to *find* their voices and advocate for stronger programs for bilingual learners in their schools and districts; we therefore made every effort to help them to engage in a problem-posing, inquiry-based, dialogic set of experiences.

The coursework required of Proyecto teachers included six required courses, three of which were taken in sequence, and for approximately half the content, they were intentionally built upon one another in a mirroring of the four-question sequence suggested by Katzenmeyer and Moller (2009) for the development of teacher leaders: 'Who am I?' 'Where am I?' 'How do I lead?' and 'What can I do?'. We first asked teachers to look at themselves, then at their own school communities and then to seek out the tools they needed to accomplish positive change. Specifically with bilingual teachers, we first asked teachers to explore their own and each other's rich cultural/linguistic funds of knowledge (Moll *et al.*, 1992) and community cultural wealth (Yosso, 2005), then to examine critically the strengths and faults and potential inequities in the programs and systems within which they worked, and finally to equip themselves to become voices for change in local and larger institutions and communities.

These same three courses along with the other three required courses were built to also support the teachers' development of a solid knowledge base in the field of bilingual/bicultural education (BBE): foundations, curriculum and instruction, language acquisition and biliteracy development, current and critical issues in research and practice, etc. (Crawford, 2004; Hornberger, 2003; Ovando *et al.*, 2006).

Program Design and Coursework

The Proyecto Maestría Cohort Master's Program participants completed the University of Texas (UT) Master's degree in Curriculum and Instruction: Bilingual/Bicultural Education (see Appendix A for Program of Work for MA/MEd program in C&I: BBE). To a certain extent by design, and then by default given the actively engaged nature of class discussions, course selection and content paid particular attention to the needs, strengths and goals of the Austin Independent School District (AISD) and other regional schools alongside the particular needs, strengths and goals of each individual teacher. Underlying the program and shared across all courses were the following principles:

- A critical perspective that acknowledges systemic and historic inequity toward Latinx- and Spanish-speaking bilingual students in US schooling and society.
- A philosophical and ideological emphasis on the importance of valuing the funds of knowledge (Moll *et al.*, 1992) and community/cultural wealth (Yosso, 2005) of the Latinx Spanish/English bilingual community.
- A clear focus on the importance of biliteracy development and an enrichment of bi(multi)lingual orientation toward language and content learning for emergent bilingual children.

To the extent possible, courses were taught bilingually in Spanish and English. In other words, we worked to normalize bilingual language practice and the use of Spanish in our graduate education courses. The teachers, especially those who were raised bilingually in Texas, frequently commented on the validating power of experiencing the Spanish language in an official US university space. Many had experienced a lifetime of policing of their language practices, with standard English the only acceptable language for use in school. Spanish in Texas is viewed as a home language, an informal language, with lower status than English. Higher education in particular in the United States has long been dominated by English except in courses meant to teach another language – even in courses meant to prepare bilingual education teachers.

The program was essentially a very intense 15-month master's degree during which participants were expected to remain employed full time by their school districts. Beginning in June, they would take four courses during their first summer, two courses each long semester, fall and spring, and four courses during their second summer. Most participants completed their degrees by August the following year. They took the following five courses in cohorts:

- **Theoretical Foundations of BBE:** Taken *first*, this course, taught to all five cohorts by Dr María Fránquiz, then Associate Professor of Bilingual/Bicultural Education at UT Austin, was the only course for which we preserved enrollment for the cohort only. The course introduced teachers to the history, politics, policies and programs for emergent bilingual students in a US context. Students learned the tools to create and defend high-quality programs and services for bilingual children and families. And perhaps most important for this course was the construction of a strong cohort community. During the first few days of the summer intensive course, which meant the first few days of their Proyecto Maestría experience, students developed a 'journey box' and a written narrative recounting their own journey to becoming biliterate (Fránquiz *et al.*, 2011; Labbo & Field, 1999). On the days these were shared, there were many tears, hugs and laughter. In groups, they also conducted a 'Neighborhood Walk' to explore and document the community cultural wealth (Yosso, 2005) of an Austin school community, connecting what they learned to classroom instruction. Of course, the course also included a wide range of background information about the history, policy, politics and pedagogy of bilingual education in a US and Texas context, which many of the students found to be intimately tied to their own personal histories and teaching/learning experiences. This course front-loaded the 'Understanding Self' piece of the teacher leadership path, and began the 'Understanding Context' piece (Katzenmeyer & Moller, 2009).

- **Teaching in the Elementary Bilingual Classroom**: Taken during the fall long semester, this was a survey course of critical current issues in the field of bilingual/dual language curriculum and instruction. Students explored the research literature in the field of bilingual education across different content areas, the teaching of English as a second language (ESL), instruction and assessment for bilingual education, critical pedagogies for social justice and other current critical areas of concern both locally and nationally. The final projects for the course included an analysis of the strengths and needs of programs and services for bilingual children and families at each teacher's own school campus, and an action plan for improvement produced in collaboration with school leadership. In this class, students also had an opportunity to craft their first column addressed to parents and community for the local Spanish language newspaper (see details about this project below). I taught this class to three of the cohorts; Dr Carmen Martínez-Roldán, who spent two years as an associate professor in our program at UT, taught this course to two of the cohorts.
- **Teacher Leadership for Bilingual/ESL**: Taken during the spring long semester and taught to all five cohorts by me, this course built directly on the previous two courses. The leadership course supported students to develop skills in mentoring, coaching, designing and carrying out presentations directed at professional development for colleagues, presenting at state/national professional conferences, engaging in reflective teacher inquiry and reaching out through publication to parents and communities. Projects encompassed all these areas, drawing on students' own action plan from the previous semester's final project to target specific needs at their own school campuses. The process of developing and improving this course over the five years of the project led me to explore the extant literature on teacher leadership, in order to build the course around the strongest pieces in this field and to seek out ways to link the field to work in the field of BBE. Teaching the course every year, I was prompted to think deeply both on my own and with the teachers to actually *define* teacher

leadership for a bilingual teacher... and ultimately to become aware of the need for this book.

- **Methods of Teaching ESL**: Offered every other summer and taught to all five cohorts by Dr Haydée Rodriguez, Clinical Assistant Professor of Bilingual/Bicultural Education, this course would bring two cohorts together; students took it during either their first or second summer, and it offered an opportunity for them to expand their professional community/network. The course introduced the experienced bilingual teacher to current theory and practice in content-based ESL with a particular focus on the importance of comprehensively integrating culturally relevant pedagogies (Ladson-Billings, 1995b) and experiences into classroom instruction. Students worked collaboratively to develop curricular units that they could use in their own classrooms.

- **Educational Research and Design**: Students took this course together at some point during their first summer. It was required for all master's degree students in the Department of Curriculum and Instruction (C&I), so usually at least a few additional students from other C&I master's degree programs took it with the cohort. Because inevitably one or more of these non-BBE students did not speak Spanish, the course was taught entirely in English. The instructor was usually a C&I faculty member with at least peripheral interest in and knowledge of the bilingual education field. The course offered an overview of the epistemological grounding for research in the field of education. Students explored qualitative and quantitative approaches to education research. They learned to search databases to locate peer-reviewed research, and to read, evaluate and interpret research studies. They talked to a range of researchers about their work, exploring the purposes, goals and outcomes of different research methodologies.

  Along with the cohort classes, students had two other required courses, two additional electives and two 'out-of-department' courses – i.e. beyond the C&I department. We encouraged students to follow their own passions and professional needs and to ask each other for recommendations for exciting courses or professors.

- **A Course in Biliteracy**: At some point during their program, students were required to take a course focused specifically on biliteracy in theory and practice. Courses offered include 'Biliteracy and New Literacy Studies', 'Biliteracy in New Technologies' and 'Biliteracy and Culture'. These courses were taken alongside doctoral students, but because they required at least some Spanish proficiency they tended to be primarily our own BBE students.

- **Theories of Second Language Acquisition**: This course served a dual purpose: it offered teachers an understanding of language/linguistics and language acquisition to support the language and content learning of their students; and it gave teachers an opportunity to carry out library research in a subfield of particular interest. Teachers learned to talk about and evaluate language and language learning and were introduced to a range of assessment tools for deepening their understanding of linguistic repertoires. It was taught by faculty members in the Foreign Language Education (FLE) program, usually Dr Elaine Horwitz. Because it was required for FLE graduate students and encouraged for other students depending upon their interests, it usually enrolled students from across the C&I programs, and was taught in English.

Elective Courses: Students selected two courses in consultation with their academic advisor. One elective many of the students selected was 'Latino Children's Literature'. Designed and taught by Dr María Franquiz, this course was technically an undergraduate course in our bilingual teacher preparation sequence. In this course, our Proyecto Maestría students – who were also taking the course for credit – served as mentors to preservice bilingual education teachers in a project in which groups created bilingual, culturally relevant children's picture books and then shared them with bilingual children. Some other common and popular electives were 'Language Policy in Education', 'Immigration Theory', 'Culture of Teaching and Teacher Education', 'The Art of the Picture Book', and 'Multicultural Curriculum'.

As per the requirements of UT's graduate school, students also needed to complete two courses outside the Department of C&I. This allowed students to explore such fields as special education, educational leadership, educational psychology, Spanish literature, Mexican-American/Latino studies, Latin American studies, theater, anthropology, history, etc.

Some teachers elected to complete a master's report in place of two elective courses. A report, supervised by a BBE or affiliate faculty member, comprised of either a literature review on a topic of interest to the student, or a classroom-based research project or curriculum development that enhanced the teachers' understanding of their practice or students.

Proyecto Maestría garnered a reputation for intensity. However, after completing the program, most participants expressed that they were glad it was structured as it was: the intensity allowed them to fully immerse, and at the same time they were glad to 'get it over with quickly'. Many asserted that it was the power of the cohort that made this possible. Students would stick together in pairs or groups as they signed up for elective and out-of-department courses; they developed nicknames for one another, routines together and strategies for sharing the burdens of graduate school – not only the intensive workload, but the challenges of navigating a very large public institution that was not particularly friendly to working professionals, and that also may be construed as marginalizing to Latinx students. The strength and power of the cohort community was one of the most consistent findings in this project. I will elaborate and share students' own words about this cohort experience in Chapter 7.

Upon completion of the program, students were awarded a Master of Education (MEd) or a Master of Arts in Education (MA) (if they wrote a report) in Curriculum & Instruction: Bilingual/Bicultural Education, and became Proyecto Maestría Program graduates, entering a corps of teachers with a growing reputation as empowered, strong, engaged leaders working hard to move local area schools and school districts forward in the interests of bilingual children and families.

Application, Selection and Matriculation Process

The broad goal of the grant was to improve the quality and increase the quantity of bilingual and ESL instruction in the Austin, Texas region. Our mechanism for accomplishing this goal was to develop a cadre of skilled and knowledgeable teacher leaders to support the professional development of their colleagues in the field. Thus, in order to participate in Proyecto Maestría, bilingual teachers were required to have at least five years' experience teaching as certified bilingual education teachers.[1] They were also required to be strong Spanish/English bilinguals, and to be current full-time teachers or coach/resource teachers in a school district within the Austin metro region. If accepted to Proyecto Maestría, participants signed an agreement that they would remain in the service of Austin area bilingual students for at least three years post-completion.

The grant supported two half-time staff members. An administrative assistant allowed us to provide applicants with guidance throughout the graduate school recruitment, application and matriculation process, while a project coordinator with professional experience in bilingual classrooms allowed us to ensure that applicants were properly screened for instructional and linguistic mastery in order that they would be able to focus in our program upon leadership skills. Both staff members supported recruitment efforts, including designing flyers and other recruitment materials and updating the website, scheduling information sessions in local school districts and disseminating materials about the project.

Interested teachers first submitted what we called an 'Intent to Apply', in order to get on our email list to receive updates, reminders and tips in support of their applications. Applicants were required to fully complete all regular graduate program application processes by the UT Graduate Admissions December deadline, including taking the graduate record examinations (GRE), seeking letters of recommendation and writing a statement of purpose. In addition, we required a statement written in

Spanish. After an initial applicant screening by faculty in January, the project coordinator visited all finalists' classrooms, observing and video recording them teach a lesson in Spanish. The purpose of this visit was to evaluate the teachers' capacity to serve as a master Spanish/English bilingual teacher. After this process was complete, the faculty would again come together to select the final cohort.

Recruitment

Despite the opportunity for a tuition-free master's degree, we struggled each year to recruit qualified teachers to participate in Proyecto Maestría. One issue we had was the difficulty of getting information out to the region's practicing bilingual teachers. Typically, school districts did not have an effective medium for communicating opportunities such as ours directly to bilingual teachers; the only means was through campus administrators. Principals, among the busiest, most harried educators in the system, often failed to disseminate our information; and even when they did, overworked teachers seemed to miss our emails. We ran information sessions in the evenings, publicizing them as best we could through a range of means. We spoke at principals' meetings, shared flyers at district-wide events and made efforts to have the program publicized through the AISD district website, each strategy succeeding to a limited extent. One of the lessons learned as we struggled each year to recruit was the inherent lethargy and bureaucracy of a large urban school district, even filled as it was with engaged and interested educators and leaders at all levels. Our partner district, meanwhile, became aware of the need to build a communication strategy to support bilingual teachers across all its schools. By the end of the grant period, there were far more mechanisms in place to accomplish this, including officially appointed bilingual teacher leaders on each school campus and email lists of teachers run by the Department of Multilingual Studies.

Many external programs and opportunities vied for the limited attention of busy local teachers; few were as huge a gift as ours, which was essentially a nearly full scholarship for a master's degree at a major research university. Yet, inquiries never flooded our office. At the same time, we maintained a high standard for participants, and ultimately were able to recruit excellent teacher participants into each cohort.

The 53 Proyecto Maestría Teachers

The five cohorts of teachers who participated in Proyecto Maestría during the grant years broke down as follows:

- Cohort 1: 9 teachers
- Cohort 2: 12 teachers

- Cohort 3: 11 teachers
- Cohort 4: 13 teachers
- Cohort 5: 8 teachers

The 'pilot cohort', two years prior to the grant's award (i.e. in 2005), comprised 12 teachers.

Each cohort developed a professional learning community, and each grant-supported cohort engaged with at least one other cohort for at least the length of one class. All but one of the teachers who entered as a Proyecto Maestría participant completed their degrees; that final teacher had some personal issues that impeded completion just two courses away. Most completed their degrees within 15 months, while five required extra semesters. Seven of the 53 teachers opted to write a master's report or thesis, thus earning an MA instead of an MEd.

Of the 53 grant-funded teachers:

- 12 were men, 41 were women.
- 48 self-identified as Latina/o, 4 self-identified as white, 1 as Asian.
- 34 said they were primarily from Texas, 7 from Mexico, 2 from other US states, 3 from Puerto Rico, 2 from Spain, 1 from Costa Rica, 2 from Colombia, 1 from Panama and 1 from El Salvador.
- Nine held positions in districts or schools outside AISD (all within driving distance); 44 worked at one of the over 80 elementary schools in AISD.
- 48 were classroom teachers in bilingual pre-kindergarten through fifth-grade classrooms; five were campus-based teacher coaches, supporting colleagues in math (1), literacy (1) or bilingual/dual language pedagogy (3). All worked as full-time teachers in a school context throughout their time in the program; this was a requirement for participation.

In order to better and more thoroughly analyze the overwhelming amount of data collected from these 53 teachers, I purposively selected one of the cohorts, Cohort 5, as a focal case, and a few teachers from across the other cohorts as focal individuals. Selection was difficult; nevertheless, I included plenty of data in the analysis that came from non-focal participants. The selection criteria included:

- Willingness to participate in the extended research project.
- Extensiveness of data on file from their time at UT and the years that followed.
- Potential to offer insight into the experiences in which I was interested, which included an openness and ability to articulate their personal experiences.
- Divergence of experience from other purposively selected focal teachers.

While I drew on the entire data set to produce the analysis in the remainder of this book, I tended to pay particular attention throughout to these focal participants. Table 4.1 provides some background information about the members of Cohort 5, including their number of years' experience when they began Proyecto, the teaching positions they held during the program and the region/district of their schools. Note that most names are pseudonyms. Teachers were given the opportunity to select pseudonyms. While many did, some participants left pseudonym selection to me, and a few asked that I use their real names. I honored their preferences.

The focal cohort, Cohort 5, had eight participants. Alondra had graduated from UT's undergraduate bilingual teacher preparation program and was still close to my colleague, Dr Haydée Rodríguez from her undergraduate years at UT. Four of the others were graduates of other Texas state institutions' teacher preparation programs, and the remaining three were certified through alternative pathways after having graduated with bachelor's degrees (in Paco's case, in education, but in Spain).

There were three men and five women in the focal cohort. Six self-identified as Latinx, one of whom self-identified as Afro-Latina. Two self-identified as white – non-Latinos. Miguel was raised in Mexico, and Julieta was raised a bilingual Latina in Austin, in the community where she was a teacher. Alondra, Gisela and Maya were Tejanas/Mexicanas from the Texas border region. Paco was from Spain, Natasha was Puerto Rican and George was a white male born and raised Dallas and East Texas. Maya was the only cohort member who was not a teacher in AISD; she taught at a school in a district to the north of Austin, along with two teachers from a previous cohort. Julieta came into the cohort having already begun her master's degree, as she was impatient to wait the requisite five years as a teacher before beginning. Four of the cohort

Table 4.1 Cohort 5: Focal cohort

Name	Age	Years teaching	Certified	Grade level/position (at time of participation)	District/school
Paco	29	6	Alt. Cert.	K bilingual teacher	AISD (east)
Alondra	28	6	UT	Second-grade bilingual teacher	AISD (south central)
Gisela	29	5	UT other[a]	PK bilingual/DL teacher	AISD (south central)
Maya	33	11	UT other	Second-grade TWDL teacher	Suburban district north
Natasha	40	7	Alt. Cert.	PK bilingual/DL teacher	AISD (southeast)
Julieta	27	5	State Col.	Second-grade DL teacher	(northeast) AISD
Miguel	46	6	State Col.	Third-grade bilingual teacher	(southeast) AISD
George	34	12	Alt. Cert.	First-grade DL teacher	(southwest) AISD

[a] A different UT campus, in the border region.

members wrote master's reports at the end of their program: Paco, Miguel, George and Natasha.

The cohort had two courses with me, both long semesters, and the reason for their selection as the focal cohort was simply that I had kept a clear record of their exchanges with one another in online (Blackboard) discussion boards for the entire year, and had a complete set of several of their course assignments. Most of the members of this cohort also participated in follow-up interviews and post-graduation activities such as the ¡Adelante! Conference, a local teacher-run conference (see Chapter 7). I therefore had a great deal of data related to the experiences of members of this cohort. Finally, by the time this cohort went through the program, the courses were well elaborated – these teachers benefitted from the improvements we had made to the program along the way, and in a sense provided the most complete windows into the experience of developing bilingual teacher leadership.

Individual Focal Participants

From Pilot Cohort: Leti

Although the pilot cohort is not officially part of this project, I chose to include data from one of our participants from that cohort of 12 students for two reasons. First, Leti embodied a broad spectrum of what Proyecto Maestría turned into; in fact, it was working with Leti in that pilot cohort that most guided my writing of the grant with the focus I did. Also, Leti's success moving from the role of bilingual teacher to that of a principal in a school with a strong bilingual education program led the AISD administration to support continuing the project beyond the grant years, although in the end funding was not found. Second, I actually had a substantial amount of data from Leti's experiences in Proyecto and following, given her own investment in the project and her commitment to encouraging the teachers at her school to participate.

When Leti went through Proyecto, she was a third-grade teacher at a school in southwest Austin where many of our UT undergraduates were carrying out their practicum experiences. She was a cooperating teacher for our bilingual teacher preparation program and a good friend of my clinical faculty colleague Dr Haydée Rodriguez, the director of our bilingual teacher preparation program. She had three small children; the youngest was a baby in 2005 when she began the master's program. She also had a very clear goal: to be a school leader. Leti drew what she needed from every class she took in order to forward her professional goals. She was a leader in her cohort; when the teachers would come together to work out how to survive an intense summer course, she would be the one to take charge, giving everyone their marching orders for readings and assignments. After graduating, Leti accepted our invitation to serve on Proyecto Maestría's advisory board for the grant-based program.

In total, she supported three of her teachers to apply to Proyecto, and hired at least six program graduates to come to her school, including her assistant principal (Lupe, Cohort 2), whom she mentored into leadership.

From Cohort 1: Mariana, Leila and Raquel

Mariana, who immigrated to California from Mexico as a middle-schooler, began Proyecto Maestría as a soft-spoken, newly minted literacy coach at her large elementary school in north Austin. She had been a teacher for eight years, some in California and some in Texas. She had a calm demeanor and gentle interactional style. She had one young child and was open about the struggles she faced in balancing family and career, especially during the intense 15 months of the master's degree program. In the years that followed Proyecto, Mariana would go on to have two more children, and to become an assistant principal at her school. As of this writing, she has recently left Texas to return to her home state of California, and continues her work there as a school leader.

Leila had taught for more than 20 years when she began Proyecto. She had a particular passion for social studies and had been a leader in this area. She had also served as a mentor to novice teachers. She was a second-grade teacher at a very large school in southwest Austin in which approximately half the students were bilingual. Like all of her particular cohort's members, she self-identified as Latina, and she was a confident bilingual. But she was decidedly English dominant, generally choosing English even when her colleagues spoke or wrote in Spanish. Her own two children were in high school and college when she began the program. Leila was a clear-spoken, down-to-earth, community builder. She was the cohort member who would offer her home for gatherings, bring support to colleagues in crisis and always be ready with a friendly word or a hug. She had a clear goal from the start: to become a teacher educator. Now, several years after she completed her degree, Leila works with preservice teachers in a university-based bilingual teacher preparation program, teaching courses and supervising practicum experiences.

Raquel was in her eighth year of teaching when the cohort program began. Extremely motivated, she had already begun her master's program before learning of the grant-supported opportunity; because of her excellent fit with the program, we invited her to join the cohort after her first year in graduate school. Born and raised in Central America, Raquel came to the United States as an adult. She was a fluent bilingual. With her strong academic skills in both English and Spanish, Raquel's cohort colleagues viewed her as a resource. They frequently drew on her support in classes, for editing Spanish writing, for help navigating the complicated library resource websites and for ideas in both formal and informal conversations around graduate school coursework. Raquel taught at a medium-sized elementary school of approximately 500 students with a small bilingual program. Bilingual students made up approximately one third of the student body, and there was one bilingual teacher at each grade level. Bilingual classes at Raquel's school in general contained native English speakers, as there were not enough Spanish-dominant students to fill the classes. When she entered the program, Raquel framed her biggest challenge as that of helping bilingual families navigate the mainly English-only school context. At this writing, Raquel now works at a dual language elementary school near her home, about 45 minutes outside of Austin, where her young daughter is a student.

From Cohort 2: Lorena, Lupe and Aisha

Lorena was one of the nine participants who were not employees of Austin's large urban school district. She worked in a small rural district about an hour's drive from Austin. She had lived and worked her whole adult life in this small community and was well respected there; she engaged fully and enthusiastically in Proyecto Maestría despite her commute distance, often appealing to the responsibility she felt toward her community to explain her boundless energy. Lorena had eight years' experience as a bilingual teacher when she entered Proyecto, and was a third-grade teacher during that year. She was married with two small children, was raised Tejana on the US/Mexican border and described herself as a devout Catholic. After she completed Proyecto, she moved into an official district-office leadership role as director of bilingual/ESL education, and eventually moved to another nearby rural district to take a position as an assistant principal at an elementary school.

Lupe, who primarily grew up and still had family on both sides of the border in the region around El Paso, was a bilingual coach in a large, predominantly bilingual school in south central Austin the year she went through the master's program. She was the parent of two children, one of whom had special needs. She had her eye on leadership from the start, and soon after graduating she sought her administrative certification. She currently serves as the assistant principal at Leti's school in southeast Austin.

Aisha self-identified as Asian American, of an intraracial Pakistani and Filipina background. She grew up around both Urdu and Tagalog, and learned some Arabic as a child, but was not a productive speaker of these languages. She was married to a Mexican-American man and spoke Spanish fluently. She had been through UT's certification program five years before. When she began Proyecto Maestría, she was a fifth-grade bilingual teacher, team teaching with Lila, another member of Cohort 2, at a small school in south central Austin. A few years after completing her master's degree, she began a doctoral program in elementary social studies education with a focus on Asian American history in elementary curriculum and instruction. She is now an assistant professor in a tenure track position at a public university.

From Cohort 3: Sofia and Christine

Sofia took an extra year to gain entrance to UT Austin; she was originally accepted to be a part of Cohort 2, but because of a mix-up in her transcripts, which were translated from Spanish since she was educated in her native country El Salvador, the graduate school refused to admit her. While she was willing to wait out the year for a range of reasons, her elation was indescribable the following spring when she and I walked into the actual office of Graduate Admissions and worked out the details in person, allowing her to become a graduate student at UT Austin.

Not one to sit still or sit down, Sofia was an outspoken advocate and a fighter from her first day of classes and she only grew stronger as she gained the skills of leadership and background knowledge in her courses. Sofia began Proyecto as a fourth-grade teacher at a large school in north Austin with an almost entirely bilingual population. Although she has moved schools and grade levels several times since, she remains in the classroom and continues her work as an advocate and activist leader. She is active in the teacher's union. She has one son who was in elementary school during the time she was a UT student.

Christine is a white woman, the daughter of a teacher who also worked in Austin with the Mexican-American community. When she began Proyecto, Christine was already well known and highly regarded within and beyond the district, with several years' experience as a successful fourth-grade teacher of recent immigrant students in a school in the heart of the Latinx community. Christine had one young child when she was going through the program, whom she and her husband were raising bilingually. The year after she completed the program, Christine was recognized as the Elementary Teacher of the Year for all of AISD's 80+ elementary schools. This tremendous honor came, as Christine explained, with a certain untouchable character in the year or two that followed, which allowed her to be an even more vocal and outspoken advocate for equity in the community. She has nevertheless found herself needing to move schools recently as her activism has bumped up against administrative discomfort.

Christine and Sofia contrived to work together as a team several years after graduation, and during their time together developed a number of valuable digital tools for professional development, including a website they developed in partnership with a school librarian full of resources for using culturally relevant bilingual literature in the classroom, a comprehensive unit on immigration for fourth graders and a workshop that they enthusiastically take to conferences nationwide.

From Cohort 4: Patricia, Mireya, Lucia and Emma

Patricia and Mireya were dual language teacher coaches at two different schools in a suburban district to the north of Austin. Having spent six years in the classroom, Patricia's year in Proyecto coincided with her very first year as a teacher coach, as she took on the official leadership role of 'Dual Language Coach' for her school. Thus, she was exceptionally receptive to discussion of leadership and a particularly powerful informant for me about the impacts of different assignments, conversations and aspects of the program. A self-identified Latina, Patricia was raising her own three children bilingually with the support of the dual language programs in her district. While this book was being written, Patricia and her family moved to California due to her husband's career, and she is currently engaged in professional development and teacher preparation for dual language teachers in that state.

When she began Proyecto, Mireya was an experienced teacher coach who had already been serving as an instructional leader promoting her district's 50/50 dual language program. She was a strong and articulate advocate for additive dual language bilingual education programs. She was also Latina, raised in the border region, with two children. Mireya has taken on a range of official and unofficial leadership roles in the years since she graduated, and is currently working as a curriculum specialist for language arts in her district's administration. Patricia and Mireya both carried out master's reports at the culmination of their program.

Lucia, a fourth-grade math/science teacher whose language arts/social studies team teacher had just gone through the Proyecto the previous year, was an enthusiastic participant in the program and a community builder in her cohort. Lucia always seems to have her eye on opportunities. Even before completing her master's program, she participated in the Tejano History Project (Salinas et al., 2015), and after graduating she became a dedicated Academia Cuauhtli teacher (Valenzuela et al., 2015), both programs that have engaged Proyecto teachers with UT faculty around language and culture revitalization for Latinx bilingual students in Austin (more detail in later chapters). Lucia recently changed schools and grade levels seeking new growth opportunities. She has also taught writing and ESL to adults at a nearby community college, an experience she relishes both for the rewards of working with immigrant adults, and for the extra income, which she explained allows her to stay in the classroom as a teacher while actually making ends meet and saving for her future.

Emma was an extremely organized kindergarten teacher with five years' experience when she went through the master's program. She was raised in a bilingual home in the border region, and had graduated from UT's bilingual teacher preparation program. She had served as a cooperating teacher for UT as well. She had one young son. After completing her degree, Emma changed schools and grade levels, moving to a school with a prominent dual language program, and giving second grade a try. For a time, she and Lucia became team partners at this school. At this point, Emma has completed her administrative certification and is now an assistant principal at a school with a large bilingual population.

These were the teachers whose data figured most prominently in the following chapters. All of the teachers, and all of the data, informed the analysis.

Data Collected

Each cohort took at least one class with me, while three of the cohorts took two classes with me. Archived data from participants' time in my courses were included in this analysis, including their reflections in weekly online discussion boards related to readings and topics, and some of their other written assignments. For many participants, I have occasional recordings of them participating in outside-of-class, primarily post-graduation activities such as presenting at professional conferences; speeches in front of undergraduate students or other local audiences; and informal study-group conversations in participants' classrooms, which we held monthly for a couple of the project years. I and several of our project employees, including particularly Monica Valadéz and Blanca Caldas, interviewed many of the program graduates individually or in focal groups; these interviews were transcribed. I also have some artifacts from program experiences or administrative materials, and occasional field notes or reflections of my own from experiences interacting with program participants and graduates.

Data analysis was best described as idiosyncratic. I took a grounded approach to theorizing in this project (Strauss & Corbin, 1997), by which I mean I began with the data, and at least part of my purpose was to develop theory – a theoretical framework for bilingual teacher leadership – *from* the data. As it turned out, the theories of Freire and Bakhtin strongly supported my understanding of the data, but these entered the analysis only after several rounds of open thematic coding.

I experienced the project alongside the participants, as their teacher and the project director, and as such had many initial thoughts around my research questions even before I sat down to carry out data analysis. I also had many thoughts related to all of the issues of program design, curriculum development and alignment, teaching and pedagogical principles, organization and recruitment, etc., which are detailed in the first half of this chapter. Although it turned out that many of these aspects were aligned with and ultimately relevant to the findings of the research study, these thoughts needed to be set aside for my initial data analysis to ensure validity. Therefore, in order to ensure fidelity to the data, as well as the range of experiences beyond my own, I wrote down my initial thoughts and made a supreme effort to set them aside.

I then organized all the data by participant and cohort year, loaded them into NVivo and thoroughly read through them with as open a mind as I could. Using NVivo, a widely available qualitative data analysis software tool, I began to code data in a method resembling constant comparative (Glaser, 1965). I moved among the different data sources and enhanced my collection of codes and subcodes, theorizing along the way, until I felt satisfied that they consistently and comprehensively reflected the full data set and that my developing understandings about bilingual teacher leadership were clearly reflected in the teachers' experiences. NVivo allowed me to pull up all examples of each code and subcode generated, from which I inductively developed four primary themes as I coded along with many sub-themes. These themes turned into the following chapters, in which I explore the aspects of bilingual teacher leadership that appeared most salient to participants across the data: reflexive praxis, cultural/linguistic identities, collaboration/community and advocacy/activism. Of course, the themes overlap and are interconnected; this is, in fact, my primary argument – that all these elements come together to create the possibility of powerful bilingual teacher leadership.

At this point, I drew on the theoretical frameworks that seemed most to suit these themes; theory further enhanced my understanding of the themes, and I believe contributed to a more robust understanding of the work of bilingual teacher leaders. Because theory did not enter into my analysis until after I had identified the major themes, and my selection of theoretical frame was driven by the nature and organization of the data themselves, I am calling this a grounded approach. By this I mean, I let the data speak for themselves and only after the bulk of the analysis was complete did I bring theory into the picture.

It is important to note that, although my initial thoughts about the data prior to my thorough analysis were relatively aligned with the final data analysis, the thorough analysis produced a far more complex accounting for participants' experiences, and therefore I believe allowed for a more useful and theoretically grounded definition for future researchers and practitioners. That said, this analysis is but a bare beginning; I hope to continue this work with more teachers, and I know that the teachers who participated in this project are continuing their work in their own contexts too.

Another disclaimer: while these 53 teachers provided a wealth of data in a range of forms, and while these four themes were dramatically consistent throughout the data, the definition that I am proposing for bilingual teacher leadership was developed in just this one context: in one urban center in Texas, with a group of powerful and vocal elementary school (PK-5) Spanish/English experienced bilingual education teachers. It is of course quite conceivable – even likely – that more, fewer or different themes would have emerged were I carrying out this work in a different context or with different teachers. I welcome others to explore these questions with teachers in contexts beyond Austin in order that we may continue to develop our understanding of bilingual and ESL teacher leadership for excellence in education for emergent bilingual students.

Note

(1) There was some disagreement among faculty members about the wisdom of this requirement; many highly qualified teachers, for various reasons, leave the field before they reach the five-year mark. I personally believe that three years' experience would have sufficed, and would have supported the participation of some teachers who might otherwise have left the profession. That said, the five-year requirement ensured that our cohorts were packed with dedicated and deeply experienced teachers – these were the teachers who did not leave the field.

5 Bilingual Teacher Leaders are Reflexive Practitioners

Teachers and students (leadership and people), co-intent on reality, are both Subjects, not only in the task of unveiling that reality and thereby coming to know it critically, but in the task of re-creating that knowledge. As they attain this knowledge of reality through common reflection and action, they discover themselves as its permanent re-creators. (Freire 2000: 69)

Natasha (Cohort 5), a dual language pre-kindergarten teacher from Puerto Rico, read aloud the above quote from the first chapter of Freire's *Pedagogy of the Oppressed* in front of an audience of professors and education students at my institution as she closed out her acceptance speech on the occasion of winning an award for Early Childhood Educator of the Year. She explained how she began to connect her practice with theory:

It wasn't until I came to UT that I really started to realize, 'Oh, my goodness! These are real things that I do in the classroom and they have a theory.' So I started to put the theory to my practices instead of relying only [on] my practices. Because I started to think, 'Oh, when I do this, it goes with Freire's humanizing... when I do this, it goes to funds of knowledge, and when I...' So, I was like, 'Wow! These things I didn't invent. They're real out there!'

We hear frequently in the field of teacher education that we need to make our coursework more 'practical', that what teachers most need in order to succeed in the classroom is an emphasis on practice, on *how* to teach, with less focus on theory or research or 'foundations' (Zeichner, 2006, 2016). The Proyecto teachers consistently projected the opposite message: they valued the ways that theory informed their practice, allowed them to more powerfully understand and justify their professional decisions and gave them ammunition and legitimacy when they had to defend their decisions and advocate for their students. They felt the ground beneath them firm up as professionals as they came to understand the theoretical constructs and develop a broader perspective on the research upon which their practices were built.

Natasha vividly illustrated the power of theory to strengthen and inform her practice in a presentation she made at the ¡Adelante! Conference for Dual Language/Bilingual Educators in 2015. I crafted the following description from my field notes that day:

> I walked into Natasha's presentation just as she was beginning. There were about twenty teachers sitting at five large round tables. Natasha presented in Spanish, and had such a powerful presence and clear articulation. I was riveted. She credited Proyecto Maestría with transforming her teaching, explaining that this was in part because UT classes exposed her to a series of theoretical frameworks that allowed her to see her students and her role as their teacher through different lenses. She presented four frameworks, illustrating each with a direct connection to teaching in an early childhood bilingual classroom: Humanizing pedagogies (Freire, 2000), Funds of Knowledge (Moll *et al.*, 1992), Culturally Relevant Pedagogies (Ladson-Billings, 1995b) and Community/Cultural Wealth (Yosso, 2005). To illustrate Humanizing Pedagogies, she shared two photos: the first of children sitting silently working, the second of children leaning over to talk together about their work. She explained that children construct knowledge in collaboration, sharing their ideas in dialogue with others; they are not merely vessels for a teacher to fill; acknowledging their humanity meant allowing them to be themselves in her classroom. For Funds of Knowledge, she talked about valuing her students' parents as teachers and connecting each element of the official curriculum with the vast knowledge children come in with from home. To explain Culturally Relevant Pedagogies, she talked about choosing curriculum and instructional strategies that 'include our own kids' stories so they see themselves in the classroom.' In illustrating Community/Cultural Wealth, she described bringing the resources of our surrounding community in to support her students as they learn.
> All four of these frameworks came together in the practice example she shared: using Pancho Rabbit and the Coyote (Tonatiuh, 2013) as a homework assignment in her dual language prekindergarten classroom. She explained that she sends the book, which she translated into Spanish for families (Spanish text taped in to each page), home with a shared class journal to a different family every few days. She asks families to sit together and read the book, and then discuss – and write down in the journal their reactions to the story. She shared on her power point some of the journal entries from families, connecting the activity and the kinds of responses from families to the four frameworks she had introduced. Her choice of this text, a story of a young rabbit's effort to cross the border and find his father with the sometimes-dubious help of a coyote, is an example of a Culturally Relevant Pedagogy given the immigrant experiences of many families in her school. Sending it home to be discussed between children and their parents is a way to engage family funds of knowledge. The kinds of stories that came out of the experience, and the empathy

that this shared journal built among her diverse families across her classroom, is a beautiful illustration of humanizing pedagogies; the deep knowledge that some families shared as they connected their own lives to the immigration experience and other aspects of Pancho Rabbit's family and community life were illustrative of Community/Cultural Wealth. The stories, emotions, and reflections that parents wrote down after sharing and discussing this book with their children were incredibly powerful. Natasha explained that in her view, the learning that occurred around this shared literacy experience was so multilayered and significant because of the ways it interwove these four theoretical frameworks. (Field Notes, ¡Adelante! Conference, March 2015)

In this intuitive and practice-oriented presentation, Natasha made concrete connections to aspects of her classroom, illustrating four theoretical frameworks that were central to her master's program: humanizing pedagogies (Freire, 2000), community cultural wealth (Yosso, 2005), culturally relevant pedagogies (Ladson-Billings, 1995) and funds of knowledge for teaching (González et al., 2005). Natasha's articulation of the links between theory and practice was vivid and explicit. While not all the teachers were as articulate as Natasha was in this presentation, the habit of connecting theory to practice to action in this deeply reflexive way was one of the major themes that ran through teachers' post-program interviews. This level of reflection and engagement with critical theory seemed a necessary characteristic of teacher leadership for teachers working with bilingual children and families. George (Cohort 5), a first-grade, two-way dual language teacher who would ultimately go on to the doctoral program, affirmed in an online post toward the end of the spring semester the importance and relevance of theory and research for his classroom practice:

> Going into [graduate school] I worried that what I would be learning might feel disconnected from my daily experience as a classroom teacher. On the contrary, I've found the broad scope of educational context we've been learning about to be directly tied to what I do as a teacher. Now it seems everything I read gives me ideas for research topics that I would like to pursue because they're things that interest me in how they relate to teacher practice.

Alicia's (Cohort 1, fifth grade) comment, exemplary of many throughout the data, summed it up:

> I was kind of self-reflective before, but not to this extent, once I had all the history and everything to back up what I was thinking and learning, but, like Mariana, I mean, I had that metamorphosis, complete metamorphosis.

Alicia's self-described 'metamorphosis' led to her involvement in a research project with a doctoral student related to funds of knowledge in science in her fifth-grade bilingual classroom (Fránquiz *et al.*, 2013). She then shifted into an official leadership role as a teacher coach, and ultimately became a school principal; critical reflexivity played and continues to play important roles in her work.

The power of reflexivity

Teachers offered a range of reasons why developing deeper connections to theory and research had expanded and improved their practice and supported their growth as leaders. In an online discussion board exchange (more thoroughly presented and analyzed in Chapter 7), Alondra (Cohort 5, second-grade bilingual) expressed why she believed reflection to be important in education, and how her experiences engaging with theory and research have more securely grounded her in the profession:

> The education world is constantly changing. Year after year we are given different resources to try with our students. Once we have become familiar with a resource, a new one comes out. This instability requires us as teachers to be researchers. We often ask ourselves: what is best for our students? Being in Proyecto Maestría has allowed me to see things through different eyes. The researcher in me has evolved. I pay more attention to quality over quantity.

In the same exchange, Miguel (Cohort 5, third-grade bilingual) directly linked the increased reflection in his and his cohort colleagues' practice to new knowledge and new perspectives learned in graduate school courses, expressing that this increased perspective about the theoretical foundations of the field comes with a responsibility:

> The fact that we all are part of the Proyecto Maestría indicates that we want to change our practices for the good of our students. In the last few months, we all have expressed how the classes we have taken so far have changed our vision about education. We all have shared how our practices in the classroom are different compared to previous years. At the same time, the new knowledge we have acquired compromises[1] us to keep reflecting and redefining what we do in the classroom.

Emilia (Cohort 4, pre-K bilingual) in an interview similarly expressed that the increased reflection that she engaged in with colleagues in her master's degree program led to stronger practice, stating, 'That is something that really made me a better teacher because I reflected on my practices with other teachers'.

Lucia (Cohort 4, fourth-grade bilingual math/science) explained that the habit of engaging in reflective practice also gave her the cognitive and emotional tools to manage failures along her career path:

> **Lucia:** So I think that's another thing that the project taught me is that we're always learning, you know. So when I didn't get the jobs instead of being destroyed, you know, 'Oh, I didn't get this. I'm not good enough'. I was mature enough to be, 'Well, I do need more experience', you know, in certain things, you know'.
>
> **Me:** You were self-reflective about it.
>
> **Lucia:** Right. Because of grad school. We reflected. We would constantly be talking about... we were always talking about learning, you know. That was a big theme. That was another thing that the project gave me. That no matter... your growth doesn't stop, you know. You should always be learning. You should always be growing. So, that's something that also stuck with me with the project. So, when I didn't get those jobs, that kind of mentality set in, you know, I have to learn more and grow more.

Thus, for Lucia, having a mindset that situated herself as a continuous learner in ongoing dialogue with a larger professional field, what Alondra (above) called 'the researcher in me', allowed her to be proactive and resilient even in the face of failure.

Thus, the teachers broadly asserted that deep, critical reflection and engagement with the theory and research that made up the foundation of their field, supported their improved practice, confidence, agency and ongoing sense of belonging to the profession. For bilingual teachers, reflexivity allowed them to bring together the deeply practical with the profoundly theoretical, in the interests of forwarding radical visions for change. Reflexivity led to radical engagement with pedagogies of hope.

Developing Reflexivity

How did teachers develop critical reflexivity? Many of the teachers began Proyecto as already deeply reflective practitioners, which was one reason the program attracted them. After a minimum of five years in the field, the teachers who entered Proyecto had proven their status as 'master teachers', having achieved a certain level of reflection and confidence. At the same time, this was a group of teachers seeking more: they were thirsty for new challenges or hungry for new ideas – they were the teachers who were not satisfied to stay still, and so returned to graduate school in search of something more in their professional lives. When they entered the program, a few of the teachers already had well-developed critical pedagogical visions for social change; but many more left the program describing themselves and their work in these terms. When interviewed post-graduate school, many teachers – even those who may be described as having entered with 'ideological clarity' (Bartolomé & Balderrama, 2001) – described their experience as 'transformative'.

In that sense, this group of teachers offers the perfect window into the process of moving from merely *reflective* (thoughtful, continuously improving their practice based on their observations) to critically engaged and *reflexive*. I am defining 'reflexive' in Freirean terms: teachers who are critical pedagogues consider larger structures of power and the struggle for liberation in their daily decision-making around curriculum, instruction and professional interaction, and they engage dialogically with other professionals and with parents and students to act on behalf of justice. There is value, therefore, in understanding how teachers can move to develop their *reflexivity*, to engage more deeply with critical consciousness and to broaden their understanding of the structures of power that govern schooling.

Leila's (Cohort 1) experiences during her two long-semester courses with me in the master's program can help to illustrate the process by which teachers *developed* reflexivity, and the ways in which critical theory became increasingly integrated into their own thinking and talking about their teaching. This process unfolded differently across participants, of course, depending upon each teacher's contexts, life experiences and identities. However, Leila's particular case, with her extensive experience in the field prior to entering the program, makes a good window for understanding the process and the possibility.

A second-grade bilingual teacher with over 20 years' experience in the field when she came into graduate school, Leila had worked in a range of schools and grade levels. She had a longstanding interest in social studies and had pursued a great deal of professional development in this area, but was interested in new ideas in all areas in order to enrich her instruction in the classroom. She was the most experienced member of her cohort, and a frequent and outgoing participant in group discussions. She came into graduate school 'with conditions' imposed by the university due to her low undergraduate grade point average. However, her tremendous amount of professional experience outweighed her academic record and she performed well in her classes. One outstanding quality of Leila was that she was warm and friendly to all, almost always positive in her outlook and meticulously polite. Yet, she was not afraid to speak her mind, even to professors with whom she disagreed. This seems to be an excellent beginning to developing critical consciousness and reflexive praxis.

An example of Leila's direct but friendly interaction style occurred in one of her fall semester classes when a professor, who was a member of the Curriculum and Instruction (C&I) faculty but not in our bilingual/bicultural education program, was exhibiting a subtractive orientation toward 'poor, urban students'. Leila raised her hand and asked the professor whether it was possible that there may be other factors involved in urban school failure than just willful disengagement, as the professor was evidently implying. The story was told and retold both by Leila and by her classmates as an example of the challenges they faced as practicing bilingual teachers (in this particular cohort, all Latinas) in a large mainstream research institution's graduate school. While presenting at the annual conference of the National Association of Bilingual Education (NABE) in 2009, a presentation that Leila unfortunately had to skip because she was ill that day, one of Leila's cohort classmates told the story in this way:

> Leila … actually had the guts to question our professor [who was saying] 'Well these kids don't want to learn…' And very respectfully my colleague [Leila] said, 'well do you think that there's more there than that they don't want to learn, do you think that there's a lack or gap in meeting their needs?' just throwing it out there to make her – an educated person, you know, our superior – think. But you know to have just that perspective, and to also have the guts to feel secure to question somebody like that, to feel secure in your beliefs and to question someone who is your professor!

Leila's 'guts' and 'security' to speak her mind, her confidence in herself, emerged from her many years' solid experience in education. Certainly, her cohort classmate constructed her as a brave and clear-spoken professional; these are all qualities of strong leaders and advocates.

Leila appeared highly respected on her campus as well. She had strong relationships with both bilingual and monolingual personnel, including her principal and assistant principal. Her school, one of the largest elementary schools in the district, had over 1000 students from pre-kindergarten to Grade 5. Approximately a third of them were Hispanic and a quarter were enrolled in bilingual or English as a second language (ESL) programs. She described her biggest challenge in her efforts to strengthen her school's services to bilingual children as helping the non-bilingual education faculty and students to 'own' and respect the growing bilingual community at the school. She began graduate school focused upon how to improve student learning in her classroom, and how to improve relationships and engagement at her school. She did not necessarily begin with an understanding of the deeper issues of power and inequity in the lives of Latinx and Spanish-speaking children. Graduate school, though, was a space of growth for her in terms of developing reflexivity. Leila grappled with more critical understandings of the systematic and inequitable nature of structures of opportunity in schooling.

Early in her fall course, Leila was confronted with several readings grounded in a critical paradigm that pushed her to look at the power structures of schooling and society. Among these were two chapters from Freire's (2000) *Pedagogy of the Oppressed*, in which among other things Freire argues that the 'banking' model of traditional education disrespects students' own ideas and resources. Leila's ambivalent response reflected a lifetime of experiences in school, both positive and negative, both as student and as teacher, in which this was the dominant paradigm:

> I'm not too sure that I felt completely oppressed by this style of teaching. The 'banking concept of education' according to Freire has the potential to severely harm the human race. I do believe that because of the 'banking method' I missed out on the richness of a quality education, but I don't think that I was permanently damaged in any way.

She seemed to contradict herself a few times in this statement, as she struggled to reconcile Freire's arguments with her own experiences. Acknowledging that the main paradigm that drove most of her own schooling was rooted in what Freire would describe as 'banking education', she was 'not too sure' that she felt 'completely oppressed' by it; she agreed that she 'missed out on the richness of a quality education' but could not agree that she was 'permanently damaged'. A little later in the same thread of discussion, Leila spoke with pride and patriotism about the history of the United States, attributing the country's power to the strength of the education system:

> ...When I think about the successes of this country and how we quickly established ourselves to become a leading nation, well, it is evident that something positive had to have happened in our educational system. If learning had not taken place, where would we be know [sic]? I feel that our ancestors were taught to respect and not question the professor/teacher during lesson, but the human mind never stops working and although the mouth is silent the mind is not. Is it not human nature to learn?

Not surprisingly, considering the constructivist philosophy that guided her teaching, Leila agreed with Freire's assertion that learners should be engaged in 'problem-posing' for optimal learning, and she agreed with Freire that it was 'in human nature to learn'. Interestingly, she seemed to imply that it did not matter whether schools engaged children in problem-posing or merely 'banking', because 'the human mind never stops working'. She did not make a connection between opportunities to engage with problem-posing and social justice. She was not ready to concede that the 'banking' method is grounded in oppression, and this reflection did not note that some echelons in society experience less opportunity to engage in problem-posing than others. Based on her own experiences, she seemed to frame schooling as a great equalizer. She had enjoyed school and was a relatively successful student, and her education opened doors for her to a fulfilling profession.

Later in the semester, in response to Sofía Villenas' (2001) article 'Latina Mothers and Small-Town Racisms', Leila again experienced dissonance. She attempted to reconcile her lifelong efforts to educate Latino families (along with her own conflicted views of her parents' involvement in her schooling) with Villenas' assertion that these families' own skills, resources and cultural values are often not respected by school personnel. Villenas cautions educators not to frame immigrant mothers from a deficit perspective and in so doing engage in 'benevolent racism'. Leila reacted:

> I do think that we need to continue to educate our parents so that they can help and volunteer at our schools. With time comes change and hopefully we will continue to see our parents as advocates for our children.

While she still asserted a need to 'educate' parents so they can fit better into existing school structures, she also acknowledged a need to 'see our parents as advocates for our children'. Throughout, she described parents and children as 'ours', reflecting her long career working within her own Latinx community.

Leila revisited her struggles repeatedly in this way as she confronted each new article or idea, drawing on the support of her cohort. She carefully read and frequently responded to their reflections on the weekly Blackboard forums. Her responses often seemed meant to reassure them that things were still all right, to in a sense depoliticize the political revelations of her cohort colleagues, as can be seen in the following two responses from September:

> Hello Alicia, I enjoyed your writing and I can relate to your feelings about our educational system. I was educated in the U.S. and yet I experience the same thing, but look where we are now...something worked right? Hugs, Leila
> Hello there Lisa, I agree with [your] position on teaching, yes it is very difficult when 'your hands are tied', but like you, I strive to do my best and keep thinking about the children! Hugs, Leila

Leila made many comments simply to offer positive feedback; she was invested in building and maintaining a positive community in her cohort, as in the following from November:

> Hi Alicia, I enjoyed reading your reflection, I like the way you extended your references and made major connects to your experience and interpretations.

But other responses were more substantive, as in the following response to a colleague from an October discussion board in which she described an inequity she was noticing at her school:

> I am also concerned about the huge gaps in achievement, something is not working. When you mentioned the ESL teachers, I just found out that there are only 2 ESL certified teachers in my grade level, that's 2 out of 7 (me being one). That leaves just one teacher for all the kids...It's nuts, but, GT [gifted and talented]? Everyone is certified...interesting...they are a super team, I just don't think they realize how important it is to be able to understand and help the kids.

In this critique, even as she shared what she had recently learned about an inequity on her school campus, Leila maintained a positive attitude toward her coworkers: 'they are a super team'. She asserted that they just must not 'realize' the importance of ESL certification when a large and growing portion of students at their school were English language learners. Leila began to frame herself as a change agent in more critical terms as the first semester came to a close, in the following comment in late November in response to an article asserting the need for teachers to develop ideological clarity (Bartolomé & Balderrama, 2001), and another authored by me and two of the pilot cohort graduates that described their efforts to effect change at their schools (Palmer *et al.*, 2006). Leila asserted:

> I think that we need to insist on change on our campuses in order to help all of the kids respect each other... I am inspired to move my school forward to ensure that our kids feel ownership and a sense [of] worth. Being a bilingual teacher is not easy, it requires more than just speaking Spanish, you have to be tough, professional and as the article states 'develop a clear but flexible philosophy that helps you understand what you are doing and why, because you will be asked to defend it' (p. 79).

Leila made the assertion here that bilingual teachers not only need to 'speak Spanish' but also need to be 'tough' and 'professional', and they need to be well-grounded and prepared to defend their convictions, because the larger society will challenge them. This implied, if not outright stated, that teacher leaders do need to engage with larger forces of power as they work toward change: despite her own initial misgivings, she seemed in this reflection to be putting forth a philosophy well-aligned with Freire's critical pedagogy.

Of course, like all human endeavor, teachers' struggles to understand structural inequality are messy. It is not a simple task to uncover particular moments of transformation, either in Leila's experiences or in any of the teachers'. But many other teachers' data reflected similar struggles: grappling with class readings and discussions, bouncing ideas off cohort classmates and connecting their readings and discussions to their practice. The particular texts they were asked to take up mattered a great deal; the opportunity to reflect in safe spaces about these texts also mattered. The intellectual work of connecting the *words* they were reading and hearing in graduate school with the *world* they were engaged in beyond graduate school led many of the teachers to embrace a cycle of action and critical reflection as a part of their professional identities. They came to articulate Freire's praxis cycle in multiple ways, and to illustrate it in their classroom practice and in their descriptions of their classrooms. Although they all read several chapters of Freire in the beginning of their first long-semester course with me, not all of the teachers embraced these ideas directly beyond the expectations of my course (Natasha was obviously an exception, as was Miguel). Yet, most of the teachers articulated that one of the lessons they took from their time in the cohort was the importance of reflecting and linking their actions as teachers to those reflections in order to advocate for social justice.

Raquel (Cohort 1), a native Spanish-speaking and Spanish-educated Central American, provided another window into the process of developing critical consciousness. Raquel was a first-grade bilingual teacher in a small, diverse school in the core of the city. Because her school was predominantly populated by white middle-class students, and because their families were the most visible at the school, when she first entered graduate school Raquel stated that one of her hopes was to increase the involvement of Latino families in the governance structures of her school. She recognized the considerable efforts undertaken by the English-speaking parent community at her school to involve bilingual families in school governance, and noted that bilingual families have not responded well to these efforts. She explored possible reasons for their reticence during class discussions, noting that the structures themselves (parent-teacher association [PTA] and other schoolwide committees and events) were foreign to many bilingual – especially immigrant – families.

A crucial text for Raquel's journey was Moll *et al.*'s (1992) *Funds of Knowledge*. She enthusiastically embraced a fund of knowledge perspective and fought to maintain it. This lens shaped her subsequent experiences and became the impetus for some powerful reflection throughout the year.

For example, in keeping with her goal to increase bilingual parents' involvement at her school, Raquel took advantage of one fall semester assignment to write a column directed at parents for the local Spanish-language weekly, *¡Ahora Sí!*, to write about the PTA, letting Spanish-speaking families know about this important organization, how it works and how they might get involved. Then, a little later in the semester, Raquel identified a problem with her original framing of her goal to help bilingual families navigate her school, realizing that this represented a perspective that reinforced the white, English-speaking parents' management of school structures and governance and expected bilingual Latinx families to fit into previously existing mainstream structures. She wrote in her online discussion post to her cohort colleagues:

> La pieza de Ada y Zubizarreta (2001) me pareció muy inspiradora, no sólo presentó un 'problema' o asunto delicado desde la perspectiva del capital social sino que también presentó soluciones prácticas y muy enriquecedoras. ¡Tengo más ideas sobre qué le podemos agregar a la Noche de Lectura de mi escuela! Me llevó también a re-evaluar mis actitudes y entendimiento con respecto a las familias de mis estudiantes, y hasta cuestionarme sobre mi columna de PTA. Mi pregunta al respecto es ¿Qué tan importante es que los padres de nuestros ELLs, que tienen una percepción de la educación culturalmente diferente a la de los padres 'blancos-Europeos', aprendan sobre y se integren en las prácticas del sistema educativo de este país? *[The piece by Ada and Zubizarreta [2001] I thought was inspiring, it didn't just present a 'problem' or delicate point from the perspective of social capital but rather also offered practical and very enriching solutions. I have more ideas for our Literacy Night at my school! It also led me to re-evaluate my attitudes and understanding with respect to the families of my students, and even to question my own PTA column [for the newspaper]. My question on that is how important is it that the parents of our ELLs, who have a culturally different perception of education from the 'white European' parents, learn about and become involved in the practices of the education system of this country?]*

Raquel referenced a chapter from Reyes and Halcon's (2001) volume *The Best for Our Children* that draws on the words and thoughts of Latinx parents to interrogate mainstream theories of parent involvement, and goes on to offer alternative possibilities for authentic parent engagement for Latinx parents in US schools. This chapter prompted Raquel to reflect in several directions. First, the chapter gave her some ideas for improving the structure of an evening literacy event she took charge of at her school; she appreciated that the chapter had not only presented a problem but had also proposed some concrete, practical, exciting solutions. Next, she began to question her own advice from her newspaper column, wondering about whether it was truly appropriate or necessary to ask Latinx bilingual parents to engage in such mainstream, white-dominated organizations as her school's PTA. Ultimately, she began to ask questions that would lead her to explore the creation of alternative structures for involvement that might better match the cultural experiences and expectations of bilingual families. Looking back in reflection on her learning process in the spring semester, Raquel commented:

As I was reading this week's papers, I definitely reflected on my deficit views, and how much they've changed from the beginning of my master's a year ago, and how much they have to change as I experience new challenges, new groups of students, new attitudes in people, and my own personal limitations as a human being who was raised in a culture that, like any other culture in the world, has prejudices about others' behaviors and attitudes that are different from mine.

Raquel pointed out that the experience of transformation, and the process of embracing critical praxis, is a complicated one, with many forward and backward steps; one's journey is never complete, and each teacher explored these questions about power and privilege, justice and the purposes of education, in a different way.

I also must point out that such an open and honest reflection about one's own journey was only possible within the safety of Raquel's cohort community; feeling safe to question her foundational beliefs, Raquel actively worked to develop her critical consciousness and interrogate biases as she dialogued with texts and cohort colleagues. She went on to support transforming her school's engagement with families by becoming a vocal proponent of her school's moving from a transitional to an enrichment two-way dual language bilingual education program in the years following her graduation. She also embraced critical pedagogy in her classroom, developing units of study that would engage all students in her linguistically and culturally diverse classes in learning from one another. She worked to offer all her students a transformative set of experiences, including preservice teachers from our bilingual teacher preparation program, as she was a frequent mentor teacher for undergraduate teacher preparation students.

The process of developing reflexive practice was individual in that it was different for each individual teacher and intensely personal and self-reflective. At the same time, this process was communal and collective in that teachers interacted with each other, with texts and with professors as they developed their ideas about the world in which they worked, lived and struggled for positive change.

Making New Knowledge: Teacher Action Research

There is a growing body of evidence that empowering teachers to seek out their own answers to questions that emerge in their practice has tremendous potential to release agency and leadership skills, as well as to support reflexive practice and ultimately improve educational experiences for their students (Altrichter et al., 2013; Cochran-Smith & Lytle, 2015; Mertler, 2016). As Alondra's comment above articulates, epistemologically reflective teaching and action research are intimately connected.

The Master of Education (MEd) degree program of work did not require a culminating research project; students could complete the degree with 36 hours of coursework (12 courses), and this was the path that most chose. There was an option to replace two elective courses with a one-semester report, and earn a Master of Arts (MA) in Education rather than an MEd. For a few, a master's report or thesis, which counted for three courses and had to spread over two semesters, made sense given their interests and/or schedules.

Regardless, I made some experiences with teacher action research an explicit part of the two long-semester courses for all the cohorts. A major assignment in the fall semester was for each teacher to carry out and report on an assessment of the strengths and needs of their own school campus in terms of services and supports for bilingual students, however they decided to define these. Their reports needed to be based on data, broadly defined as information they found or collected. The second part of this assignment was to create a vision and a plan for improvement. Teachers who shared a campus did this project together. Then, in the spring semester, one of the assignments in their Teacher Leadership course asked the teachers to look at the plan they had written, choose one action item and design a professional development experience for their campus to begin to address it. Lorena (Cohort 2), who was a third-grade transitional bilingual teacher in a rural community outside Austin, described the ways in which this pair of assignments triggered processes of change: the experience allowed her to develop a vision, to make her voice heard and ultimately to make positive change happen in her small district:

> I know that the voice, the awareness, the knowledge that you gain from going through the program, and understanding that it's *practical*, it's not just...yeah, there's some theory in it...here's the theory and then here's the practicality of it...really just brought things home for me. Being able to, for example, one of the projects we had to complete, I think it was Dr. Palmer's leadership class, and it was like a data...campus needs assessment, I think is what it was called where we looked at the data that the campus culture, everything from culture, to language, to the demographics, everything, everything was encompassed within this report. And taking that information and saying, 'OK, this is what you have. Now, make it better. Put together an action plan. Put together some steps. Put together some goals. Have a vision for where you want to head within these areas'. I think that for me, that was really beneficial because I was able to TAKE that and bring it to the [school] district and present it and say, 'You know, these are our pluses and our minuses and this is how we're going to gain some additional pluses. Let's move our vision this way'.

Lorena asserted that having been required to develop a theoretically grounded analysis of data she collected about programming for emergent bilingual learners (i.e. a school-based action research project) gave her the tools to make her voice heard among her district's leadership. A direct result was the opening of spaces for change in her district – and ultimately, her experience with this process, which I had designed to engage in a Freirean praxis cycle, led to her own development of leadership skills. Soon after participating in Proyecto, Lorena became a district administrator. She served for several years as the director of bilingual/ESL programs for her district, and then as an assistant principal.

In addition to this guided school-based action research project, over the course of the program's five cohorts, I developed and gradually included in the long-semester courses an assignment in which the teachers wrote proposals for classroom-based research projects designed to answer a question of practice important to them. All members of Cohort 4 wrote research proposals in their spring semester, and the teachers in Cohort 5 actually wrote proposals in the fall and carried out very modest classroom-based research projects during the spring. It was then a more viable option for teachers to replace two of their final summer courses with a more extensive report, and actually fully carry out and write up their classroom-based research project, or something similar to it, on a larger scale during their final summer. Our final two cohorts included six students who wrote master's reports that emerged from their own questions of practice.

A few students chose this challenging path prior to my having built it into the program. Aisha (Cohort 2, fifth grade) was one of these students, largely due to her own professional goals, since she knew she wanted to continue on to a doctoral program at some point and wanted the experience of writing a thesis. When she was asked about her project, Aisha explained how she understood the value of what she had accomplished:

> The master's thesis was on a research project I did on our school's tutoring program. And I really encouraged the teachers that came [when I presented my thesis at NABE] to examine things that you are doing at your school that you're curious about, because I wanted to see if our tutoring program even worked. We were tutoring 4 days a week, all year long, for years and we weren't necessarily seeing any growth in the same kids. But I researched it and you know things had been improving even if it wasn't necessarily numerical. And I told the people in attendance, 'If there's something you're not sure about or you're wondering about, look into it. Research it. Find out the answers for yourself. You can do that as a teacher'.

For Aisha, although the answer to her research question about the efficacy of her school's tutoring program was important, the most important lesson she learned was about the power and possibility of research to answer questions of practice – and the fact that the tools of research were at her fingertips.

This, I would assert, was the lesson that many of the students took away from the experience, even if they only wrote a proposal and never actually carried out their project. The power of teacher research is the agency it offers teachers: they can answer their own professional questions. The types of questions the teachers posed varied. Some wondered about the challenges they had with particular students; others explored the efficacy of certain classroom routines, practices or programs; still others explored the possibilities of collaborative activities with colleagues. In all cases, the teachers' shared underlying purpose was to uncover problems or issues or inequities, and work to address them.

Mireya's (Cohort 4, dual language coach) master's report emerged from an issue she noted after reading some of my research about English dominance in US two-way dual language programs (Palmer, 2009). She explored Spanish and English use in the two-way dual language program at her school, in a suburban English-dominant district. The data she collected supported her intuition that English dominated the classrooms in her program. Although she had suspected this to be the case, having the data and her own analysis in hand had a powerful impact on Mireya. It planted a seed that in many ways drove her career from that point forward: her vision seemed to clarify around the marginalization of Spanish and speakers of Spanish in her school and district.

In the years that followed, Mireya would move from a site-based dual language coaching position, in which she had already initiated efforts to develop her faculty's understanding of teaching for biliteracy, to a district-level leadership position supporting general education language arts curriculum development. In this position, with the support and cooperation of a small but unified community of the district's dual language coaches, including two other Proyecto program graduates, she would strategically move her district to accommodate bilingual learners in three important ways. She worked to develop and make available more equitable curricular materials in Spanish, to offer dual language teachers authentic professional development opportunities in Spanish literacy and ultimately to move nearly all district bilingual programs from a 50:50 dual language program model to the more powerful 90:10 'minority language dominant' program model (Cloud et al., 2000). In Mireya's case, the master's report seemed to mark one important beginning point on a long and exciting road of empowerment and leadership.

Four of the teachers completed master's reports that related directly to the process of teaching other teachers, an important aspect of their work as teacher leaders. One of these was George's (Cohort 5, first-grade dual language) report, titled 'Video reflection in teacher professional development', which explicitly explored the potential of video to support teachers' development of reflective practice. In his concluding paragraph, George noted:

> The potential for video mediated reflection to improve teacher quality is immense... The stakes of this journey are high. A need for well-versed professional teachers becomes increasingly apparent in light of the proliferation of sterilized standardized curriculums. ... Our educational system stands to benefit greatly as a result of the continued development of reflective and professional teachers. The alternative is bleak to consider.

George's words articulated the urgency of the need to develop critical reflective professional teachers in our current neoliberal educational contexts.

Patricia (Cohort 4) who was a dual language coach in the same district as Mireya, wrote a report that also highlighted her work as a teacher of teachers. She talked about teacher empowerment and creating bilingual, culturally relevant mentor texts for the classroom. Her transformative participatory study involved a book study that she carried out with two of the dual language classroom teachers at her school. They examined and discussed the need to develop 'culturally relevant Spanish or bilingual mentor texts for use in writing workshop'.

Like Patricia, Natasha, who was a pre-kindergarten dual language teacher, worked with two other teachers to produce her report, a narrative analysis of a Freirean dialogue she engaged in with two colleagues that explored relationships between their cultural identities, language ideologies and teaching practices.

Miguel's (Cohort 5) report also explicitly embraced a critical pedagogy framework and explored the power of culturally relevant curriculum and instruction to transform educational experiences. Miguel focused on his use of literature circles in his own third-grade bilingual classroom. He powerfully asserted:

> I propose that literature circles based on a critical pedagogy have the potential of providing spaces to engage students in their own educational process in order to be academically and socially successful in their educational endeavor without assimilating to the dominant culture or even worse rejecting their language, culture, ethnicity (Valenzuela, 1999); but at the same time acquiring a second language and a second culture.

The teachers in their reports related theories of identity and critical pedagogy to teachers' professional and personal lives; they answered their own questions of practice, resolved their own challenges and explored topics of personal and professional interest. It was evident in Cohort 5's spring semester mini-research reports that generating new knowledge had a powerful positive impact upon their sense of professional agency. Like George's and Miguel's inspiring assertions above, the teachers spoke with eloquence, confidence and urgency about their findings.

Gisela, for example, having carried out a study with her pre-kindergarten grade-level team that related to intentional planning, reported: 'This process gave our team something that we were missing... Generating a focus for a lesson should be standard for any given planning session, however the piece for reflective discussion is also crucial'. Julieta's concluding statement about her exploration of her second-grade bilingual students' hybrid language practices, grounded in linguistic anthropology and theories of translanguaging and biliteracy, asserted: 'Promoting bilingualism in all forms, biliteracy, and biculturalism in the classroom continuously and understanding how it affects academic achievement, identity construction, and linguistic equality can be a powerful tool'. Alondra, having carried out a study exploring various ways to increase parents' participation in her second-grade bilingual classroom, wrote:

> Using articles from different sources to inform parents about the importance of being part of the education of their children had an impact on their participation. Parents want to be involved in their students' education and they need for us as teachers to guide them with this process... It is important that we continue looking for ways to increase parental involvement so that students thrive in the classroom and have positive attitudes towards their education.

Maya's case study of the fascinating path to biliteracy of one emergent bilingual student with attention deficit hyperactivity disorder (ADHD) in her second-grade class led her to conclude, 'Amy's case study shows the value of in-depth individual studies. This case study allowed a close look at the different factors that may affect an emergent bilingual's literacy development'. At the end of Natasha's (pre-K dual language) exploration of humanizing pedagogies that might be in tune with her particularly active group of four- and five-year-old boys, she exclaimed:

> Me encantaría continuar investigando y aprendiendo a proveer una educación centrada en las necesidades y capacidades de los niños. Estoy muy de acuerdo en la necesidad de ofrecerle a los niños Latinos una educación de calidad y de altura, en el cual se vean retados y animados a dar lo mejor de ellos. *[I would love to continue studying and learning to provide an education centered in the needs and strengths of boys. I'm very much in favor of the necessity to offer Latino boys an education of*

quality and caliber, in which they appear challenged and motivated to give the best of themselves.]

These bilingual teachers carried out powerful research about bilingual children and the kinds of pedagogies that support their success. What's more, developing the tools to answer their own questions transformed their practice.

Reflection into Action

Every teacher dreams of their students taking their learnings into their lives, applying directly what they've learned; in this way, being the professor of Proyecto teachers was extremely satisfying. There are a tremendous number of examples of the teachers applying reflexivity and praxis to their classroom practice and into their professional work in general. Critical pedagogy was a central theme in teachers' conversations through the years as they made sense of these powerful ideas for their teaching. But praxis for the teachers, as for Paolo Freire, did not stop within classroom practice; it went far beyond the classroom and beyond the teaching and learning they directed, into the *world* – a world that frequently marginalized bilingual and Latinx students and families. Thus, in many cases, the teachers' reflections led directly to activism – direct and clear action meant to advocate for equity or fairness.

Christine (Cohort 3) explained the way she saw the relationship between her activism and her job as a fourth-grade bilingual teacher:

> ...if no one is saying something at my school about something that should be said then it's like, 'Oh, then I guess I better do that.' I'm the one that would say anything. Or if something's happening in the community or to our vertical team and there was very little teacher voice or teacher representation it's like, 'Oh well now I better step forward and write some letter to the editor or contact the [newspaper] or something.' So I think what happens...I definitely want to focus on what happens right here in this [class]room but I know...I feel like as an educator I'm very aware of what happens *outside* of this room though too and I just want to help these kids find that path so that they're okay and so that they find what they want, right?

A teacher's job, as Christine described it, was to 'help these kids find that path', and sometimes that required not just focusing on what happens within the classroom but also being aware of issues impacting the community outside the classroom – and speaking up.

The year following her graduation, Christine won the honor of district-wide Elementary Teacher of the Year. Immediately following this honor, she found herself challenged to speak up about an important issue: the closing of a neighborhood elementary school in her students' community (not her school, but nearby) and the opening of an unwelcome English-only charter school in its place. As she put it, 'that's one of those kind of moments that just sort of propel me to action'.

Having a master's degree, and having the status of Teacher of the Year for the entire district, significantly increased Christine's confidence as she stepped up. She explained:

> I guess I sort of felt like especially last year that I was in some untouchable bubble...I was teacher of the year and if [district administration] is going to pull some crazy stuff (against me) it's going to look real weird...
> I really stepped out as somebody who would write and speak for this community and what they needed, and what wasn't fair, and what was done incorrectly, passing injustices and things like that. And it's perhaps now that I feel like, 'Well I have a Master's! So you should think I'm kind of smart, and maybe I can say all this and hopefully I won't get in trouble (but let me join the Union anyways because I probably will get in trouble.) But I think my leadership roles have drastically changed in the last two years based on situations and then based on like the confidence gained from doing the Master's program.

Activism for Christine in the year or two after she completed her master's degree increased significantly, partly based on circumstances, in that there were urgent things to activate against, and partly based on her own identity and confidence. In the years that followed, Christine maintained an activist identity. Even as the perceived aura of invincibility that she described began to fade, she would continue to be known as the teacher who spoke up when things were not right:

> I stay in really close contact with the union when something comes up. For example, I didn't want to give a mandated Spanish test that was badly translated and two questions about the rhyme scheme of a translated poem that didn't rhyme. Why would I give that test. But I wrote an email to the people in charge of the test, and got reprimanded by my principal for 45 minutes. These are the kinds of things I'm sure I will keep doing, but they do have consequences for me.

Christine authored herself as an outspoken, ideologically clear activist, even as a troublemaker. Not all the teachers became activists to this extent. Some did, but nearly all found their voices and spoke up in various strategic ways, from speaking their mind to grade-level team teachers about issues of curriculum and instruction, to speaking up at faculty meetings, to sharing important information with parents about community issues and events. There were many ways in which teachers brought the world into their visions for leadership.

Praxis as the Antidote to Discouragement and Burnout: Pursuing Continued Opportunities for Critical Engaged Reflection

An argument could be made that our requirement of a minimum of five years' teaching experience for admission to the Proyecto cohort master's program supported the teachers' development of such powerful reflection/action connections, and their moving more smoothly into leadership identities. The teachers were at a stage in their careers where they had firmed up their practice. They were no longer novices, and had enough experience to have identified their own strengths and needs, as well as to have uncovered plenty of challenges and issues in their contexts. Maya (Cohort 5), a second-grade dual language teacher in a suburban district, explained:

> You get overwhelmed by the system and you get used to... at least for me, where I used to teach, it was 'here's your curriculum and you are going to teach it every year' and a bunch of problems that come with it. Meetings after meetings that don't give a chance to reflect on your teaching. I found that to be different here [at UT] and this program has helped me to reflect on my own teaching and on myself as a teacher in a different way. It's given me the time and the pause. Having – teaching for 8 years and [comparing] before Proyecto Maestría and for these past 3 years that I have been teaching in my district, I feel like I've learned so many things... It comes with maturity too. Maybe in the beginning of my career I was more focused on learning how to teach that I wasn't focused on other aspects.

For bilingual teachers in particular there is a documented tendency to become discouraged by the particular set of challenges and extra work entailed in their positions. Teacher retention is a particular challenge in many bilingual contexts (Montaño & Burnstein, 2006; Ovando & Casey, 2010; Weaver, 2003) in part precisely because of the marginalization they and their students experience on a daily basis. Reflexive practice, and the development of critical sociocultural awareness, helped the teachers grapple with these challenges, understand the underlying causes and come to terms with the difficulties, such as racism and other forms of bias, structural inequities and poverty that they witnessed and experienced. As George (Cohort 5), a first-grade dual language teacher, explained, 'It can be kind of overwhelming and depressing sometimes, of being able to make sense of these things and historically'. Ultimately, critical awareness offered teachers the vocabulary and the tools to reorient themselves away from the negative and toward the possible. Christine (Cohort 3, fourth-grade bilingual) explained the affordances and challenges of critical awareness this way:

> Maybe it just happens with every cohort, but towards the end people just seemed somewhat negative about school. We would have these discussions where you become aware and more resentful of the bad stuff that happens all the time. I think in a way it makes us so critical that we become unhappy. But at the same time, I hope that many of us are stepping forward and challenging practices that are outdated or don't value children or families.

The experience of developing the language and understanding to critically engage with issues of both classroom and society, and to challenge the status quo and work for change, energized the teachers. Their positive energy in the profession visibly impacted their campuses and the leadership in the district. Gisela (Cohort 5), a pre-kindergarten dual language teacher, shared her post-Proyecto professional energy in an interview, barely containing her enthusiasm:

> A mí me gustaría pasar unos *años* en mi salón. The way I see it, I'd like to perfect my craft, what I do. Estoy como que bien ansiosa que llegue el año que entra porque ya quiero empezar a implementar cosas nuevas que se me han ocurrido. Quiero tener unos cuantos años más de eso y luego tal vez buscar otro grado u otra escuela, u otro trabajo que sea diferente pero en educación. Como que hay personas que, ok, ya me voy, pero yo quiero quedarme y mejorar unos cuantos años y seguir implementado las cosas que he aprendido y seguir aprendiendo cosas nuevas para implementar en mi salón. *[I'd like to spend years in my classroom. The way I see it, I'd like to perfect my craft, what I do. I'm like, really excited for next year to get here because I already want to begin implementing new things that have occurred to me. I want to have a few more years of this and later maybe look for another grade or another school, or another job that might be different but in education. Like, there are people who, 'ok, I'm out of here,' but I want to stay and improve for several years and continue implementing the things that I've learned and keep learning new things to implement in my classroom.]*

Thirst for ongoing, authentic professional learning opportunities brought many of the teachers into Proyecto in the first place. By many reports, the experience of Proyecto supported and expanded this thirst: Patricia (Cohort 4, dual language coach) for example, at the end of her interview several years after graduation, when asked if she had anything else to add, exclaimed, 'Wow! That was probably the best years of my academic career. It's just, it really opens your eyes to be more reflective and keep you learning'.

Not surprisingly, thirst for continued growth carried far beyond Proyecto for most of the teachers. I might even define teacher leaders as those teachers whose thirst for continued learning seems insatiable; and their manifestations of leadership are as varied as the directions their thirst might take them. Lorena (Cohort 2, third-grade bilingual) expressed in an interview several years after completing her master's, the motivation behind every one of her recent career moves: 'I know that my goal is to continue to learn and move forward'. Lucia (Cohort 4, fourth-grade bilingual math/science) in a post-program interview, explained why she decided to move to a different school, despite having built positive relationships at her current school:

> Ultimately, I guess, for selfish reasons I wanted to be in an environment where I can *learn* from people. I just… I feel like I'm at that point where I want to learn and so here [at current school] it's more, I'm the teacher, which is fine because I'm teaching other people. But, I don't have any growth. And I don't mean, I want more, you know, to be an assistant principal or anything like that. But I mean, I want to learn from other people how to be a better teacher. And I really don't have that here.

As one, the teachers recognized the potential of authentic professional learning to energize and motivate them. They saw the power and hope behind a critical pedagogy, and they did not stop after Proyecto. They continued to seek out new opportunities to learn, to grow and to contribute.

Consuelo (Cohort 4), who was a kindergarten dual language teacher in a private bilingual school during Proyecto, went on to become a certified reading teacher. Lucia (Cohort 4), who was a fourth-grade math/science bilingual teacher, moved schools and also became an adult ESL teacher at a nearby community college. Emilia (Cohort 4, pre-K bilingual), as I will elaborate in the final chapter, became a leader in the teacher's union and entered into dialogue with school district leadership on behalf of teachers' issues across her district. Many, many of the teachers have sought administrative credentials and additional master's degrees. Four of the teachers have entered doctoral programs. Several of the teachers were National Board Certified: Nicole (Cohort 1, pre-K bilingual) actually accomplished this *during* her Proyecto year, while Emilia (Cohort 4, pre-K bilingual) and George (Cohort 5, first-grade dual language) chose to go through this intensive process prior to entering Proyecto.

To make strong bilingual programs that support success for transnational Latina/o bilingual students, by necessity we must work to develop not only bilingualism, biliteracy, biculturalism and strong academic achievement, but also a critical sociocultural awareness at all levels – among kids, parents and educators (Cervantes-Soon *et al.*, 2017). This comes from engagement in the cycle of reflection and action to acknowledge the dominant structures of power in the worlds inside and outside our schools. In order for teachers to develop the 'ideological clarity' required to lead this charge, to counter the dominant hegemonic forces that subordinate and marginalize Latinx and other bilingual learners in our schools, they must develop the tools for reflexivity – for critical praxis. While reflection is a key characteristic of successful teacher leadership in all contexts, bilingual teachers by necessity take this reflection further: in reflecting on their conditions for work, they develop critical awareness. Successful bilingual teacher leaders' reflection leads to praxis; their action–reflection cycle turns political and their work to improve their own and others' practice in schools and classrooms becomes advocacy and activism. As Christine (Cohort 3, fourth-grade bilingual) explained:

> I think we get pretty radical and subversive here in my classroom sometimes. I think that was happening before Proyecto but I think it happens on a deeper level now. My first year of teaching we did a unit on gentrification but I was just making up stuff and asking kids what their thoughts were. They wrote some really cool poetry, but it was not like what we do in Proyecto—connecting with other teachers to really work through units of study and make them systematic. What am I pushing children to think about, to do, to say? And so through the relationships I've made we would meet in a small professional learning community to really develop a unit on identity texts where we used picture books that are culturally relevant that reflect the authentic experiences of children of color. We used those as a way to help kids start expressing themselves. Units become richer through the relationships I've made during my Master's.

From Christine's explanation and others, it is clear that community, collegiality and collaboration play a central role in empowering teachers to embrace leadership identities. It is also clear that cultural relevance and critical pedagogy go hand in hand in master bilingual teachers' classrooms; the link between cultural/linguistic identity and professional identity is what I will take up next.

Note

(1) I believe Miguel means 'commits', which is directly translated from the Spanish 'compromiso' or commitment.

6 Bilingual Teacher Leaders are Cultural/Linguistic Brokers

I started thinking when we started with your class. My way of thinking changed just from that, you know, from, I guess **getting to know myself a little bit more**, and the way I was thinking. Como la mayoría de la gente piensa *[like the majority of people think]*, you know, estos, es la culpa de los padres *[these, it's the parents' fault]*. You know, I had that mentality. (Mariana, Cohort 1 bilingual literacy coach, after graduation in conversation with Dr Fránquiz, professor of her first cohort course)

One of the most powerful differences the teachers and I noted between their own paths to leadership and the paths of monolingual, mainstream teachers was the central and primary role that awareness of linguistic and cultural identities played. In line with what Moraes (1996) argues is necessary in any bilingual education context, the Proyecto teachers' particular brand of reflexive practice was necessarily married to an accounting for cultural and linguistic identities – their own and their students'. As would be expected, participants came into the program along continua in terms of critical multicultural awareness, or a coupling of awareness of their personal cultural/linguistic identities and understanding of the larger structures of society that stratify these (Bartolomé & Balderrama, 2001; Freire, 2000). But they consistently described their experiences in the program as furthering their journeys in this way. As Mariana expressed above, 'getting to know [themselves] a little bit more' and interrogating their own ways of understanding their histories and those of their students began the change process, leading many to identify and to question their own deficit assumptions. This self-interrogation turned out to be essential to their embracing of leadership identities.

This was true not only for the participants who themselves shared a cultural/linguistic identity with the majority of their students (i.e. Mexican-American or immigrant Latinx teachers who grew up bilingual or speaking primarily Spanish in their homes), but with *all* the teachers. Whether they shared their students' backgrounds or not, nearly all the teachers echoed the sense that their own growing understandings of themselves and their own place in the world supported their work as teachers and leaders in dialogue with and for bi(multi)lingual Latinx children. As the reader might imagine, among 53 teachers there was a wide range of experiences; the consistency of this theme in all of their narratives of their experiences in the program was striking.

Admittedly, this was not necessarily by accident; several class assignments across their cohort courses explicitly supported teachers' explorations of their own and their families' linguistic and cultural identities. This was strongly supported in the literature on the development of teacher leadership (Katzenmeyer & Moller, 2009) and bilingual teacher preparation (de Jong, 2011; Ladson-Billings, 1995b; Lucas & Villegas, 2013; Nieto, 2002), and as I have articulated, we intentionally made cultural/ linguistic identity a central theme in the program. Furthermore, both during the application process pre-matriculation and when we interviewed the teachers post-graduation, we explicitly invited them to share the story of how they became bi(multi)lingual, and how this has impacted them as teachers. This, of course, brought out their personal histories and cultural/ linguistic identities. Nevertheless, this emerges as an important part of the journey toward bilingual teacher leadership because of the force with which the teachers seemed driven to share their stories and to make links between their own identities and the work they did as teachers, leaders and advocates. The links and connections, and the vehemence with which they shared them, came from the teachers.

In this chapter, I will share some of the participants' rich and powerful descriptions of their personal journeys through the educational system and their developing understandings of their linguistic and cultural identities and critical multicultural consciousness. Linked to these narratives, I will share some articulated (i.e. in teachers' written or spoken words) and embodied (i.e. in their classroom and professional practices) examples of the central role cultural/linguistic identity played in teachers' practice. These examples will bridge the connection between teaching and being, which was ultimately for these teachers the process of constructing oneself as an advocate/activist and leader.

Developing Awareness of Cultural/Linguistic Identities: The Proyecto Experience

Dr Alba Ortiz, project co-director, gave an inspiring and very personal keynote speech at the 2016 teacher-organized ¡Adelante! Conference in Austin. Her talk was a richly painted tapestry of her own cultural and linguistic heritage, a Tejana raised in San Antonio with Spanish and English all around her, linking each fascinating, funny, heartwarming and eye-opening detail to its value for educational success. Her choice to share these personal stories took me – and many of us, I think – by surprise. I knew she had such stories to share; her amazing mother, then having achieved centenarian status without losing an ounce of acerbity or wit, was the subject of many shared moments of laughter and admiration over coffee in the kitchen of the Office of Bilingual Education at the University of Texas (UT). But Alba had nearly always stayed on-message in public talks that I had witnessed, using every offered venue to push the central message of her career, that emergent bilingual children require and deserve equitable access to special education services when – and only when – they need them. So I, like all the other listeners that evening, was mesmerized by Alba's narratives.

The next day, in the corridor outside the exhibits, I was catching up with two Proyecto graduates, Lorena and Margarita (Cohort 2). Lorena, previously a third-grade bilingual teacher but at this point a bilingual/English as a second language (ESL) coordinator for her small rural district, made the following connection:

> [Dr Ortiz' message] reminded me of this one book – I was actually pulling it out from the shelves – *The Sleeping Giant* (Katzenmeyer & Moller, 2009) book that was part of our program. And I thought to myself, 'I don't want to be sleeping'. Right?!

Margarita, who was about to begin an administrator certification program, agreed with her, asserting: 'We are going to go in there and we are going to wake up!' Lorena and Margarita saw an instant link between Dr Ortiz' talk about her own cultural/linguistic heritage and identity, and 'waking up' – activating and advocating for bilingual children in schools.

The 'first stage' described by Katzenmeyer and Moller (2009) for developing teacher leaders is to learn about 'Self'. The stages that follow are to learn about one's context and what needs to change, and then to gain the skill set to enact positive change. This connection between culture/language and engaged, critical advocacy emerges also in Yosso (2005), Ladson-Billings (1995) and Moll *et al.* (1992), all of whom the participants read and discussed early in their program. In particular, the students in Proyecto read about funds of knowledge for teaching; they read a range of work that has emerged from this framework, and they engaged in funds of knowledge research themselves in several of their courses.

Literacy journey boxes

The very first assignment teachers had when they began their master's degree program with Dr María Fránquiz was to create a literacy journey box (Fránquiz *et al.*, 2013; Labbo & Field, 1999) in which they pulled together photographs, memories and images to build a box and write a narrative explaining their journey to biliteracy. The second time they met as a cohort, they began by sharing these journeys, and this experience supported their bonding as a cohort. Emma (Cohort 4, K bilingual) explained:

> I still remember the first summer we were in the program. Everyone was in tears with Dr. Fránquiz' class with journey boxes, I want to cry now, it was – it just – all of us cried because we hadn't realized we had dug back into our past, and why we're here, and why we're truly doing what we're doing. It was amazing.

As Emma explained, the literacy journey boxes assignment supported students' initial dig into funds of knowledge: their own. It supported their co-construction as a community of bilingual teachers, it deepened their understandings of their own personal cultural/linguistic identities and it awakened them to why this was important.

Raquel (Cohort 1, first grade), having grown up in an elite family in Central America, described the importance of journey boxes for her developing her understanding of the cultural and linguistic resources of her first-grade students:

> All the things [my cohort colleagues] shared about their personal life taught me so much about bilingual education in this country it was so like… you went through this? and this is because they're from different regions of Texas and they all had so many rich experiences and their perspectives as learners and bilingual students in Texas, it's just so *rich* to me and more meaningful than going through several books of history. And I'm not, I used the book as references because they have good information. They're nice to me and answered a lot of questions that I had in relation to the background of my students in their families, in their families' history in this country so I think it was just completely an eye-opening experience. And they are still you know …every class we get to share a little bit more about something else in a different area so there is always something else to learn about them. To me that's one of the most important things about the cohort – that we're there to support each other and learn from each other. (field notes, NABE Conference, Feb 18–21, 2009, Austin TX)

At information/recruitment sessions, at the above-referenced National Association of Bilingual Education (NABE) Conference presentation in 2009, at meetings with faculty and the new incoming cohort, Raquel articulated repeatedly that in her view the most important lesson she learned in Proyecto was taught to her in the first week of the first summer session, when she heard her eight cohort colleagues share their own personal histories with language, literacies and cultures through the journey box project. Listening to her classmates, she explains, her eyes were opened and her vision transformed. She developed a renewed understanding and respect for the rich mixing of languages and cultures in Texas – and most importantly, a better understanding of her own young students, border dwellers, whom she had before thought of as having 'deficits' in their Spanish and their English.

I asked George (Cohort 5), a white, male, first-grade dual language teacher, what he most remembered about Proyecto after he finished. He immediately offered:

> How quick it seemed to gel… it's like, people that you've known for ever. It happened within the first two weeks of Proyecto. I remember doing the Journey Boxes… and having everybody go around and share in class. I still very, very, you know, it seems like it was yesterday. I still remember certain things that people talked about their experiences.

In a focus group interview in response to 'what was eye opening' in Proyecto, Gisela (pre-K) and Alondra (second grade) from Cohort 5 had the following exchange:

Gisela:	Para mi fue eye opening cuando tuvimos la clase con Dr. Franquiz porque fue donde dije, 'Ah, sí. Es cierto. Nosotros nunca tuvimos libros. Ah, sí, el catecismo'. Fue cuando empecé a ver esas piezas que tuve como literatura. Yo nunca había pensado en la lotería como literatura pero ya analizando bueno, sí es cierto, crecí con la lotería. Eran como mis primeras palabras. Era el juego familiar y empecé a verlo de otra manera; y los cuentos de mi papá. Se la pasaba contando contándonos cuentos todo el día y aprendí muchas cosas académicas por medio de sus cuentos pero nunca pensé que me estaba enseñando algo. *[For me it was eye opening when we had the class with Dr Franquiz because that was where I said, 'ah yes, it's true. We never had books. Ah yes, catechism.' It was when I began to see those pieces that I had as literature. I had never thought of Lotería (Mexican bingo-type game) as literature but looking at it closely, yes it's true, I grew up with Lotería. Those were like my first words. It was the family game and I began to see it in a different way; and the stories of my dad. He passed the time telling stories all day and I learned many academic things by way of his stories but I never thought that he was teaching me something.]*
Interviewer:	¿Qué pasó en la clase de la Dra. Fránquiz? *[What happened in Dr F's class?]*
Alondra:	Teníamos que escribir un ensayo sobre nuestra adquisición de la lectoescritura. *[We had to write an essay about our acquisition of literacy.]*

Gisela: Biliteracy journey. Tenías que irte hasta atrás. Como
             aprendiste a leer en tu primer idioma, de los dos, pero lo
             más que te puedes acordar. Teníamos que traer la cajita llena
             de objetos. *[Biliteracy journey. You had to go back in time.
             How did you learn to read in your first language, in both,
             but as much as you could remember. We had to bring the
             box full of objects.]*

In that first assignment, these two teachers explained, their definitions
of literacy expanded to include the kinds of family and community activities
they had participated in as Latina children in Texas bilingual homes near
the border; they began to see the educational value of the games, stories
and religious practices they had taken for granted. And they realized they
had been essentially tricked by the dominant society that led them to believe
that no books in their homes meant no literacy. They had to 'go back,
to how [they] learned to read'. This, they explained, was so eye-opening
because of the implications it held for their own literacy teaching in their
primary-grade bilingual classrooms. Later in the interview, in response to
the question 'Anything else you have modified in your practice as a teacher?'
Gisela explained:

Han sido varias cosas. Como este, el proceso de aprender; la literatura, los
libros que escogemos. Yo creo que no le estaba poniendo tanta atención
a los libros que estaba escogiendo porque para empezar donde trabajaba
antes tenías que seguir el curriculum que te daban y no lo cuestionaba.
No había sido consciente que era diferente. Siento que sí he notado desde
Proyecto Maestría la diferencia y la necesidad de por qué usar cierta
literatura con nuestros estudiantes y las diferentes maneras en que los
estudiantes se pueden involucrar. En la clase que aprendimos de literature
circles y que ellos pueden tener una discusión que se inicia por ellos mismos,
no por nosotros y lo que puede salir de esas conversaciones. *[There have
been various things. Like, the learning process: literature, the books we
choose. I think that I wasn't giving much attention to the books that I was
choosing because to begin with, where I was working before you had to
follow the curriculum they gave you and you didn't question it. I hadn't
been aware that there was anything different. I feel like yes, I've noticed
since Proyecto Maestría the difference and the need for why we should
use certain literature with our students and the different ways that the
students can be involved. In the class where we learned about literature
circles and that they can have a discussion initiated by themselves, not by
us, and what can come out of those conversations.]*

The teachers linked this particular assignment and others that followed
to their own transformed practice, to an emphasis on culturally

relevant and sustaining (Ladson-Billings, 1995b; Paris, 2012) books and materials, engaging activities that center children's own narratives and ideas and an intentionality to their professional choices that had been less present prior to their being in graduate school. This is critical multicultural awareness: reflexive practice infused with the intention to center (hooks, 2015) their students' cultural and linguistic identities. Gisela went on to explain that in the process of creating and sharing their own literacy journey boxes, they 'let down the walls' between each other as cohort colleagues. This, in turn, led to them deliberately taking down the walls between themselves as teachers and the parents of students in their classrooms:

> Yo creo que también entre nosotros dejamos caer la muralla que uno pone naturalmente cuando conoce a una persona que es nueva porque no los conoce. Nosotros la dejamos caer cuando empezamos a presentar nuestro journey of biliteracy... Dejamos caer nuestros murales y nos llegamos a conocer entre nosotros y creo que Lupe (Palmer *et al.*, 2006) habló como ella con sus niños era bien honesta y siempre bajaba ese mural para que ellos la llegaran a conocer mejor a ella y así ellos pudieran bajar sus propios murales. Creo que fue algo así con los padres. Como que yo bajé mi mural con los padres. Que sepan todo de mí, de donde vengo, quién soy, etc. También con los niños. Les abrí las puertas a quién soy yo y cuáles son mis debilidades. *[I believe that also between us we let down the wall that naturally gets built when one meets a new person because one doesn't know them. We let it fall when we began to present our journey of biliteracy... We let our walls come down and got to a place where we knew each other and I think that Lupe talked about how she with her students was very honest and always took down this wall so that they could get to know her better and that way they could take down their own walls. I think it was something like this with the parents. Like I took down my wall with the parents. That they learn everything about me, where I am from, who I am, etc. Also with the children. I opened the doors to them about who I am and what are my weaknesses.]*

Gisela provided a beautiful and poetic description of the process of learning to engage in Freirean dialogue in their cohort, and carrying that dialogue into their relationships with families, thus humanizing the relationship between teacher and parents.

Finally, when asked directly by the interviewer, 'Do you think it was necessary to uncover who you are?' Gisela unhesitatingly responded, 'yes'. The interviewer asked her to explain why, and she responded:

> Then it brings back why you became a teacher and why you wanted to teach with this population. What can you do to make a difference? It

brings back the whole 'you are here because...' You know. The whole reason of why you became a teacher.

Gisela confirmed that the purpose, for her, of learning to value her own past experiences and develop a deepened sense of her own cultural and linguistic identity, was to connect herself with her professional identity; *who* she was personally and culturally formed the basis of her understanding of *why* she was a bilingual teacher.

Preguntale a la maestra: *Ask the Teacher*

Another major assignment that seemed to spur the teachers to talk about their personal cultural and linguistic identities was the column that students wrote in their long-semester cohort courses with me or Dr Carmen Martínez-Roldán as their professor, for a local Spanish weekly, *¡Ahora Sí!*. This was an assignment all of the students had to complete in their fall and spring long-semester cohort courses. Thanks to the hard work and outreach of one of our project coordinators, Elizabeth Villarreal, we had an arrangement with the editors of the *Austin American-Statesman*'s Spanish-language weekly to publish our teachers' columns in a series titled 'Pregúntale a la maestra/Ask the teacher' (or 'al maestro' when it was a male teacher). Most of the teachers became published authors through this collaboration, and the column itself won a prestigious bronce/*bronze* José Martí award in 2009 for 'mejor serie de articulos/*best series of articles*'.

Lorena Pacheco (Cohort 2), who traveled an hour each way to classes on campus to participate in Proyecto, was one of the teachers who shared a Tejana background with many of her students in the rural town where she taught third grade. In the fall semester, she wrote her column for *¡Ahora Sí!* about the important role of storytelling in developing literacy and cultural identities for bilingual Tejanx children.

Lorena's column was titled 'Cuentame Otro Cuento.../*Tell me another story...*' and the rough draft she handed in to me began:

Estas eran mis palabras cuando mi papá acababa de contar sus cuentos de los tiempos pasados. Muchos de sus cuentos incluían cuentos acerca de leyenda de la Llorona o cuentos acerca de la mano pachona. Recuerdo también que mi papá tenía la habilidad de capturar la atención de todos que prestaban atención a sus cuentos. Mi papá nos contaba comó era nuestro pueblo antes y de la gente que vivía allí. También nos contó comó mi abuelita le había dado a luz dentro de un vagón de tren durante los tiempos que eran migrantes porque no había hospitales y aunque si los hubiera su familia no tenía el dinero para ir a ellos. Recuerdo que contó de los tiempos en que su familia viajaba atravéz de los Estados Unidos como trabajadores migrantes. Los cuentos de mi papá han permanecido conmigo atravéz de mucho tiempo. Y siempre cuando los recuerdo siento respeto y aprecio por las experencias que ha compartido mi papá conmigo. Lo más importante que he logrado en descubir es de la importancia de no dejar que estos cuentos mueran. *[These were my words when my dad would finish telling his stories in times past. Many of his stories included stories about the legend of the 'Wailing Woman' or stories about 'The Fuzzy Hand.' I also remember that my dad had the ability to capture the attention of everyone who listened to his stories. My dad told us stories about his town in the past and the people who lived there. He also told us how my grandmother had given birth to him in a train car during the times when they were migrants because there were no hospitals and even if there had been his family didn't have the money to go to them. I remember that he told of the times in which his family would travel across the United States as migrant workers. The stories of my dad have stayed with me across many years. And also when I remember them I feel respect and appreciation for the experiences that my dad shared with me. The most important thing I have discovered is the importance of not letting these stories die.]*

Stories from her father, Lorena explained, helped her to know who she was, where she came from and how her ancestors had survived and thrived. They communicated cultural norms and practices, along with the histories from her own community that remained lamentably absent from the official narratives found in textbooks. Referencing Gerald Campano's (2007) work, which she had read in one of her classes, Lorena went on to explain to her audience:

Las historias orales nos enseñan mucho acerca de las realidades que fueron las historias de nuestros antepasados. Nos ayudan a conocer una historia que desafortunadamente han sido omitidos de los textos academicos. Cuando compartimos historias orales estámos compartiendo recuerdos y eventos que son importantes para nuestras propias familias, para mantener tradiciones orales en nuestra cultura y para desarrollar nuestro sentido como individuos. Las historias orales son importantes porque son lo que hemos sobrevivido. *[Oral histories teach us a great deal about the realities that were the stories of our ancestors. They help us know a history that unfortunately has been omitted from academic texts. When we share oral stories we are sharing memories and events that are important for our own families, to maintain oral traditions in our culture and to develop our sense as individuals. Oral histories are important because they are what we have survived.]*

Ultimately, she assured parents (and anyone reading her column), oral storytelling traditions would help their children thrive in school and in life and build strength and resilience in their family and community.

These were messages Lorena had heard herself in her courses, and they were profound messages for her, given her own background and history (see below). Lorena's articulation of these ideas for an audience of parents and community was a clear example of engaging in Freire's dialogue: bringing a thoughtful idea into the community, offering people words for phenomena that potentially shape their reality and the tools to name and transform that reality. In a Bakhtinian sense, she had taken the words/ ideas that seemed powerful to her, shaped them into her own and sent them back into the world expanded and changed to reach a new audience. In a sense, she was dialoguing with her professors and texts, and then forming a bridge from the theory and examples in the graduate school scholarly texts to the real and concrete realities in the larger Spanish-speaking community in the region. This type of intellectual bridge-building was a feat at which the teachers were particularly strong.

The column came out several months later in the newspaper. Shortly thereafter, bringing tears to our eyes, Lorena shared in class and later at a professional conference an extraordinary experience that, she explained, affirmed a thousand-fold the truth in what she had argued in her column. An elderly Spanish-speaking Tejano gentleman had tracked her down. He had come to her school, having driven a significant distance from his own rural Texas home, asking to talk with her. He had a neatly folded copy of her column in his hands. He told her that he just wanted to thank her for putting into words what he knew deeply to be true: that his stories, and the stories of his elders, were valuable and that his children and grandchildren would learn from them. He just wanted to thank her. She was awestruck by his visit. And so, the dialogue continued, sometimes reaching beyond our own perception into communities we never imagined.

The ¡Ahora Sí! column was an open-topic assignment, with students encouraged to respond to any real or imagined questions they felt parents would appreciate. Many columns covered topics directly related to navigating the education world or advocating for the needs of one's child, such as the potential consequences of absenteeism; the purposes and limitations of state-mandated standardized tests; the inside scoop on state and district class size regulations; what to do if a child is being bullied; ensuring your child is college-ready; seeking college scholarships and other resources for undocumented students; and how to access gifted/ talented or special education services. Others dealt with education in a broader sense, such as ideas for kitchen mathematics, advice about the importance of good nutrition for young children or resources/special events in the community.

But it is worth noting that Lorena's was one of a number of columns – at least a couple every year – that directly addressed links between Latinx cultural/linguistic identities and success in school and life. One column, for example, by Jennifer (Cohort 2, K) was titled 'Transmite el orgullo por tu cultura para que los niños aprendan mejor/*Transmit pride for your culture so that children learn better*'. Another by Ileana (Cohort 4, fourth grade) was titled 'Cuida tu cultura en tu corazón/*Care for your culture in your heart*'. Alicia (Cohort 1, second grade) wrote a column titled 'Cuenta anécdotas a tu hijo/*Tell stories to your child*' that reminded parents of the power of sharing their memories for building up children's understanding of themselves and their families/communities/cultures. She explained, 'La historia de tu vida refleja ricas costumbres y el orgullo por ser quien eres [*The story of your life reflects rich customs and the pride of being who you are]*'. Patricia (Cohort 4, dual language coach) wrote a column titled 'Lo hermoso de ser morena/*The beauty of being brown*', springing from her four-year-old daughter's questions about race and ethnic identity; she wrote:

> Me di cuenta de que [mi hija] ya percibía los efectos de la discriminación. Como padres, es muy importante que habelemos con nuestros hijos sobre este tema. Debemos inculcarles el valor de pertenecer a dos culturas y hablar dos idiomas. [*I realized that (my daughter) already perceived the effects of discrimination. As parents, it's very important the we talk with our children about this topic. We need to inculcate in them the value of belonging to two cultures and speaking two languages.*]

Sofia's (Cohort 3, fourth grade) title was 'Da a tu hijo aceso a su patrimonio cultural/*Give your child access to his/her cultural heritage*', and in it she defined 'capital cultural/*cultural capital*' along the lines of Yosso's (2005) framework of community cultural wealth. The final paragraph of her article read:

> Cuéntale a tu hijo las historias que te contaban tus abuelos, cocínale platillos de tu país, muéstrale fotografías de tu país de origen, si puedes busca en Internet información sobre tu país, léanla juntos y conversen sobre ella. Que nuestros niños aprendan a sentirse muy orgullosos de toda la riqueza de su cultura, para que su identidad se fortalezca y puedan así desarrollarse en todo aspecto. [*Tell your child the stories that your grandparents told you, cook the dishes from your country, show him/her photographs of your country of origin, if you can find on the Internet information about your country, read it together and talk about it. Our children should learn to feel very proud of all the wealth of their culture, so that their identity strengthens and they can develop in every way.*]

The links are clear in these columns: both for ourselves as teachers or parents and for our children, awareness of who we are and where we come from enhances our learning and supports our success, now and into the future, at school and in life.

Critical multicultural awareness across the curriculum

Other assignments throughout the program allowed space for students to engage their own and their students' cultural/linguistic identities. One of the students' early assignments, in their first class 'Theoretical Foundations of Bilingual/Bicultural Education' with Dr María Fránquiz, was a 'Caminata' or community walk (González et al., 2005). Having read both Moll et al. (1992) and Yosso (2005), teachers formed small groups and were tasked with taking on an anthropologist's stance and going for a walk in an unknown community with the aim to learn as much as they could about the community's assets and cultural wealth in a few hours' exploration. Groups presented their findings to the class, clearly expressing their respect for the communities they explored. In the Latino Children's Literature class, which many of the students took as an elective, also designed and taught by Dr Fránquiz, each Proyecto student worked with a small group of undergraduate preservice bilingual teachers to develop bilingual storybooks and read them to their classes. Many of the storybooks the groups wrote were directly drawn from their own lives, and the intensity with which they shared them – both with their students and with me on their own initiative – reinforced the importance of writing our own lives for our children's futures.

In their Teacher Leadership class with me, toward the end of the program, participants developed conference presentations: they proposed and then created 20-minute presentations that engaged colleagues in a workshop related to something they did well and wanted to share with peers. In many cases, this led teachers to share an activity, unit or set of ideas they had developed out of their readings and interpretations of Campano (2007), Ladson-Billings (1995b), Moll et al. (1992), Paris (2012), Yosso (2005), or other course-related readings that emphasized the cultural and linguistic identities of their students. Natasha, Paco and Gisela, all pre-K and kindergarten teachers in Cohort 5, put together a presentation that they subsequently brought to several conferences during and following their Proyecto year: 'Integrating Cuentos [Stories] Across the Content Areas: Making Traditional Tales Culturally Relevant for Bilingual Learners'. The presentation encouraged teachers to have their young students interview their parents about traditional tales from their own childhoods, and use these stories as the basis for an exploration of literature and fairy tales.

Sofia and Christine (Cohort 3), who a couple years after graduation taught fourth grade together at the same school, together developed a website and presentation around a unit they created on immigration that began with students learning the stories of their own families' entry to Texas. They drew on rich, bilingual, culturally relevant children's literature and engaged the children's family and community resources throughout the unit (see sites.google.com/site/bordercrossingstories). Their presentation always begins with Sandra's in-depth introduction of herself, her own immigrant identity and experience, and the path that brought her to teaching young immigrants and children of immigrants. They have a fully articulate and ideologically clear rationale for immersing their classrooms in culturally relevant and critically engaging children's literature. As teachers, they offer presentations full of real stories from their own teaching, including examples of their own students' thoughtful and creative responses to their materials (field notes, NABE Conference, Dallas, TX, February 22–25, 2017). They continue to present their materials at professional conferences and expand the scope and depth of the website.

Lila (Cohort 2) put together several very powerful presentations based on the curricula she developed in her fourth- and fifth-grade bilingual classrooms, merging culturally relevant and critically engaged science and social studies units of study with the language arts. Lila worked for several years in collaboration with doctoral students, including participating in the Tejano History Project (e.g. Fránquiz et al., 2013; Salinas et al., 2015), before entering a doctoral program herself to continue carrying out research on using rich, culturally relevant children's literature in bilingual classrooms. She was generous enough to share her ideas and materials with my undergraduate classes on several occasions, and my students always vividly remembered her talks because of the powerful way that Lila illustrated theory in her practice. She offered rich connections between her teaching and her own life experiences growing up on the US/Mexico border in a bilingual home; she shared her students' elaborately detailed and sometimes deeply personal work products; and she linked everything she did to wonderful, critical culturally relevant children's literature. We invited her to give a keynote talk to open one of the ¡Adelante! Conference Saturday seminars in Fall 2013. She has presented her curricular work at a range of conferences, and at this point she is moving into the academic world as a researcher.

These many examples illustrate the ways that teachers took up our invitations to reflect upon their own and their students' cultural and linguistic identities, to express their understandings of the importance of identity to the project of education for liberation and then to share these reflections with others.

Personal Cultural/Linguistic Identities: Schooling as Connection or Disconnection

Participants' own narratives of their lives as students – collected primarily in interviews conducted after they had completed the program – are very telling in terms of the kinds of connections they felt to school and to teachers, and the kinds of disconnections they experienced. For participants, their own schooling and early life experiences were one of their primary go-to sources of information for what kinds of teachers they wanted to be. They would identify moments of connection in their own past as moments that informed them how to be as a teacher; conversely, they would identify moments of disconnection, microaggressions (Kohli & Solórzano, 2012; Yosso *et al.*, 2009) or particular difficulties for guidance on how best to support their own students to have positive schooling and learning paths. As Emma (Cohort 4, K bilingual) succinctly explained:

> I think having grown up in the [Rio Grande] valley [on the border] and coming from grandparents and parents who spoke Spanish and who are uneducated and who are migrant workers, I feel a strong connection to the kids and their situations and their stories. I feel like I can relate and have a deep connection with them and the families.

When the interviewer asked Lorena (Cohort 2, third grade) what prompted her to become a bilingual teacher or leader, she responded, 'I think as far back as I can remember, it always starts with my mom and my dad'. She went on to describe the dedication her parents had for their children's education, despite having had very few opportunities to attend school themselves. About her father in particular, she explained: 'he only made it up to the third grade, but he was very motivated... He always talked to us about education first from the very beginning'. Expressing the ways that both her parents set her up for success in school and college, Lorena went on to explain, 'And it's funny because my parents, even though they were not the most educated people in the world, they knew a LOT, enough to help them build a business...'. Describing how she majored in Spanish because of a passion for learning about 'my language', and then took an alternative route to teacher certification, Lorena went on to connect her own past to her reasons for staying in the field: 'I think the families, and the language, and wanting for the kids what I wanted for myself'. She explains:

> ...being a bilingual teacher, how could you not want to have kids really, truly bilingual, biliterate, and bicultural in both languages? You know, and I don't see that. I see a lot of kids wanting to still erase their backgrounds and their language and not see the value of that and move into mainstream American culture. That's what I work against a lot and even with teachers because some teachers will have that same mentality. But, you know, it's about growing and helping people see what could be instead of what they think it is. And for me, that's what keeps me here.

Thus, for Lorena, her deepest motivation for doing the hard work of countering deficit narratives in her school community about bilingualism, Spanish and the dedication of Mexican-American families to education, came from her own parents and her own path through childhood, college and career. Her narrative lent strength and commitment to her work. Even as she described her own path to deepened critical awareness, through her major in college and through her years of struggle in her first teaching assignment, she articulated a clear philosophy of critical pedagogy, as she maintained a dialogue with those around her to help them 'see what could be instead of what they think it is'. Because she was linking her teaching to her own past, Lorena's philosophy of teaching and learning in her context was a profoundly critical one.

Lucia (Cohort 4), who taught math and science to bilingual fourth graders, similarly volunteered her own life history in response to a question about what she had in common with her cohort colleagues. She explained, 'the commonality with all of us was a passion for teaching', and went on to explain 'A big, you know, a big part of also the sense of community you know, my peers that I felt with community, was finding our...'. She seemed about ready to fill in 'past', but instead launched into a narrative of her own life history:

> I wasn't born in Mexico. I was born here but just that whole Gloria Anzaldúa (1987), caught between two borders, you know, that's huge, you know, that identity because, you know. I didn't really travel much when I was a child and grew up in this town that's all minorities in Laredo; so to me that's all I knew, you know. That was my world. All these minorities where everybody looks... I feel like I'm in Mexico, but I'm not. And I grew up with all these Mexican traditions and meals, and customs. And my parents speak Spanish all the time to us, so I was... And then I came to UT and I was a business major and I was the only minority, you know, and I just felt so out of place, very confused, you know, of who am I. You know, I don't feel like I'm American because I don't feel very white in my complexion or in my customs, but then I'm not Mexican, you know, definit... you know, I'm not Mexican. So, where do I fit? And I think what happened for a lot of us was doing with Dr. Fránquiz the Journey Box, which I want to do at [my school]. I think that was really... that I think it's what connected us all when we did our Journey boxes. I mean, we were all crying, you know, very emotional and I think that everybody kind of talked about that, you know, where do I fit in? And I think, not just that one class, but the whole program, you know, helped me find where I fit in into this world.

For Lucia, the identity work she and her classmates did from the very beginning of their program – and all the way through – was intimately connected to her sense of both personal and professional belonging and community. It was through validating and acknowledging her own life history and the value of her borderlands identity that she claimed a place in the professional community of bilingual teachers. In one of her spring semester online reflections, after reading the opening chapter of Rebecca Freeman's (2004) *Building on Community Bilingualism*, Lucia remarked:

> I very much related to Ch.1. On page 12, they reference the effects of bilingual parents rejecting their own native languages when speaking to their children. That's exactly what happened to me. I started to believe that I had to reject that part of me to participate in a monolingual world. It's unfortunate that a native language is lost after three generations in the US but I see that happening with my own family. Peyton (ref. unknown) argues that a national policy needs to view heritage languages as something to be preserved and developed rather an [sic] as obstacles to overcome. I agree with Freeman that this change in policy and practice needs to begin at the local level. It's ridiculous that we have a subtractive language policy for the primary grades then in high school it's OK to learn a second language. Freeman presents a strong argument for bilingual education. This chapter is one that I would reference in promoting bilingualism.

Lucia's response to the readings drew on her own experiences growing up in a Spanish-dominant bilingual home, impacted directly by the phenomena she read about. Then she talked about how she would use this chapter in the future for her own advocacy work 'promoting bilingualism'.

Lupe (Cohort 2, bilingual coach) identified 'two catalysts' that led her to become an engaged educator: first, her own and her sisters' early experiences immigrating from Mexico and facing an English-only schooling context in New Mexico; then having a child with special needs and feeling the urgency to advocate on her daughter's behalf:

> First of all, I was born in Mexico and came to the United States when I was in 3rd grade. We moved to New Mexico where it was just an [English] immersion program. I was the oldest of four. My youngest sister struggled a little bit more than I had in education because I believe at that time I had a really good foundation of the [Spanish] language where my sisters didn't. I felt that we didn't have support as bilingual students back in New Mexico. And I remember getting pulled out for speech and that's what we received instead of any kind of ESL, it was speech. And so, I always felt like, looking back, it was unfair and my sisters struggled. Both of them are college graduates but it took them a long time. They got their degree after they were married. And I always thought the school system kind of failed us somehow. So that was always like in my heart. We could have gotten our education faster if we were kind of geared in the right direction, my parents not being college graduates as well.

Lupe's and her younger sisters' experiences were, as she put it, 'always... in my heart' as she moved into teaching, coaching and ultimately into school administration. Becoming a parent of a special needs child also played a role in her decision to 'become an administrator that makes a difference':

> And then with my special needs child as well. It was that and also knowing you had a child with educational challenges. And I thought *we really need to understand the education system*. Not only be the teacher that makes a difference, but then in the decision of becoming an administrator, being an administrator that makes a difference, that really welcomes parents in, that is able to take the time to explain and to be an advocate for bilingual education and special education. Those are the two catalysts I think that really that drove me to where I am today.

Lupe, Lucia, Emma and Lorena all described themselves as sharing characteristics or experiences with the Latinx bilingual students and families in their schools, and linked their own experiences to the strength of their desire to advocate on behalf of their students. It may not be terribly surprising to see that their cultural and linguistic identities supported their professional identities as bilingual teachers; furthermore, when they interrogated their own pasts, they easily made direct links to their students' lives.

Not all of the teachers came from the same background as their students, however. Several powerful teacher leaders actually spoke eloquently about how *different* their own backgrounds were from those of their students, and in articulating these differences reinforced the importance of their own self-knowledge as they approached their work as teachers of Latinx, bilingual and immigrant students.

Aisha, for example, expressed that her Asian American background set her apart from her cohort colleagues:

> Because what I noticed was people would say, 'We're bilingual. We're bilingual.' But it was only Spanish and English. And even in Proyecto they would always say, 'We as Latinas need to do this...' And I was like, 'I am not a Latina. We cannot say that because we are not all Latinas.' It is 'you all Latinas', and then me.

Yet, for Aisha, who grew up an English speaker in a multilingual home, just as profoundly as for her classmates, the importance of promoting and developing students' cultural and linguistic identities figured centrally in her motivations for becoming a teacher. She explained:

> That's why I decided I wanted to become a bilingual teacher. It wasn't because I had any experiences of my own in bilingual ed. I just became very passionate about the idea of promoting multilingualism and maintaining students' identities and cultures and language. So that's basically how I decided I wanted to do it.

After she graduated from Proyecto, Aisha participated enthusiastically in the Tejano History Project with her fourth graders (Salinas *et al.*, 2015). This project engaged fourth-grade students in the development of curricular materials about Tejano history, drawing from primary documents and the about-to-be dedicated monument to Tejano history on the lawn of the Texas State Capitol (Casares, 2012). The primary goals of the project were to guide the children to see themselves (or their classmates) and their families in Texas history, to use studying their 'own' history to develop their academic skills and confidence and to interrogate what narratives are missing from our textbooks – to bring necessary critique to the world. These were exactly at the heart of Aisha's passions. In fact, after completing Proyecto Maestría, Aisha went on to a PhD program in social studies education with a focus on teaching Asian American History in elementary classrooms, embracing her own Asian background to enhance a field she felt was marginalized in her own schooling *and* in her experiences in Proyecto. Her own research helps to bring culturally relevant/sustaining curriculum and instruction into the field of Asian studies, and to bring critical perspectives about the stories of Asian American children into elementary education.

Natasha (Cohort 5, pre-K) also thought deeply about her own cultural and linguistic identities in relation to her students. As an Afro-Puerto Rican who did not come to the mainland until after she graduated from college, her background was quite different from her largely Mexican-American students, even though, like most of them, she was a Spanish-dominant bilingual. She described the time when her 'eyes were opened' about the mainland perception of Latinos:

> Me fui a CA por algo de la iglesia y ahí estuve involucrada también mucho con niños. Y trabajaba mucho con niños de la comunidad y ahí fue que yo desperté a que, 'Caramba, la gente no piensa igual de mí como pensaba yo en PR de los hispanos – son gente que lucha, son gente que trabaja, son gente educada'. *[I left for California for something with the church and there I was involved also a lot with children. And I was working a lot with children from the community and that was where I woke up to, 'Wow, people don't think the same of me the way I thought in Puerto Rico of the Hispanic people – they are people who fight, they are people who work, they are well educated people'.]*

Natasha became a bilingual teacher because as a Spanish speaker, she felt more comfortable working with Spanish-speaking children; as a Latina, she felt culturally more at home with Latinx students:

> ¿Por qué en bilingüe? Pues primero porque me hacía sentido. Yo hablo español. Segundo porque decía, 'Pues a estos niños sí los entiendo. Se

parecen a mí, no entiendo mucho la otra cultura. Estoy aprendiendo la otra cultura – no es la misma cosa. Yo creo que puede ser más eficiente con los de español'. *[Why in bilingual? Well first because I felt comfortable. I speak Spanish. Second because I said, 'well these students I understand. They look like me, I don't understand much the other culture. I'm learning the other culture – that's not the same thing. I think it could be more efficient with the Spanish speakers'.]*

However, she acknowledged with a great deal of embarrassment that she fell into a trap that many teachers find themselves in: she began to view her students' parents through deficit lenses:

A pesar de venir de PR y saber que los hispanos somos educados también... es que lo oyes, y te convences: 'son ignorantes, no tienen interés, no les importa, es free childcare'. Te lo empiezas a creer. Te lo dicen tantas veces que te lo empiezas a creer y así los trataba. *[Despite coming from Puerto Rico and knowing that we Hispanics are well educated too... it's that you hear it, and you convince yourself: 'they're ignorant, they're not interested, it doesn't matter to them, it's free childcare.' You begin to believe it. They tell you so many times that you begin to believe it and that's how I treated them.]*

During her first summer in Proyecto, Natasha deeply interrogated her views about parents. Her experiences in class, including texts and conversations and projects, supported her on this path, but mostly she found transformative the experience of carrying out home visits to all the families whose children she would have in class in the fall: all 30 of them. When asked what helped change her perspectives, she reflected:

Ver la realidad que han pasado sus padres. Yo no los entendía. También no puedo negar que como puertorriqueña nací ciudadana. Vengo aquí, me miran con otros ojos que con los ojos que miran a los mexicanos, a los salvadoreños, ellos no son ciudadanos. Entonces, cuando yo empiezo a ver todas sus luchas te tienes que quitarte la capa, y quitarte el sombrero y decir, 'Ud. tenga' a los padres porque ellos han luchado por tanto para llegar aquí que ya de entrada el que ha luchado para llegar te demuestra que sus deseos son, por sus hijos y por ellos, de mejorar, de ayudar. *[To see the reality that their parents had lived. I hadn't understood them. I also can't ignore that as a Puerto Rican I was born a citizen. I come here, they see me with different eyes from the eyes that see Mexicans, Salvadorans, they are not citizens. So, when I begin to see all the struggles you have to take your hat off, and take off your hat and say, 'You sir, take it' to the parents because they have struggled so much to get here that already coming in he who has struggled to get here shows you that his desires are, for his children and for themselves, to improve, to help.]*

She went on to describe the transformation that home visits offered her:

Aprendí de Emilia (Cohort 4, pre-K) lo de visitar a los padres en las casas y de mala pata que este año yo empecé con 30 estudiantes y yo visité 30 hogares antes de que empezara la escuela. Sábado, domingo, cuando pudiera, cuando ellos estuviesen disponibles. Pero lo hice y lo voy a volver a hacer y ando reclutando maestras que lo quieran hacer también. Porque me abrió los ojos a la realidad particular de cada estudiante y no lo puedo comparar con nada. *[I learned from Emilia about visiting parents in their homes and as luck would have it this year I began with 30 students and I visited 30 homes before school began. Saturday, Sunday, when I could, when they were available. But I did it and I will do it again and I am trying to recruit teachers who want to do it also. Because it opened my eyes to the particular reality of each student and I cannot compare it with anything else.]*

Natasha's reflections moved both into areas she had in common with her students, and ways in which they differed; one thing remained constant, that Natasha's own identity mattered for her teaching, and when she began to think more carefully about the attitudes she had toward her students' families, and to engage across the borders she herself had begun to create, she felt herself to be a much more effective teacher.

The white teachers who came through Proyecto Maestría were also reflective about the question of cultural and linguistic identity, although their path to embracing its importance in their own lives was different. George, a first-grade dual language teacher in Cohort 5 who grew up a monolingual English speaker in a middle-class home, explained his personal motivation to move into bilingual education in this way:

I worked really hard to learn Spanish in high school and in college... and... My mom was an ESL teacher in my high school and so... And I had friends that were in her classes and I played soccer with a lot of older guys I had friends from like Guanajuato that played in a soccer team. So, I was just interested in the language first, I guess, and learning Spanish for whatever reason (laughs) I really don't remember how that came about, but I had a knack for it. I was a strong student in Spanish when I was in high school and then in college, I stuck with it. I went abroad. I went to Madrid and then when I graduated college I did not want to be a teacher because my mom was a teacher and lots of teachers in the family. They weren't... they didn't actively discourage me, but they didn't exactly encourage me to become a teacher (laughs) and then I just... I moved out to the Austin area and needed a job at the beginning and I saw 'bilingual teacher'. 'Oh, my god. I can do that', you know. And I got into it...

This seems to be a somewhat standard narrative from a white bilingual teacher. Success in a traditional foreign language program in Spanish in high school, combined with some academic and personal connections to primary speakers of the language and an opportunity to study abroad, ultimately gave George the skill set to consider using his 'knack' for the language in a career – and the option of being a bilingual teacher conveniently presented itself. It stands in stark contrast to the strong personal investment prevalent in Latinx and especially Tejanx participants' experiences.

However, during his first few years in the classroom, as a teacher in several different schools, George did make personal connections to the centrality of cultural identity to his students' success, and then to his own professional identity. He contrasted his and his students' experiences at schools in which bilingual students were the minority, versus schools in which bilingual students were the majority:

> I worked at three schools in AISD, and the only one that I felt kind of in the inside part of the group was when I worked at P_ and that's, that's mostly bilingual students, mostly bilingual teachers. And I felt that I was seen as a good teacher there. The other schools that I worked in Austin, I always felt kind of on the outside... and my students too were kind of on the outside.

When I pushed him to explain a little more about what made his experience at P_ different, he explained:

> Just being bilingual was normal (laughs). Speaking... I mean, having so many people there it was rare to be monolingual there. And so, really, the school was easy to navigate if you were bilingual as opposed to if you were monolingual which is the other schools I worked at, so... you know. I think it was just the culture of the school where languages were appreciated.

As a bilingual teacher with primarily Latinx students in his class, George experienced marginalization at his first two schools, whereas at P_ he found that his and his students' bilingualism was normalized.

It was finding himself again in a school that was not majority-bilingual that pushed George to apply to the Proyecto master's degree program; he sought a community of shared interests where he could learn about these 'language issues' that were intriguing him. One of the most powerful things about Proyecto, he explained, was that he developed a critical awareness, which he essentially described as a vocabulary to better understand and talk about the marginalization he and his students were experiencing in his school:

> Then I think as I went through the process I became more comfortable with, you know, those critical issues of power and oppression that I think really affect the students that I was working with and affected me as their teacher.

He drew connections to the history of marginalization of the Latinx community in Texas and his experiences as the teacher of bilingual students:

> ...being able to make sense of these things and historically that this is... something that... bilingual ed is ... coming out of the civil rights that, you know, started out as... with issues of access and having a better school experience for these students.

Whereas before Proyecto, George pretty much thought it was 'all about the language', he began to see that in fact 'all this was about equal opportunity; making things better for people'. He found this developing critical awareness to be energizing in a way that nothing before in his experiences had. This led him directly to participation in extra-curricular projects that would extend his Proyecto experience. He became active in Academia Cuauhtli (Valenzuela *et al.*, 2015), a teacher-driven language and culture revitalization project held on Saturdays at the Mexican-American Cultural Center for upper elementary age bilingual children and their parents. He explained that the agency – the 'freedom' that the Saturday school teaching experience afforded him, outside the intense school-accountability microscope, as he collaborated with fellow bilingual teachers – was invigorating. Now, as a doctoral student in bilingual/bicultural education continuing to work intensively on the Cuauhtli project, he explains that advocating for equity through sustaining and developing children's cultural and linguistic identities as bilingual and bicultural Texans has become his primary area of focus. Beginning with a focus on the language and his own relationship with it, George's narrative led him to discover the importance of learning about and teaching from his students' cultural identities.

George's choice to pursue a doctorate in bilingual/bicultural education was particularly intriguing to me. As a white scholar myself in the field of bilingual education, I am often asked, 'what led *you* to the field of bilingual education?'. Like me, George is navigating a predominantly Latinx field as a white scholar. So, at the end of our interview, I asked him what he thought about this; I asked him how his whiteness has played into his experiences in Proyecto Maestría and as a leader. He responded:

> I think I certainly have, yeah, a unique position and sometimes I wonder, you know, there's times in which it's uncomfortable, I guess would be the word... Sometimes I struggle with that. What is appropriate for me to be doing here...

I followed up by sharing that I sometimes felt as a white person in bilingual education that I needed to purposefully quiet my own voice, to step aside as a leader and follow the lead of the scholars of color who surrounded me. I asked if he ever felt the same:

Deb: I wonder sometimes whether some of the Latino leaders in the field notice, you know, when I am... if I'm too loud of a voice. I have to... Do you ever find yourself doing that sort of tempering your own leadership in order to give space to others?

George: Yeah. I think... I generally, especially in groups, I'm very quiet... but I think that's what makes me potentially, you know, a good researcher that I can, you know, the understanding part, I feel that I do listen and I notice and I really, whatever is being said I think about it (laughs) before or I try to think about anything before I make up my mind – maybe that's my strength that I do listen. So I go in a lot of times consciously going, you know, to listen not jump in and interpret or explain other people's experiences.

George described himself as a naturally quiet person, a good listener; this was my experience with him too. He was possibly the quietest member of his cohort, rarely offering his own perspectives except when asked, but attentively paying attention to what was said. His written reflections, and his elaboration of ideas when in one-on-one conversations, were thorough and thoughtful, but in groups he largely listened and learned. He explained that he believed this disposition would help him as a bilingual education researcher, as it would ensure he did not 'jump in and interpret of explain other people's experiences'.

Christine's (Cohort 3, fourth grade) mother, too, was a teacher, who 'worked primarily with pregnant and parenting teens...women/girls of color and people in low income neighborhoods'. Christine explained that she 'always saw her (mother's) work and noticed how much time she put into it'. In college, Christine majored in journalism and in Spanish. As part of an internship, she was covering a story in the Centro Latino in a Missouri community, and realized she was happier volunteering at the Centro Latino than as a journalist; her Spanish became relevant, and she connected with the community. She returned to finish college and immediately sought an alternative certification to be a bilingual teacher. She looks at her own work as 'continuing my mother's work'. Because her mother's work and her own entry into the field were in close contact with struggles against poverty and marginalization – supporting poor women of color, working in marginalized communities – Christine developed an awareness of her own privilege long before she began her master's program. She talked openly about race and about her role as an ally to communities of color, and seemed almost amused at other white people's discomfort with the topic. When asked why she decided to participate in the Proyecto Maestría master's program, she explained:

> I think a lot about privilege and the lack of privilege. I feel like I'm coming with my backpack full of plenty of privilege so I want to step it up. The sacrifices these families make are so profound and with the sole purpose of educating their children. I've got to be the best that I can be to really serve them and help them on their journey.

As Christine described it, the contrast between her own whiteness and 'backpack of plenty of privilege', and the sacrifices that her students' families had made to be able to send their children to her fourth-grade classroom, gave her a profound sense of responsibility to provide an excellent education, to be the very best teacher she could be for them.

Although each narrative is different, all the teachers narrated their lives – authored their identities, in Bakhtin's terms – to assert the centrality of culture and language and the importance of really knowing themselves in order to best teach. Their paths to developing this critical multicultural awareness differed, of course. But they all emphasized the importance of moving from understanding themselves, to opening themselves to better understanding and appreciating the students and families they serve. This deliberate emphasis on humanizing (Freire, 2000) and culturally sustaining pedagogies (Paris, 2012) was consistently framed as essential to moving into a problem-posing educational frame.

As Erika (Cohort 1) exclaimed in conversation with cohort colleagues in a post-graduation study group, 'that very first two classes, oh my goodness, that was just... You know, it just made you evaluate, really think about *what was your background*. I think that's, that impacts everything you do today'.

For most of the teachers, a developing critical multicultural awareness led them directly toward activist leadership identities. Knowing the intensity and beauty of their students' languages and cultures, and tying these to their own growing self-awareness, they were moved to engage. It was also centrally important that the teachers' first and most formative experiences in graduate school delving into their own cultural and linguistic identities and making these links to theory and practice were *in community*. The cohort formed a solid and safe community from the beginning. Even for teachers who came into their master's program already having reflected about the importance of cultural/linguistic identity in teaching, which some teachers certainly had, community and collaboration played a crucial role in their development of leadership identities. The importance of community for bilingual teacher leadership is what I will explore next.

7 Bilingual Teacher Leaders are Collaborators

I always felt kind of on the outside... and my students too were kind of on the outside. And so, part of, you know, what was so great about Proyecto and this [current engagement with Academia Cuauhtli] too is talking and being around other people that understand and have the same, I guess, orientation towards the students, and language and all of these things that, yeah, I wasn't getting any more working at the school that I was working at. (George, Cohort 5, first grade, post-graduation interview)

Many – if not most – of the teachers, when they began their master's program, described their schools and their experiences up to this point in their careers the way George did above: as isolating, and their work as lonely. This is a well-known and frequently identified issue across all sectors of teaching: overcoming the isolated and individualistic paradigm for teaching has been a struggle taken on in several fields, including teacher education, professional development and teacher/school leadership (Lieberman & Miller, 2008). It is commonly agreed that the field desperately needs a change of paradigm, from one in which each teacher closes the door to do their work, to one in which teachers work together in engaged learning communities. It is also broadly understood that this paradigm shift will require resources, especially that most difficult to acquire resource: time. Collaboration requires time (Katzenmeyer & Moller, 2009). As Gisela (Cohort 5, pre-K) exclaimed at the end of a long post to a class discussion board about the challenges of becoming an agent of change, 'What are my limitations? I think the biggest limitation is time!'.

There was, however, an additional layer to the isolation described by the bilingual teachers in this project: marginalization, as teachers serving a minoritized community – and often, as members themselves of minoritized communities. George, himself a white male, explained above that he and his students were 'kind of on the outside' in the schools where he had worked. Mireya (Cohort 4, dual language coach), a Tejana, echoed this feeling, describing how leadership in her suburban district dismissed the needs of the bilingual kids who were her primary concern: 'There's nobody up there (district level) that really knows about the needs of bilingual students, educators and curriculum. ... Nobody up there ever thinks about bilingual students first. Nobody ever thinks about the children in poverty'.

Thus, it is not surprising that teachers repeatedly came back to the cohort community and the larger networks of community they built as a result of their experiences, as the most powerful aspect of Proyecto Maestría. The teachers described the powerful role that their cohort had in their journeys to leadership identities. For most of the teachers, the cohort was a source of academic and emotional support that got them through the intensity of the program, especially during the short-format summer courses. The cohort also provided an ongoing source of strength as they sought to advocate for bilingual families in their own school contexts. Cohort members shared resources, continued to collaborate on professional development projects, share opportunities and ideas, recommend one another, etc. Plain and simple, the cohort was proof that they were not alone on their journeys. As Gisela (Cohort 5) explained in an interview, the best thing about Proyecto is:

> Gisela: El saber que hay otras personas que piensan igual. Que tiene los mismos valores que tú y tienen experiencias muy similares a las tuya y aquí están y si te sientes, asi como, no sé… aquí están. Eso es lo más bonito. Saber, que, pienso yo, que sé que le puedo llamar a Maya o le puedo escribir a Alondra o a Natasha y… [*Knowing there are other people who think the same. That have the same values as you and have very similar experiences to yours and here they are and if you feel, like, I don't know… here they are. That's the most beautiful thing. To know, I think, that I know that I can call Maya or I can write to Alondra or to Natasha and…]*
>
> Interviewer: Que no estás sola. [*That you're not alone.*]
>
> Gisela: Aja. [*uh huh.*]

In the focus group interview where Gisela made the above comment, the interviewer followed up with the question, '¿Cuál fue la influencia de su cohort para su aprendizaje? ¿Influyó o no?'. [What was the influence of your cohort on your learning? Did it influence - or not?] All three teachers present (all members of Cohort 5) responded:

> Maya (second grade): There were a lot of contributions that we took from each other.
>
> Gisela (pre-K): Tengo una admiración por cada uno de ellos porque como que digo, 'o, que buenos maestros. Wow que linda historia tienen. No sé. Los admiro bastante'. Hay personas que admiro ciertas características, digo, 'Hay quiero ser tan buena presentadora como Natasha. Tan organizada como Maya'. Lo que sea, no?

Como que hay ciertas características de ellos que admiro. *[I have such admiration for each one of them because like I say, 'oh, what good teachers. Wow what a beautiful story they have. I don't know. I admire them a great deal'. There are people for whom I admire certain characteristics, I say, 'Ah, I want to be as good a presenter as Natasha. As organized as Maya'.]*

Alondra (second grade):   Pues creo que ser parte de un cohort fue algo muy bueno porque nos conocimos muy bien. Nos ayudamos a salir adelante con las clases porque a veces sí era difícil. Nos ayudó mucho ese apoyo. También me dio la oportunidad que hay buenos maestros en el Distrito. Pues sí hay pero es cuestión de encontrarlos. *[Well I think that to be part of a cohort was really good because we got to know each other really well. We helped each other get through classes because sometimes yes it was difficult. That support helped a lot. Also it gave me the opportunity that there are good teachers in the District. Well yeah there are but it's a question of finding them.]*

Patricia (Cohort 4, dual language coach) expressed a similar sentiment when asked what she remembered most about Proyecto:

Proyecto, what I remember the most is something that I missed the most, is just being able to come back and talk about these things, you know. Like sometimes you need a kind of reset because the work – and that's one thing – we are struggling. We sometimes feel that we're always going uphill against the current... *A veces* [sometimes] I tell my husband, I feel exhausted because I feel like I'm always having to convince everybody over, and over, and over again.... So, that part gets exhausting as a coach and as an advocate just because we don't want to let go, we don't want to go back. So, just the conversations just coming and, not just venting, but actually hearing like ideas, or what do we do, or how.

As Patricia vividly illustrates, leadership and advocacy work on behalf of minoritized bilingual students of color in majority white spaces like her suburban school district can be very discouraging – one can feel much of the time as if one is making little progress. Allies are crucial. The cohort provided a built-in community of allies even as the coursework awakened in many teachers the very need to advocate.

In a description that is representative of multiple comments from Proyecto teachers across the cohorts and throughout the data, when asked what he remembered most from Proyecto, George provided a stark contrast with his experiences on his school campus described above:

> I feel that our group really stuck together and helped each other in a lot of different ways and… everybody had their strengths and we knew what these were and, you know, we would go for certain people, you know, (to) help with whatever, you know, we were trying to do with assignments. Even, you know, talking about what was going on at our schools. You know, ideas with instructional practices, everything. So, I think it was… That's what I remember the most about it, the relationships we all made with each other and how much I certainly learned from everybody that was in there. So, even now, I still see Miguel two or three times a week with Cuauhtli. I still talk to Paco all the time and I see Julieta at the District a lot… Gisela… I see mostly everybody except for like Maya, who's somewhere north. I don't see Alondra so much, but ah… I mean, yeah, the relationships is what I remember the most about. And how quick it seemed to, like, gel… It's like, people that you've known forever. It happened within the first two weeks of Proyecto.

George's was one of the last interviews I conducted. I acknowledge that I may have influenced his response, but at this point having heard this from many teachers, I remarked, 'The cohort. That's probably the most powerful piece of it, eh?' and George echoed, 'Yeah. Yeah. Absolutely'.

Learning From and with Others: Co-Constructing New Identities, Developing Reflexive Practice, Becoming Advocates

The cohort was above all a space for dialogic peer learning and a source of support throughout the intensity of graduate school. Lorena (Cohort 2, third grade) described this clearly:

> And I wouldn't have been able to have felt so confident … had I not gone through the training with the Proyecto group, with my cohort, and learning from…my gosh, the stuff that I was able to pick up from my peers in my cohort, I mean I would leave and my little brain was just going and going with all the conversations and all of the discussions that we had had. You know, it just made you hungry for more of it.

When asked which aspects of Proyecto made the most impression on her, Consuelo (Cohort 4, K) replied (emphasis mine):

> Well definitely the **community** that developed out of it and around it that I just remember that really intense summer. It was such an amazing **group**

of people. We all had different experiences, but we were **coming together and sharing ideas, experiences, and talking and learning together** and really getting to know each other and respect each other in our work and we are still good friends and we get together and we talk about things. I mean, I feel like that was just one thing that this is a beautiful moment of all these people coming together, and you know, building really a nice community. And it was just great to have that for two years to be going to the classes together. A year and a half, I guess. So that's one thing. And we got involved in things together just outside direct classes, you know. We love seeing each other at Adelante.

A little later in her interview, Consuelo added:

I'm always so impressed when I see the great work that all my colleagues from Proyecto are doing too. I don't know... It's just really inspiring as well to like keep wanting to do more and like see them just grow and be successful too.

One space in which the ongoing dialogic relationships between cohort members were visible was in their online discussion boards, a weekly assignment in both their long-semester cohort courses with me. Cohort 5's fall semester online discussion boards illustrate the culture of sharing resources and learning from one another that the teachers describe in their interviews. Admittedly, I required the assignment, and I gave the teachers explicit instructions with the intention to support dialogic engagement. I described it thus in the syllabus:

Blackboard/Canvas Reading Reflections: Each week upon completion of the required readings, please write up your reactions and post a reflection to the corresponding online Discussion Board. Do not summarize readings; rather, offer your colleagues your reflections about the readings, connecting the ideas to your practice and personal development as an educator, to other readings (both in the class and outside), and to the larger field of education. Reflections should be at least a few rich paragraphs in length, and incorporate all the readings in some way. The goal is to synthesize, react, connect, critique, &/or reflect. A successful reflection will do at least some of the following:

o   *Refer to specific ideas, theories, stories or research described in the text*
o   *Pick out the most important concepts for your own work/research/ thinking/teaching*
o   *Include connections to your own experiences or to other things you've seen or read on the topic*
o   *Mention themes previously discussed in class*

    o   *Relate different readings/authors to one another*
    o   *Go into depth about one or two ideas that particularly strike you*

Please also read and respond to colleagues' postings. Strong participation will be rewarded in your grade. (20% of course grade)

These discussion board conversations made visible the teachers' learning and supportive professional relationships. The large amount of relational work that occurred, and that was only required in the sense that I asked participants to 'please also read and respond to colleague's postings', hinted at the powerful role that interpersonal connections played in learning for the teachers. In their discussion boards, the teachers supported each other's co-construction of ideas in visible ways. They reframed and revoiced language and ideas from their readings and course texts, appropriating the words as their own and developing internally persuasive discourses. In articulating the ideas of educational theorists and researchers, they built upon one another's ideas; they posed questions; and they shared connections both to other Proyecto-related experiences and to their own workplaces/classrooms. These reflections illustrate the facility with which the members of Cohort 5 negotiated the borderlands between reflection and action, pulling new ideas into their classrooms and making links to what they'd seen, tried and planned to try with their students and colleagues.

Let's take for an example, because the self-referential nature of including this particular dialogue in this book intrigues me, the first posted thread of the online conversation that Cohort 5 had early in the fall semester after reading two key chapters of Paolo Freire's (2000) *Pedagogy of the Oppressed* and a well-known article by Moll *et al.* (1992) titled 'Funds of Knowledge for Teaching: Using a Qualitative Approach to Connect Homes and Classrooms'. This was actually a part of the cohort's first online conversation for my classes, and it took place between the first- and second-class sessions in September. The cohort had just completed one entire summer – four courses – of experience together in graduate school. Their already strong relationships, described above by George and Gisela, are evident in their dialogue. For reasons of space, I will primarily share just two threads of a multi-thread conversation, in which the various threads reference one another and overlap in fascinating ways. In total, this week's discussion board had four threads. Miguel's thread, titled 'Freire and Moll', was the first one and received five responses, three of which were sufficiently elaborated and original to be considered the participants' own reflections rather than merely responses, and one of which was Miguel himself rejoining the conversation. The second thread was titled simply 'Maya'; it began with Maya's reflection and received 10 responses, some of which were brief affirmations or questions. The third thread was titled 'Week 1' and consisted of George's full reflection; it did not receive responses. The fourth and final thread was offered by a master's student who was not a Proyecto participant (in all except each cohort's very first class, non-Proyecto graduate students were enrolled alongside Proyecto students). This thread received one response, from Miguel.

Miguel (third grade) began his thread in Spanish, which was his stronger and primary language, talking about Freire's chapters. He explained that reading Freire helped him make better sense of last summer's research course in which they learned about the transformative paradigm for research. He also directly connected Freire's description of the 'oppressed' to the children and families in his own and his colleagues' classrooms, and vehemently advocated for change for them, and for women in US society. He wrote with a rhythm and a passion that in many ways echoed the language of Freire:

Las ideas presentadas tanto por Freire como por Moll me parecen innovadoras, transformadoras y revolucionarias. Me parece fascinante el poder escuchar acerca del poder que debe de tener la educación de luchar contra la alienación. También me satisface sobremanera el leer acerca de la educación como cambio, transformación y humanización. Recuerdo que en el verano anterior cuando estudiábamos acerca de los diferentes paradigmas en trabajos de investigación uno de ellos era el Transformativo. En ese momento no me quedaba muy claro las pretensiones de este paradigma, además de que no había leído acerca de ningún autor en particular con ideas transformativas. Al leer a Paulo Freire me queda mas claro las ideas y pretensiones de quien profesa un paradigma Transformativo. Como ejemplo quiero citar un párrafo del capítulo 2 'Es verdad, lo que pretenden los opresores es transformar la mentalidad de los oprimidos y no la situación que los oprime' (p. 75). Solamente alguien con deseos de transformar la realidad se atreverá a cambiar la situación de discriminación y exclusión que viven muchos de los estudiantes en nuestros salones de clases y sus familias. Solamente alguien con deseos de cambio se atreverá a cambiar la situación de alienación que viven muchas mujeres en nuestra sociedad. *[The ideas presented by Freire and Moll seem to me innovative, transformative and revolutionary. It is fascinating to me to be able to listen to the power that education should have to fight against alienation. It also satisfies me exceedingly to read about education as change, transformation and humanization. I remember that in the summer when we were studying about the different paradigms in research one of them was Transformative. At that point the implications of that paradigm weren't totally clear to me, not to mention that I hadn't read about any particular authors with transformative ideas. Upon reading Paulo Freire I'm much clearer about the ideas and pretensions of someone professing a Transformative paradigm. As an example I'd like to cite a paragraph from Chapter 2 'It's true, what the oppressors intend is to transform the mentality of the oppressed and not the situation that oppresses them' (p. 75). Only someone with desires to transform reality will dare to change the situation of discrimination and exclusion that many of the students in our classrooms and their families live. Only someone with desires to change would dare to change the situation of alienation that many women in our society live.]*

The next section of Miguel's reflection wove together Moll *et al.* (1992) and Freire (2000), noting that Moll's innovative proposition that we should build upon children's cultural and linguistic funds of knowledge contrasted with Freire's image of 'banking education' in which children were perceived as empty vessels needing to be filled:

> Por otra parte las ideas de Moll me parecen innovadoras en el sentido de aprovechar los fundamentos del conocimiento los cuales se encuentran en las familias de los estudiante, los recursos culturales y el bilingüismo como el punto de partida para la enseñanza. Como maestros debemos de construir sobre lo que los alumnos poseen y aportan al salón de clases en lugar de escudriñar y señalar sus carencias. *[On the other hand the ideas of Moll seem to me innovative in the sense of taking advantage of the funds of knowledge that can be found in students' families, the cultural resources and the bilingualism as the point of departure for teaching. As teachers we should build upon what the students have and bring to the classroom instead of scrutinize and point out their shortcomings.]*
>
> Now let me talk about banking education. Since I read the article in English, I am going to talk about it in English. Banking education is a practice that still exists in many classrooms. According to this approach, students are merely empty vessels in which teachers just have to deposit knowledge. Teachers are the subjects (experts) of education and students are the objects (do not know anything) of such education. Such practice deprives students from innovation, creativity, and transformation for they are only docile listeners and not critical thinkers.

It seems important that Miguel shifted from Spanish to English in the middle of this part of his reflection; he claimed that because he had read Freire in English, he found it easiest to talk about these abstract ideas using the language he had just read them in. As with most bilingual language practice, though, his shift is more interesting than it appears. Miguel had also read the Moll *et al.* (1992) article in English, yet had just finished talking about it in Spanish. And in the opening passage above, he reflected beautifully upon Freire's ideas in Spanish. Regardless of why he chose to articulate his ideas in one language or the other, it is important to note that Miguel knew already that both Spanish and English contributions were equally welcomed and valued in our classroom community. By opening his thread in Spanish, Miguel illustrated and reinforced my desire to support just such a transgressive translanguaging community. There is a growing body of evidence supporting the power of translanguaging pedagogies to support bilingual learners' critical reflection (García & Wei, 2014; Gort, 2014; Palmer *et al.*, 2014a; Sayer, 2013). Although when Miguel was writing these passages in 2012, I had only just begun to theorize this as translanguaging pedagogies, as an instructor I had learned from prior experiences with Proyecto cohorts and with bilingual education undergraduate students the intellectual and ideological power behind engaging bilingual students bilingually.

Miguel then closed his reflection by connecting what he just described, the distinction between problem-posing/funds of knowledge education and banking education, with what he had seen and experienced as a bilingual teacher, and by making a commitment to work toward problem-posing pedagogies in his classroom:

> I do not want to point fingers to any teacher, but unfortunately this practice is still common in classrooms. It is possible that at some point even our classrooms exhibit pieces of this practice. The perfect classroom is impossible to exist for there is always room for improvement. I see this practice every year in many students coming to my classroom. Such students are used to be told what to do in reading and what to read, math is just memorization of facts, and students are always prompted what to write about. They do not feel responsible for their education, they do not take ownership of their learning, they are not independent, and they have not become critical thinkers yet. As mentioned in chapter three, banking education exists where there is absence of dialogue and just narration. This practice is obvious where students do not participate in conversations with the teacher and classmates in whole, and small group conversations and inquiry. If we want for our students to take ownership of their education, they need to be in a constant conversation and reflection about their learning. Freire mentions in chapter three that the difference between animals and ourselves is that we are able to re-present and reflect about the world around us. This is going to be the challenge of my classroom this school year.

Miguel's '2–3 meaty paragraphs' (as per my assignment description) sparked immediate and direct responses from his classmates. Alondra (second grade) responded with her own reflection, building her thoughts directly upon Miguel's. She opened by throwing support behind Miguel's 'challenge':

> Estoy de acuerdo con Miguel: nuestra meta como maestros es tener el salón perfecto, y aunque es algo que tal vez nunca se puede lograr, siempre hay que estar buscando maneras para mejorar. Como seres humanos que

somos, muchas veces se nos olvida que lo que nuestros estudiantes traen de su casa a nuestra clase es un tesoro. Si nosotros tomamos el tiempo para valorarlos, ellos van a ser mucho más exitosos académicamente. *[I agree with Miguel: our goal as teachers is to have the perfect classroom, and even though that's something that maybe can never be achieved, we always have to be looking for ways to improve. As the human beings that we are, often we forget that what our students bring from their home to our classroom is a treasure. If we take the time to value them, they will be much more successful academically.]*

Then Alondra offered her own metaphor for Moll, that we should 'treat our students like plants'. She explained:

Después de leer la lectura de Moll, pienso que debemos de tratar a nuestros alumnos como plantas. Hay que darles solo suficiente agua para que ellos logren florecer. A veces los inundamos con información con la que no saben que hacer. Los maestros sólo proveemos la base de su educación pero hay que dejar que ellos aprendan de lo que viene de ellos. *[After reading the article by Moll, I think we should treat our students like plants. We need to give them just enough water for them to flourish. Sometimes we inundate them with information that they don't know what to do with. Teachers just provide the base of their education but we need to allow them to learn from what comes from them.]*

As Alondra explained, 'this brings me directly to Freire', which she connected to early literacy instruction and the distinction between decoding and comprehending words on a page:

Esto me lleva a la lectura de Freire. Las palabras son valiosas solamente si le enseñamos a los estudiantes a entenderlas completamente. Es muy fácil enseñar a un niño a descifrar palabras para que lea con fluidez, pero eso no es lo más importante. Necesitamos abrirles las puertas al mundo de la comprensión donde ellos sean capaces de llevar la información que están leyendo al más allá. *[This brings me to the readings by Freire. Words are valuable only if we teach students to understand them completely. It's very easy to teach a child to decipher words so he/she can read fluently, but this is not the most important thing. We need to open for them the doors to the world of comprehension where they can be capable of bringing the information that they are reading to the next level.]*
Por ejemplo, utilizando la Taxonomía de Bloom y haciéndoles preguntas de más alto calibre les permitirá a nuestros estudiantes pensar críticamente. Una vez que ellos se sientan más seguros de sus ideas y pensamientos, entonces van a ser capaces de producir diálogos con otras personas... y si los guiamos por el camino correcto, lograrán hacerlo con amor, humildad

y esperanza. *[For example, using Bloom's Taxonomy and asking them questions of a higher order will permit our students to think critically. Once they feel more sure of their ideas and thoughts, then they're going to be capable of producing dialogues with other people... and if we guide them along the right path, they will succeed in doing so with love, humility and hope.]*

Connecting Freire to Bloom's Taxonomy, Alondra expressed her understanding of problem-posing education as supporting students to develop reading comprehension and critical thinking skills in order that they can gain the confidence to engage in dialogue and ultimately 'do it with love, humility and hope'. Although not expressing the level of understanding of transformation that Miguel had articulated, Alondra made the readings make sense to her; in a Bakhtinian sense, she formed the words to her own meanings, which is the ongoing process of dialogue.

Then Alondra followed Miguel's example and set a goal for herself for the coming school year: to focus more on the questions she was asking her students, and push them to think more; to allow them to take more responsibility for their learning – to, in the terms as she's understood it, embrace a problem-posing pedagogy in her classroom. She built directly upon Miguel's challenge, elaborating more on the details.

Este año escolar, quiero enfocarme más en las preguntas que les hago a mis estudiantes. Voy a poner más empeños para que sean a un nivel que los haga pensar más. También quiero permitirles que se hagan mucho más responsables de su aprendizaje para que yo no termine siendo la única persona que les está dando información. Esto se puede lograr dándoles oportunidades para que trabajen con otros compañeros, ya sea en parejas o en grupos. Lo importante es que ellos estén frecuentemente involucrados en conversaciones con los demás. *[This school year, I want to focus more on the questions I am asking my students. I will put more effort into ensuring they are at a level that makes them think more. Also I want to let them take much more responsibility for their learning so that I don't end up the only person who is giving information. This can be achieved by giving them opportunities to work with other classmates, in pairs or in groups. The important thing is that they be frequently involved in conversations with others.]*

Following Alondra's lengthy response, Maya jumped in with a connection she made:

Tu respuesta me hizo pensar en problem-posing como lo presentó Freire y lo comparé con Problem-based learning (PBL) como lo a presentado Gomez & Gomez. Me parece que son la misma cosa, no? Este año pensamos implementar PBL en las dos clases de 2o grado de DL, asi es que talvez podemos colaborar ya que las dos enseñamos segundo grado. *[Your response made me think of problem posing as Freire presents it and I compared it with Problem-based learning (PBL) as the Gomez & Gomez team have presented it (Gomez & Gomez, 1999). It seems like they are the same thing, no? This year we are thinking of implementing PBL in the two second grade DL classes, so maybe we can collaborate since we both teach second grade.]*

Maya expressed her idea that Freire's conception of 'problem-posing' appeared to resemble an approach to planning and teaching called project-based learning (PBL, which she here called 'problem-based learning'), which had been presented to her in her school district as a key aspect of the dual language program they were implementing. Taking the theory immediately into her current practice, she invited Alondra to collaborate with her in reaching her goal, since they both worked with second graders and since Maya also expected to be working toward similar transformation in her own classroom.

Natasha's post came next, offering her own reflections on the readings, laced with a clear indication that she had read what preceded her. She began by stating she was in agreement with both Miguel and Alondra, that banking education prevailed in many current school contexts, and that – like Alondra – she wanted to be more aware of her own work in the classroom:

Perdon por llegar tarde a la discusión, no me percaté de que habíamos comenzado este diálogo... estoy muy de acuerdo con ambos. Al leer a Freire cuando habla del maestro que se ve como fuente de toda sabiduría y cuyo deber es llenar a los estudiantes como si fuera un vaso...tengo que confirmar que desafortunadamente aún vemos esto en las escuelas. Estoy de acuerdo que esto representa una filosofía limitante y atrofiadora. Los estudiantes no tienen oportunidad de tomar control de su aprendizaje ni de definirlo. Al igual que Alondra yo quiero estar más conciente de mi labor en el salón, quiero ser más una facilitadora de aprendizaje y no una 'bomba de incendios' que apaga el deseo de aprender de mis niños. Al contrario quiero que mi salón sea una continuación de su vida y de su realidad. *[Sorry to arrive late to the conversation, I didn't realize that we had begun this dialogue...I'm very much in agreement with you both. Upon reading Freire when he talks about the teacher who sees himself like a fountain of all wisdom and whose job is to fill the students as if they were a glass... I have to confirm that unfortunately we still see this in schools. I agree that this represents a limited and atrophied philosophy. Students don't have the opportunity to take control of their learning nor to define it. Like Alondra I want to be more conscious of my work in my classroom, I want to be more a facilitator of learning and not a 'fire engine' that shuts down my children's desire to learn. On the contrary, I want my room to be a continuation of their lives and of their reality.]*

Natasha then seamlessly moved into a description of several experiences in her classroom that reflected efforts to engage family and community funds of knowledge rather than following this banking approach:

> Veo el beneficio de que en el salón de clases los niños se vean a sí mismos y a su cultura representada. Parte del fracaso de los estudiantes de minorías se debe al enfoque de las maestras en pensar que ellos no saben nada y que con sólo escuchar una catedra diaria van a aprender y también se debe a no valoramos el conocimiento y experiencia que los niños traen de sus casas. Al contrario, muchas maestras terminan reemplazando la cultura de los estudiantes por otra. El año pasado durante el tema de trabajadores de la comunidad y durante el tema de las plantas las maestras de nuestra escuela incluímos a todos los padres en pláticas con los niños. Nos dimos cuenta que mientras los niños no sabían vocabulario de ciertas profesiones, eran expertos en las profesiones que ejercían sus padres y les permítimos no sólo apreciar, sino compartir sus conocimientos con sus compañeros. Fue una experiencia enriquecedora para todos. Los puntos eran relevantes y reales para los niños y ganaron cierto orgullo por sus padres y lo que han aprendido de ellos. *[I see the value of in the classroom children seeing themselves and their culture represented. Part of the problem of minority students is due to teachers' focus on thinking that they (students) don't know anything and that only by listening every day to a professor will they learn and also it's owed to us not valuing the knowledge and experience that children bring from their homes. On the contrary, many teachers end up replacing the culture of the students for another. Last year during the unit on workers in the community and during the unit on plants the teachers in our school included all the parents in conversations with the children. We noticed that while the children didn't know the vocabulary of certain professions, they were experts in the professions that their parents practices and we permitted them not just to appreciate but also to share their knowledge with their classmates. It was an enriching experience for everyone. The points were relevant and real for the children and they gained a certain pride for their parents and what they had learned from them.]*

Like Miguel, Natasha embraced Moll's funds of knowledge and in general an assets-oriented approach to the children and families she served. She referenced home visits, which are a prominent feature of the Moll *et al.* article, and described her own experiences with this practice:

Yo pienso que es totalmente erróneo pensar que por venir de un trasfondo humilde y por tener experiencias diferentes, los niños son totalmente ignorantes. Pienso lo mismo acerca de pensar que los niños sean problemáticos por hacer las cosas diferentes o tener reacciones inesperadas. Es importante tomar el tiempo para conocer a nuestros estudiantes y descubrir todas las riquezas que pueden aportar a nuestro salón. Debemos comenzar por apreder acerca de la cultura del país que provienen hasta la cultura que tienen como familia. Al leer a Moll se me confirmó mi deseo de visitar a mis estudiantes en sus hogares. Este año, a raíz de mis visitas a las casas de mis estudiantes, he visto los beneficios de conocer de dónde vienen nuestros estudiantes. Siento que abrí una ventanita por la que veo y entiendo algunas de sus reacciones, también he comenzado a establecer relaciones positivas con los padres y ver cómo los puedo integrar a las actividades y lecciones que tenemos en clase. Es mi gran deseo este año crear la confianza (Moll, 1992, p. 19) con los padres, facilitándoles la participación activa, en cuanto sea posible, en la educación académica de sus hijos. Quiero crear una conexión entre el salón y el hogar que le de poder a los padres para aportar su conocimiento y para que ayude a los niños a apreciar más a sus padres. Me parece que muy pocos maestros hacen esto, y pienso que hasta cierto punto la falta de esta visión crea una limitación en las posibilades de aprendizaje y de progreso de nuestros niños. *[I think it's totally erroneous to assume that because they come from a humble background and have different experiences that children are ignorant. I think the same about thinking that children are problematic because they do things differently or have unexpected reactions. It's important to take the time to know our students and discover all the riches that they can bring to our classroom. We should begin by learning about the culture of their country of origin including the culture of their family. Reading Moll confirmed for me my desire to visit my students in their homes. This year, because of my visits to the homes of my students, I've seen the benefits of knowing where they come from. I feel like I've opened a little window through which I can see and understand some of their reactions, also I've begun to establish positive relationships with their parents and to see how I can integrate them into the activities and lessons that we have in class. It's my big desire this year to create trust with parents, facilitating their active participation as much as possible, in the academic education of their children. I want to create a connection between the classroom and the home that can give power to the parents to share their knowledge and so that this helps the children to better appreciate their parents. It seems to me very few teachers do this, and I think that after a certain point the lack of this vision creates a limitation in the possibilities for learning and progress for our children.]*

Home visits, Natasha exhorted, 'opened a little window' into her students' lives, offering her insight into their reactions and allowing her to build positive relationships with parents. This led to shifts in her curriculum to take account of the wealth of resources parents offer – which in turn led to that 'confidence' that Moll described.

At this point, Miguel returned to the conversation to reinforce Natasha's positive description of home visits with his own:

> Natasha, mas vale tarde que nunca [better late than never]. At my school it is like a tradition to do visits at the beginning of the school year. All the teachers go and visit their students (the majority) to welcome them to the new school year. From my experience I can tell you how great and beneficial it is. You can see the students' excitement when they open the door to find out that it is a teacher coming over to visit them. I remember that on my first year one family invited me to dinner. This was the beginning of a wonderful relationship that to this day I am still in touch with them. Families open their doors and hearts to show you how important you are in their life. In addition to this, such experience gives us the opportunity to extend learning beyond the classroom. As we have learned from the readings, the fundamentals of knowledge start at home.

Beginning with a Mexican expression that translates to 'better late than never' (in reference to Natasha's beginning, 'perdón por llegar tarde a la discusión'), Miguel switched into English for the remainder of his description of how home visits happen at his school. Paco, meanwhile, a kindergarten teacher from Spain, responded next with his own lengthy reflection, beginning with a direct reference to Alondra's plant metaphor and extending – perhaps even clarifying – her metaphor:

> Me encanta la analogía de la planta que has usado para describir el proceso de aprendizaje de nuestros niños, Alondra. Es cierto que, en ocasiones, más que facilitar el conocimiento a nuestros alumnos, lo que hacemos es anegarlos con un mar de ideas y conceptos que difícilmente son capaces de asimilar, en lugar de conectar primero con sus conocimientos previos, y ser más un facilitador y un guía para el desarrollo de sus conocimientos y de su pensamiento crítico. [I love the analogy of the plant that you've used to describe our children's learning process. It's true that, sometimes, more than facilitate the learning of our students, what we do is negate them with a sea of ideas and concepts that they're barely capable of assimilating, instead of connecting first with their prior knowledge, and being more a facilitator and a guide for their development of knowledge and critical thinking.]

Paco's explanation of Alondra's plants metaphor more clearly linked the conception of drowning the 'plants' in a 'sea of ideas' to banking education, and contrasted this with problem-posing in which a teacher's role is more a facilitator and guide. He expanded upon Alondra's original idea.

Then Paco went on to agree with Miguel's initial assertion that many teachers engage in 'banking education', and with everyone's connection between Freire and Moll. He offered the idea that younger teachers may be more open to transformation. He also suggested that teachers' surprise at parents' high levels of expertise may be due to unexamined prejudice, and offered that we might want to reflect on this – beginning with himself:

> También estoy de acuerdo con vosotros en que, en efecto, todavía quedan muchos profesores que convierten su labor docente en una vía de un único sentido, en la que el educador es quien enseña, y los educandos los que son enseñados, exclusivamente, como critica Freire, aunque tengo que decir que, afortunadamente, he conocido a muchos más maestros como 'educadores problematizadores' que como 'bancarios', en términos freireanos. En mi experiencia, por lo general la edad influye en este concepto – la mayoría de nuestros colegas coetáneos están abiertos a la metodología moderna –, así como el campo de trabajo – me he topado con un porcentaje mucho más alto de profesores tradicionales en el entorno universitario que en el escolar, al menos en España –. *[I'm also in agreement with all of you in that, in effect, there are still many teachers who convert their job as teacher into a one-way street, in that the educator is the one who teaches, and the educands (students – Freire's term) the ones who are taught, exclusively, as Freire critiques, even though I have to say that, fortunately, I've known many more teachers who resemble 'problem-posing educators' than 'bankers', in Freirean terms. In my experience, in general age influences this concept – the majority of our contemporaries are open to modern methodology –, as well as the field – I've come in contact with a much higher percentage of traditional teachers at the university level than in the schools, at least in Spain.]*
>
> Y qué decir de los fundamentos del conocimiento. Estoy seguro de que todos tenemos la experiencia de cuán enriquecedor es contar con el apoyo y la participación de los padres en la educación de sus hijos. Por un lado, citando a Moll, con frecuencia los padres de nuestros alumnos tienen mucho más que aportar de lo que a veces creemos. Reflexionando sobre el porqué de esta idea, es posible que esté tan extendida porque, como el propio Moll cita al principio del capítulo 1, en los Estados Unidos los programas bilingües se han desarrollado en familias trabajadoras o pobres, lo cual es un dato que todos conocemos. Tal vez estemos más influenciados por nuestros prejuicios de lo que realmente creemos, lo que nos lleva a sorprendernos cuando nos encontramos con padres con

conocimientos avanzados sobre ciertos temas. Quizá sea un punto sobre el que podamos reflexionar, empezando por mí mismo. *[And what to say about the funds of knowledge. I'm sure that we all have experience with how rich it is to count on the support and participation of parents in the education of their children. On the one hand, citing Moll, frequently the parents of our students have much more to bring than we sometimes believe. Reflecting upon the why of this idea, it's possible that it may be so widespread because, as Moll himself states in the beginning of Chapter 1, in the US bilingual programs have developed in working class or poor families, which is something we all know. Maybe we are more influenced by our prejudices than we really believe, which brings us to be surprised when we find ourselves with parents with advanced knowledge about certain topics. Maybe that's something we can reflect about, beginning with myself.]*

Paco's insight here, that the necessity to learn about Latinx bilingual families' 'funds of knowledge' pointed to a discrepancy in teachers' assumptions about their students' parents, moved the conversation to a decidedly more critical level, and to a deeper understanding of Moll.

Paco then in a sense reframed this insight in a positive light. He offered that if teachers begin to take account of the funds of knowledge of their students' parents, they will broaden the value of this type of knowledge, both within and beyond the community. He connected this idea to a comment that George made on one of the other threads of the discussion board, about beginning a parent workshop on teaching writing by asking parents first for their own strategies before offering ideas. Paco ended with an observation that often parents, observing his students, had quicker insights than he:

Por otro lado, contar con las fuentes de conocimiento de las familias de nuestros alumnos es también una manera de motivarlos y de convertir su aprendizaje en significativo. A este respecto, me ha parecido interesante la idea que George ha comentado de preguntar primero a los padres en su taller de escritura por las estrategias que usan en casa para enseñar a sus hijos a escribir, en lugar de mencionar directamente las que él usa en la clase. *[On the other hand, counting on the funds of knowledge of our students' families is also a way to motivate them and make their learning meaningful. In this respect, George's idea seems interesting, to ask parents first in a workshop about writing to share the strategies that they use in the house to teach their children to write, rather than mentioning directly the ones that he uses in the classroom.]*

Un ejemplo personal del uso del conocimiento de los padres de nuestros alumnos es que, en más de una ocasión, he tenido a un padre en la clase que ha sido capaz de observar y detectar en pocos minutos características de mis estudiantes de las que yo no me había dado cuenta en semanas. ¡Pa que luego digan que los maestros son los únicos que sabemos! *[A personal example of the use of parents' knowledge is that, on more than one occasion, I've had a parent in the class who has been more capable of observing and detecting in a very short time characteristics of my students that I hadn't noticed in weeks. Who says teachers are the only ones who know!]*

The five participants in this dialogue supported one another's understanding of the text, building one upon the next so that by the end the group's understanding of the ideas presented in the texts seemed to go deeper and connect more thoroughly to their experiences as bilingual teachers in Texas public schools. They also repeatedly and continuously built rapport with one another, doing relational work throughout their reflections. Some examples follow of relational work that I pulled out of the various reflections on the above thread:

- Estoy de acuerdo con Miguel/*I am in agreement with Miguel* (Alondra)
- Tu respuesta me hizo pensar en ... asi es que talvez podemos colaborar ya que las dos enseñamos segundo grado./*Your response made me think of... so maybe we could collaborate since we both teach second grade.* (Maya)
- Al igual que Alondra yo quiero .../*Like Alondra I want...* (Natasha)
- Me encanta la analogía de la planta que has usado para describir el proceso de aprendizaje de nuestros niños, Alondra./*I love the analogy of the plant that you used to describe the learning process of our children, Alondra.* (Paco)
- También estoy de acuerdo con vosotros en que.../*I am also in agreement with you all in that...* (Paco)

This relational work was part of the co-construction of understanding that took place within the exchanges. In this thread, ideas built upon other ideas in a Bakhtinian dialogue that deepened everyone's understanding of the readings. Take, for example, one of Miguel's central arguments: that Moll *et al.*'s (1992) 'funds of knowledge for teaching' offers a contrast and remedy to Freire's 'banking education'. This idea was provocative; it traveled through several people's reflections, expanding each time in a new direction. Alondra created her own explanatory metaphor, children as plants who need nurturing, to illustrate and further theorize Miguel's connection; then she brought in Bloom's Taxonomy and her own teaching practice, suggesting that the specific task of posing questions to our students is one means to move her pedagogy away from 'banking' and toward 'problem-posing'. Maya linked Alondra's connection between problem-posing and questioning to project-based learning, which supported her understanding of Freire. Natasha then picked up and echoed Alondra's and Miguel's commitments to move their own pedagogies in the direction of problem-posing education, amplifying the idea that doing so would imply drawing on children's linguistic and cultural funds of knowledge. She articulated in detail some of the units of study in which she had been attempting to bring in family and community participation. Finally, Paco affirmed and clarified Alondra's plant metaphor, and revoiced the link several people had made between Moll *et al.* and Freire, adding his insight that drawing on community funds of knowledge could actually have a transformative impact upon broader school and society perceptions of the value of these types of knowledge – thus bringing the ideas full circle. Each teacher's reflections deepened the group's understanding of transformation and the ways that education had the potential to transform.

Another example of an idea that traveled and was expanded in the dialogue was the role of home visits in children's and teachers' education. Natasha first brought this up as part of her own reflection on Moll *et al.*, describing the ways that home visits have enhanced her relationships with families this year and confirming her desire to keep up this practice. Miguel then specifically returned to the conversation to agree with Natasha and to share his own experiences with home visits. Miguel affirmed that home visits begin a caring, humanizing relationship that lasts all year: 'Families open their doors and hearts to show you how important you are in their life'.

The conversation about home visits continued in another thread on this same discussion board, when Alondra offered:

> Our school also has a Community Walk in which we have the opportunity to visit each student's home. I completely agree that this allows us to learn about the funds of knowledge our students have to offer. We also begin to build closer relationships with our parents so that they feel more comfortable to talk to us. What I have tried as well, has been to send a short questionnaire for both the students and parents during the first week of school. The questions allow parents to tell me more about themselves. It also allows me to see if there are any special circumstances that could be affecting or interfering in the student's academic progress in the classroom.

And Maya responded to Alondra's questionnaire idea, saying briefly: 'I like the idea of the questionnaire. There's many circumstances that affect the kids that we don't know about'. Alondra and Maya's comments, although disconnected by appearing later in the complicated threading of the online discussion board, clearly connected dialogically to the previous conversation about home visits, and extended everyone's breadth of potential practices for drawing family/community funds of knowledge into their classrooms.

Sharing resources

Another illustration of the ways that Cohort 5 built and maintained a professional community of learners was sharing resources. In the same online discussion board, a second thread was started by Maya, who introduced a connection between Freire's *Pedagogy of the Oppressed* and the requirement that children raise their hands before speaking in the classroom:

> Friere's words, 'lifeless and petrified' are excellent descriptors of what the pedagogy of the oppressed looks like. When you enter a classroom in which students are merely depositors as the teacher is 'imparting knowledge' you see in their eyes the lifelessness. Dialogue between children and adult is a skill that is hardly seen. In schools students hardly have opportunities for dialogue with adults. They are told what to do, how to answer, when to answer and they must first raise their hand! This is a spot where I will stop and make a connection with my classroom. I find it difficult to have a two-way conversation with my students when they are having to raise their hand, wait to be acknowledged, and then respond. It feels unnatural to me. Last school year I came up with a signal so that my students knew when it was ok to speak or contribute to the conversation without raising their hand. We got used to it and enjoyed many conversations and different points of view. However, some visitors, at times, reminded my kids to raise their hand before speaking; which always made me feel like a bad teacher with no discipline in place. This past week, I struggled with the idea of doing this again, since this group of kids were so polite and 'proper' raising their hand before a single peep came out of them. I held back the thought of sharing with them the signals for two-way conversations or one-way. I guess I worried that I'd be breaking their manners they learned in first grade. After reading Freire, however, I am thrilled to learn that dialogue leads to critical thinking, which leads to communication, which leads to true education. Tomorrow, I will surely show my students that they have great contributions to make and that dialogue is essential for learning.

Maya's comment about hand-raising triggered a flurry of sharing. Alondra responded, agreeing with Maya and offering a solution from her classroom practice:

> It is true that by asking our students to raise their hand before they speak, we are limiting their opportunities to engage in dialogue. In my classroom what has worked has been to begin the school year teaching them this procedure. As my students begin to understand how to hold respectful conversations, then we slowly move away from raising our hand all the time.

Then George popped in with a question for his colleagues:

> I'm interested to know what you guys do to get the students to the point
> where everyone can participate in a whole group conversation without
> hand raising. Maya, you mentioned a signal? Can you tell us more about
> what it is and how you introduce it? Alondra, what kinds of activities do
> you do to teach respectful conversations?
> I'm asking because I've struggled with the whole hand raising dilemma
> for years. For me it seems the dynamics of certain of my past classes
> allowed them to forego asking permission to participate in whole group
> conversations. However, with other groups of children in which there
> were a few very extroverted students and many introverts I've been very
> strict about the hand raising so as to provide equal opportunities for all
> to contribute. (This year I'm also putting the students' names on popsicle
> sticks and pulling them randomly to try to give everyone equal talking
> time.... but then you run the risk of calling on a student who has nothing
> to say and ignoring a student who might have more to contribute.)

Although he wasn't directly asked, Miguel responded to George's
question with an idea, further deepening their collective reflection about
participation frameworks and interactional patterns in their classrooms:

> George: although you asked the question to Maya and Alondra, I would
> like to say something. At the end of your comments you said that you
> do not want to risk on asking a question to a student that has nothing
> to say and not give a chance to another student who has something to
> contribute. I think you can solve this problem by extending a whole
> conversation into a small group conversation. On one hand we have
> students who refuse to participate in whole group conversations, but do
> well on small groups. On the other hand, we have students who want
> to take over the whole conversation. Small group conversations give
> everybody a chance to participate.

Maya then returned to the conversation to respond to George's request for
more detail:

> Hi George, last year I came to realize or accept that I hated the whole
> hand-raising thing... It just stops the flow of a conversation. That's when
> I decided to tell my students that at times it was okay to just answer or
> share a comment, make a connection, etc. I showed them that there were
> times that I needed their full attention and it was only my turn to talk. The
> signal I use is pretty simple, when I pose a question, as I am asking it, I
> hold my hand up if I expect them to raise their hand, I open my hands/arms
> as I pose a question if it is an open conversation/discussion and I explain

that they can answer each others' questions as well. Last year's class was so logical and as one person made an inference the other person would respond to their answer, etc. So conversations went Teacher-Student-Student-Student-Teacher-Student, etc. It was very interesting and they would end up going places I would not have taken them to if I had been the only one talking. I also use randomization sticks at other times, especially during Math and when they need to take turns at sharing their work.

Maya's response built on Miguel's by reflecting on the amount of student talk that occurred in her classroom when she abandoned the need for hand-raising; she also affirmed George's popsicle sticks idea, offering that it was part of her practice as well during certain times. Alondra then responded again to Maya, briefly expressing that she 'really like[d] the idea of using those hand signals'. She added that she 'also use[s] the popsicle sticks on certain occasions when no dialogue is happening at all...'. And then Paco jumped into the conversation, sharing his own practices:

> I do something similar to Maya and Alondra. I model at the beginning of the school year what a good and fluid conversation looks like, and encourage them to participate in discussions as much as they can, especially in times like shared reading, read aloud, math core lesson, or science. What I stress is that they cannot interrupt anyone who's talking. In case they hear somebody say something and they make a connection, then they can raise their hand if that person hasn't finished, or simply wait till they do.
>
> To encourage everyone's participation, I usually keep track of who has shared out thoughts in the conversation, and then call out kids who haven't, but after reading Freire's chapters and your sticks idea, I believe I'm going to rethink my method.

After sharing his own methods, Paco confessed that this dialogue and his reading of Freire have led him to 'rethink' his method of 'call[ing] out kids'.

Presumably responding to George's original question, Alondra then offered her own explanation of how she taught her students to have 'respectful conversation':

> During the first few weeks of school, I model what a respectful conversation looks like. Then as a whole group we create a list of what it should look like. For example, one of the things on the list is 'Espera tu turno' ['wait your turn']. The students do not learn it right away but with practice they become better at it.

This thread then closed with one more brief affirming comment from Maya, 'Thanks for sharing Alondra'. The cohort managed in this online dialogue, using Freire's own writings about *dialogue* as a jumping off point, to discuss how to teach young children to engage in authentic, rich dialogue together – and to articulate the benefits of doing so.

The courses, and the cohort structure itself, reinforced and supported the cultural practice of sharing resources and ideas; this seemed to matter for teachers, as they took up the practice and amplified it on many occasions. It would be safe to assert that sharing resources with communities of professionals is an essential feature of teacher leadership, and in bilingual education where good resources are so scarce, this practice becomes critical.

One minor assignment in the fall cohort course was for each teacher to select a 'resource to share', to post these resources to an online discussion board titled 'Recursos Compartidos/*Shared Resources*', and then sign up for a class period at some point during the semester to take five minutes (which often stretched to 15) to share them in class. The idea was that the teachers, knowing who their colleagues were and what contexts they taught in, would engage in course readings throughout the semester and choose to share resources that were both responsive to their contexts and useful in achieving their shared goals. This online discussion board grew each week as an additional teacher would post what they had shared in class, and others would occasionally respond to it. Here is a sampling of the resources that Cohort 5 shared, as evidenced on the discussion board, with some of the accompanying online commentary:

- George shared a link to information about the National Board Certification process (http://www.nbpts.org/), explaining that he saw 'a lot of similarities between what we've been learning in Proyecto Maestría and the tenets of National Board'. He encouraged his colleagues to consider going through this intensive certification process 'in the future' as he believed it 'would be beneficial to anyone interested in improving their effectiveness as a bilingual teacher'.
- Maya shared two books related to teaching math facts in primary grades, explaining 'The suggested activities are hands on, open-ended, short and sweet and it includes a lot of games. There is also a book for multiplication and division for higher grades'.
- Paco shared the link to a blog titled 'I Teach Dual Language' (http://iteachduallanguage.blogspot.com/), explaining that it 'is a resourceful website for teachers in bilingual programs. I've found some good ideas for centers there, and researching some of those ideas on Google, I've ended up surfing other interesting bilingual sites around the web'.
- Miguel shared the link to latinopia.com (http://latinopia.com/), explaining that it was 'a great resource for primary sources about Latinos. You can find art, films, music, food, literature, and theatre related to Latinos, but specially Chicanos'.

- Alondra shared the book *Teach Like a Champion* (Lemov, 2010), explaining that it was 'a great resource for new teachers and a great review for experienced ones. It provides teachers with many different strategies that target different things such as setting high academic expectations, creating a strong classroom culture and challenging students to think critically'.
- Gisela shared two websites: an introduction to QR Codes and an online English vocabulary game with charity incentives called 'Free Rice' (http://freerice.com/#/english-vocabulary/1557). In class, she showed the group how to use both. In response on Gisela's thread, Paco voluntarily posted an additional resource that he believed connected with Gisela's: 'mobile mouse' (http://mobilemouse.com), explaining it was a 'Programa para controlar la computadora con el smartphone *[Program for controlling the computer with the smartphone]*'.

I offer these details as a small taste of the amount and kinds of sharing that took place; this cultural practice became a part of daily experience and a central feature of the teachers' interactions. On multiple occasions far beyond the course expectation, participants would ask permission to take five minutes in class to share something, and many of the teachers continue sharing resources on social media even several years after they've graduated. They also indicated that they continued to broaden the network of teachers with whom they shared ideas and resources.

Christine and Sofía (Cohort 3) are perhaps a pinnacle example of this, developing an open-access website of resources on culturally relevant children's literature and curricular materials related to a social studies unit on immigration, and then voluntarily taking their resources to professional conferences to actively recruit interest in their ideas. These moments and spaces for sharing supported the building and deepening of relationships between the teachers, and illustrated some of the explicit learning that occurred among the teachers.

Carrying Cohort Relationships into Post-Graduation Professional Lives

Emma (Cohort 4, Kindergarten) described in her post-graduation interview how her cohort continued to meet for breakfast from time to time, sharing their ideas and their practices. The value for her, she explained, was not only in maintaining the relationships they had built, but also the comfort level she had with them, and the wide range of ideas they shared. They continued to learn from each other precisely because they were in such a range of contexts, and yet had had the opportunity over 15 months to develop deep and powerful relationships. She explained that going into the program, 'I was interested in meeting different people at different areas in different you know levels, it totally pushed me to analyze what I was doing and do more'. Describing her cohort colleagues, Emma said, 'I don't think I've come across people as passionate or you know hard-working than the people I've met through the program'. She described the group's ongoing professional learning community:

> We've already, we're trying to start something... we're meeting at the end of this month. Just projects that we talked about during the program and that now that we have a little bit more time we're trying to act upon them – and the majority has been showing up, we miss about two or three people because they can't, or I know some have dropped off completely. We're not sure what happened to them, but the majority of us are getting together, I do definitely see us continuing 'cause I think there was an emotional and a personal connection. During the program we got together socially a lot so we got to know each other's spouses or families or kids and I feel like because we made those connections you know those personal connections will continue.

Emma's cohort (4) maintained ongoing gatherings for at least a year past their graduation, which was more than most. But in all the cohorts, teachers have organized ways to continue sharing. Cohort 2 has its own Facebook group that one of the teachers started when a group of them saw each other at the Fourth Annual ¡Adelante! Conference. At this conference, a full six years after their graduation, they picked up relationships as if they'd never separated. Several teachers from Cohorts 3 and 4 organized to work together as colleagues at the same schools and to propose presentations together for state and national teacher conferences, including Sofía and Christine (Cohort 3), Emma and Lucia (Cohort 4) and several teachers from both cohorts who chose to work together at Leti (pilot cohort) and Lupe's (Cohort 2) school. Three of the nine Cohort 1 members came together four years after graduating to work on the first ¡Adelante! Conference, and at least three others of the nine total members attended. Cohort 5 colleagues currently populate both Academia Cuauhtli (Valenzuela *et al.*, 2015) and the board of the Austin Area Association for Bilingual Education, which puts together the ¡Adelante! Conference every year. As one of the few people with the privilege to know all participants across all cohorts, I continue to hear about and support ongoing collaborations, which at this point have gradually extended to teachers far beyond the original five (plus pilot) cohorts.

Building Professional Community Beyond the Cohort: Local, Regional, State/National

Being a part of a Proyecto cohort spurred teachers to continue to seek out and build professional community beyond their initial university cohort. As Patricia Nuñez (pilot cohort teacher and grant staff member) explained:

> But I think that's kind of what happens with Proyecto, you know? You, all of a sudden, first of all, the fact that you're in a cohort, and then the fact that you're getting all this information and all this knowledge, and you're like, 'I want to spread it'.

Teachers experienced firsthand the power and potential of strong professional relationships, and as Patricia Nuñez went on to explain, they sought these out in whatever professional spaces they occupied:

> I know that every single cohort member that I've met so far, um, I know that one of the main qualities that we all possess, or the idea, the knowledge of understanding that a relationship is a very important thing to have, and to establish with your teachers.

Leti (pilot cohort, third grade), who moved into a principalship soon after completing the Proyecto master's and went on to hire a number of Proyecto Maestría graduates to teach at her school, explained how her experiences building powerful professional relationships in Proyecto profoundly influenced her leadership style:

> You know, you go in, and you start it in, we started in June, ¿verdad, [right?] in June? And by the time we were done the next August, I wasn't the same person. Some-something along the way changed. I think a big part of it, is what we've talked about today – is the information, the knowledge, you're, you're researching around people who are exploring and uh, and learning, and, we're **collaborating**. And that **team** portion of it, I think, became really important, and I began to *look* for that. One of the things that I've discovered is the fit – is the way that you get through those days, then those months that are, you know, sometimes hellacious, is the fit. You work with people who are like-minded and going in the same direction, and you work together, and you do the job together, and you do what, **everything that it takes, you do it together**. Um, all of that, I think, um, has brought me to the point where what I'm looking for as far as an administrator is not to be an administrator, but to be a part of a *team* that works well together, because, when that happens, then good things happen on the campus.

Lucia (Cohort 4, fourth bilingual math/science) explained that Proyecto taught her that working in collaboration was better:

I think I was so used to working alone, you know, so much that Proyecto Maestría showed me that, no, you need to work with your peers. Not that you need to, but you benefit more. You know, you can learn more. You can grow more. You can share ideas. You can bounce things off each other. So, I think that having a community, like, that it's really important.

The teachers caught the contagion of collaboration: working in solidarity, learning about one another's histories, passions, philosophies and pedagogies, realizing they were not alone. Most found ways to carry these connections forward and continue to grow new professional networks.

Several local projects grew directly or indirectly out of Proyecto Maestría professional communities and involved Proyecto teachers working in collaboration with one another or with university professors, including the Tejano History Project (Salinas *et al.*, 2015); Academia Cuauhtli (Valenzuela *et al.*, 2015); and the ¡Adelante! Conference.

The ¡Adelante! Conference

The ¡Adelante! Conference (http://www.aaabe.org/conference.html), now in its fifth year, actually began as a direct result of two Cohort 4 teachers' desire to maintain and grow the community they had developed in Proyecto. As Consuelo (Kindergarten) explained, she and her cohort colleague Amanda (second grade) had an assignment for a class with Dr Ramón Martínez during their final semester in Proyecto, to develop a project that would allow them to 'take agency' in their 'life as a teacher'. Consuelo explained:

So we talked about, you know, a few ideas and one of them was having a **teacher-led conference** and [now] it happens! And ... we put together the proposal and the ideas, but I do feel that it has always maintained that very teacher driven. And it's wonderful because teachers have *so* much to share and learn from each other. It's really great.

What Consuelo and Amanda drafted in a short proposal for a class assignment became, through financial support from Austin Independent School District (AISD) leadership, a conference that attracted over 400 teachers in its first year, and between 300 and 700 in each of the years since. After the first year, since we still had some remaining grant monies, we ran a few follow-up Saturday seminars on the University of Texas (UT) campus. Also, thanks to the dedication and determination of several teachers and UT doctoral students, beginning in the first year the conference has supported a bilingual parents' program. That program has grown into its own sister conference, with parents not only attending but participating in the planning and presentation process.

Presentations for the teacher portion of the conference are solicited, screened, organized and presented almost entirely by local bilingual and dual language teachers. Formats have shifted as teachers' ideas have evolved, and as different individuals enter and exit the process. Several agreed-upon policies support the continued centering of teacher voices and agency at the conference. First, while non-teachers (including researchers) are invited to submit proposals, priority is consistently given to teachers' proposals; we recommend to researchers that they invite a teacher to partner with them in order to strengthen their proposal. Second, commercial interests are invited – actually, encouraged and recruited – to sponsor tables in the exhibit hall, but are not permitted to take up presentation rooms or spaces. Third, for most years the conference organizers have maintained a tradition of creating informal conversation spaces, typically over the lunch hour, around specific topics, with conversation leaders assigned. This has allowed participants to meet new colleagues with common interests and share ideas, questions, strategies and materials. AISD is the primary financial sponsor of the conference, paying per teacher who attends and promising to send a minimum of several hundred teachers. Although the conference is open to teachers from anywhere, the vast majority of attendees are local bilingual teachers. Among planners and organizers of the conference, there has consistently been participation by representatives from the university, AISD administration and Education Austin – the Austin teacher's union, which co-sponsors the event. The core leadership for the conference has been teachers.

In the first year, at the end of the final keynote in March 2013, we took a photo with 22 Proyecto Maestría current participants and graduates who had been among the organizers, presenters and attendees that day. In the third annual conference in spring 2015, two years after the last Proyecto teacher graduated, I documented and described in field notes the conversations I had with 16 Proyecto graduates – and at least nine inspired teachers who had joined the community of professionals to help organize and participate in what was by then well known as the ¡Adelante! Conference.

The story of the ¡Adelante! Conference could be its own chapter, which there is not space for here. The key point I wish to make is that the conference, born to satisfy Proyecto Maestría teachers' commitments to expanding and developing teacher agency and professional networks of community, lives on as a teacher-run conference centering the voices of professionals, and giving Proyecto teachers and many, many others an outlet and focal point for sharing and disseminating their creative, culturally sustaining, critical pedagogies. As such, it consistently garners high ratings from attendees; as Consuelo explained above, 'teachers have so much to share and learn from each other'. This points to the central role community and collaboration play in teachers' development of leadership identities.

Teaching Other Teachers

Extending beyond the cohort and the experience of *learning* from other teachers, most of the participants were or became *teachers* of other teachers. They created and presented professional development workshops at conferences and at their schools/in their districts; they mentored colleagues both formally and informally; they became coaches, mentor teachers to novices and teacher educators. All of these practices were introduced and scaffolded in their course assignments toward the end of the master's program; it was impressive, however, how many of the teachers continued the practices beyond graduation. They *became* teachers of other teachers.

Mentoring

As part of their spring course on Teacher Leadership, participants mentored a colleague at their school. This could be a student teacher or novice colleague they were already officially mentoring, a teacher they already had a relationship with, such as a member of their grade-level team or a colleague who they already partnered with in some way, or someone they did not yet know. I encouraged them to invite someone from whom they could learn, and to make sure the person they chose was interested in taking this journey with them. Some of the teachers already had a great deal of experience mentoring while others had never done it before; a handful had actually received training in how to support colleagues in a mentoring role, and were able to enhance my own repertoire of tools on the subject. This was an example of me teaching something in which I was by no means an expert, and I welcomed their support and ideas as we collectively explored this idea.

Regardless of their starting level of experience, my goal with this assignment was for teachers to explore some of the literature about mentoring, to interrogate their own assumptions and reactions to mentoring and to reflect upon the experience. The guidelines for actually mentoring their colleague were very loose; this was all that was written in the syllabus:

Mentoring Project: Throughout the semester, you will work one-on-one with a colleague at your school, preferably a novice, first-year, or second-year teacher. You should ask someone who might be interested in volunteering to go through this process with you. Using the Cognitive Coaching strategies we will be learning in class, you will develop a relationship with this colleague, working towards offering support in whatever areas they most need. You will document the experience

*with a final reflection paper due 5/7. More details [about the paper] will
be provided.*

I asked only that they 'develop a relationship' and left the form and
logistics up to them. As the semester progressed, I asked them to share
their experiences and reactions in a range of formats, relating it at times to
specific mentoring-related readings (Glickman *et al.*, 2005; Lindsey *et al.*,
2007) and at times drawing on their range of experiences with mentoring
to enrich in-class activities. Finally, I required a narrative reflective paper
offering an overview of their mentoring experience guided by five questions:
Who is your mentee? What happened? What (if anything) changed for
them? What are (or would be) your hopes or next steps? and What did
you learn? The mentoring experience was a powerful one for many of the
participants, and provides a window into their process of constructing
themselves as teachers of other teachers.

As Alondra (Cohort 5, second grade) explained in the following online
reflection in the middle of the spring semester as she was preparing to
mentor her colleague, it was clear to these experienced teachers why strong
mentoring was important in the field of teaching, and why it was now their
turn to mentor:

> Throughout the years, I have witnessed how new teachers come into
> my school, teach for a year or two and then leave the profession often
> disappointed and burned out. Chapter 8 got me thinking about why this
> happens. When I started off as a new teacher, I was given a mentor. This
> mentor spent a lot of her time making sure I was prepared to teach every
> single lesson. She also would come in and model lessons for me. After that,
> she would observe me teach a similar lesson and give me feedback. There
> were many sessions where we would sit and reflect on my practices. If it
> wasn't for my mentor, I do not think I would have survived my first few
> years of teaching. Even after seven years, I still go to my mentor when I am
> stuck on something. Now that I have acquired more experience, it is time to
> pay it forward. I plan on using a lot of the strategies provided in the book.
> It is very important to support new teachers, and as we are teaching them
> new things, we are also gaining more experience for our own classroom.

Alondra explained that mentoring saved her in her first year; it kept her
in the classroom, allowed her to feel confident enough to continue every
day. The job of serving as her mentor, as Alondra framed it, was time
consuming, detail oriented and extremely important. Her mentor also
built a relationship with Alondra that continued even after seven years to
provide her with needed supports. And now, Alondra seemed to embrace
the opportunity to 'pay it forward' and to willingly take on the identity of
mentor for someone else.

George's (Cohort 5) end of semester mentoring reflection articulated some connections between what he had learned by trying his hand at mentoring, and his evolving understanding of teacher leadership in general. He identified ways in which he was developing as a teacher leader, both through his participation in Proyecto and in other professional development experiences, and tied them to his experiences with his mentee:

> As I was working through the many logistical concerns of Dual Language scheduling and planning this year with Louisa I think it likely I learned just as much as she. The relationship benefitted me by forcing me to develop an informed knowledge that I could articulate clearly to another person. This ability has come to shape my role as a bilingual teacher leader on my campus. As my knowledge base has grown through my National Board experience and Proyecto Maestría, as well as my role as a campus based mentor, I see myself becoming a more effective leader. I've learned things such as the importance of follow up and continued support for new teachers as well as the need for specific and targeted goals for both mentors and mentees. I believe in the future I'll continue to work with Louisa with hope that she come to see herself as a leader and future mentor of other bilingual teachers.

George's and Alondra's reflections about mentoring were thoughtful and well aligned with the literature on the benefits of skilled mentors and the challenges involved in mentoring (Lipton & Wellman, 2003). However, as with every other aspect of bilingual teacher leadership, the experiences of the Proyecto teachers with mentoring require the addition of a layer of critical analysis to our understanding of the process. In other words, in thinking with Proyecto teachers about what it meant to mentor other teachers, I realized over and over that it is not just professional experiences that matter when mentors sit down with mentees in schools. The race, class, culture, language and gender – i.e. the personal identities of a mentor and a mentee matter deeply in forming and enacting this complicated relationship, and society and the structures of schooling are often laced with bias when it comes to positioning some teachers as experts and others as novices. The picture is always complex: women mentoring men, teachers of color mentoring white teachers, bilingual teachers mentoring monolingual teachers – whenever members of a dominant group must listen to members of minoritized communities, this power relation can shape and challenge the already-complex teaching/learning relationship. This came to light in many instances when I asked Proyecto teachers to claim identities as mentors, or to talk about their experiences claiming these identities. In their school contexts, many of the teachers had already experienced mentoring other bilingual teachers before they entered the master's program. Strangely, however, it was much less common for bilingual teachers to serve as mentors for general education or English as a second language (ESL)-designated teachers. It was also less common for Latinx mentors to be assigned to white novices.

Mariana (Cohort 1, literacy coach) was the first teacher to bring this up in relation to the mentoring assignment. Although Mariana was already an experienced mentor, she found herself in a new and somewhat uncomfortable mentoring situation during her Proyecto year: for the first time in her career she was assigned to mentor a monolingual white teacher. During her teacher leadership course, whenever readings addressed issues related to mentoring (Lindsey *et al.*, 2007; Lipton & Wellman, 2003) or adult development (Glickman *et al.*, 2005), Mariana devoured the readings, sharing more than usual in class (especially in small group discussions) and reflecting often with her cohort members outside class discussions in her efforts to make sense of this new experience. Reflections on mentoring someone different from herself appeared several times in her written work as well. In a March discussion board posting, Mariana wrote:

> I was a little apprehensive to work with a white teacher. I have been always working with the Bilingual teachers and even if they are white we still have the language background. I guess we both came into the mentee–mentor relationship in a forced way. I had to come out of my comfort zone. ... I can now say that she is doing much better and her students have benefited too. I have learned to be more tolerant and how to interact with teachers of other cultural backgrounds.

In her final reflection on the experience, Mariana again emphasized the growth she experienced in learning to mentor a teacher whose cultural background was so different from hers; in particular, she talked of the strangeness of mentoring a teacher who was a member of the mainstream culture:

> I will confess that during my years in [my current school] I grow [sic] closer relationships with the Bilingual teachers. I just never felt that the Caucasian teachers needed me, until now. When I arrived at [my current school] they [Caucasian teachers] were the ones in power and the ones who were models for the rest of us... I never imagine[d] I was going to support a Caucasian teacher. It had been the other way in previous years... My biggest concern with this activity: how was I going to relate to a Caucasian, young, ESL teacher? I have learned that I can also support Caucasian teachers.

It was empowering for Mariana to move from embracing an identity of mentor *to other bilingual teachers*, to embracing an identity of mentor to *any* teacher who needs support. Mariana's confidence and strength grew as a leader. And given Mariana's expertise in the area of teaching emergent bilingual students, her having begun to mentor teachers more broadly would ultimately benefit more emergent bilingual students in the schools where she worked.

Lupe (Cohort 2, bilingual coach) experienced similar insecurities – at first – around her capacity to mentor mainstream teachers, but was able to leverage her experiences in graduate courses to support her own authoring as a general education instructional leader with specialized knowledge in many areas. She explained during a presentation with other program participants and graduates at the Texas Association of Bilingual Education (TABE) state conference in El Paso in 2010 (emphasis mine):

> After a few years of being on my campus, my principal who was Anglo, noticed that we had a lot of Hispanic students with the population that is basically bilingual students. So she asked me to step into a curriculum specialist position **so that I could help the teachers develop their ESL component** and of course I felt a little bit – I was very happy to do that, but **I didn't feel that I was capable.**

Lupe's lack of confidence was not mere insecurity; it seemed to be tied to two factors. First, she needed to gain the skills and knowledge to mentor and coach in the area of bilingual/ESL, as she went on to explain:

> I think I had the heart for it and I had the hard work and the ethics, but I just didn't really have the content and the research that goes behind and just the confidence in being able to go into the school to become the teacher leader that my campus needed and the students needed and the parents needed. So ah going through this course, I learned a lot of the research, the bilingual research and I really felt the – especially the component of mentoring.

As she explained, Proyecto Maestría's courses helped prepare her in these important ways. The second factor had to do with her principal's view of her, which she herself was able to shift:

> So because as Curriculum Specialist I did mentor most of our new teachers, so I felt that I was capable. And I had structure, and I had a plan, and during Proyecto Maestría we had to develop a campus goal. Like what things in my campus can I improve as a teacher leader. And so, I got together with my principal, and so I felt that my principal didn't see me as…just helping with the bilingual kids, but now I was actually a leader in helping make some decisions on our campus.

Although her principal had originally asked Lupe to step into an instructional leadership role specifically in the areas of bilingual and ESL support, Lupe drew on her experiences in the master's program – specifically, the expectation in her long-semester courses that she would develop and then carry out a goal for schoolwide improvement on her campus – to expand her own professional identity. After completing her master's degree, Lupe began an administrator certification program. She has since moved into an assistant principal position at a large elementary school campus with a thriving dual language program.

Emma (Cohort 4, Kindergarten) shared in an online post in the middle of the Teacher Leadership course some reflections about a similar challenge she envisioned as she contemplated who to mentor for her course assignment. She began by asserting the importance of having all professionals 'on board' in the effort to develop children's biliteracy:

> In a bilingual setting it is very important to bring all on board in order to support and nurture the children into becoming successful and bi-literate young adults. The message for English only is all around us, so it is much more difficult.

She then described some of her colleagues' – including one potential mentee's – attitudes about bilingual Latinx families, tying her own very different reactions directly to her personal experiences growing up as a bilingual child:

> I've had conversations with peers and some are so tired of the struggle, or tired of the lazy 'culture' and want to go somewhere else. I on the other hand lived this way growing up, with parents that were migrants and were absent from a lot of school functions due to work. It's not that they did not care, it's that school is intimidating and they trusted that I was doing my job and so were the teachers. I guess that's why I get along with parents and the kids so well (or because I'm happy and not bitter) is because I see some of me and my family in them.

She then directly reflected about the possibility of coaching or mentoring one of these deficit-oriented teachers:

> So when I think about having to coach someone who is different from me, it really makes me sit back and ponder. I have someone in mind that I would love to coach (my 'guinea pig') and know that it would be extremely difficult. As I was reading the sections [of *Culturally Proficient Coaching* (Lindsey *et al.*, 2007)] I was focused on how to deal with her. What would make it easy is that she seems approachable and open to conversations and others' opinions. Could I turn her around by the end of the school year?

No. I believe that it takes time, these teachers didn't learn to think the way they do in a year's time, it was their entire life building up to now. So coaching takes time, patience, and determination. In general, I think that if you have good people skills and you respect diversity already in your everyday dealings, then you would be an excellent coach. With some guidance and initial coaching for yourself of course.

Emma did not offer any personal details about this possible mentee, but she did make clear that this teacher had expressed deficit perspectives about Latinx families. As a skilled bilingual teacher and advocate, and as a Latina herself, Emma knew she would be challenged by this mentee. She did not express high hopes about transformation, although the reflection did lead her to draw some conclusions about what was required for good mentoring: patience, time, determination and 'good people skills'. Emma was involved in several official and unofficial mentoring relationships during her year in Proyecto; it is possible she may have tried mentoring this teacher for part of the semester and, as she predicted, did not make much progress with her. In any case, when she wrote her final reflection about the mentoring experience at the end of the semester, Emma described a different teacher: a young bilingual teacher who worked on her grade-level team, with whom she had been working closely as an official mentor since Emma had mentored her student teaching two years previous.

Emma's reflections about the challenges inherent in mentoring a teacher 'who is different from' herself and holds deficit perspectives about families like hers, point both to some unique challenges for bilingual teachers becoming mentors, and to some of the assets bilingual teachers bring to the task. When the teachers embraced their own cultural/linguistic identities and developed the skills to express these critical components of curriculum and instruction, they became better mentors for it. They included in their mentoring not merely the kinds of guidance around basic issues of classroom management that so often dominate mentoring relationships for new teachers, but inspiring and critically important messages about centering students' identities in curriculum and instruction. Emma's final reflection of the spring semester, in response to a prompt asking how her definition of teacher leadership may have changed, expressed this expansion clearly:

Previously I thought I was a 'good leader' because I was organized and able to move meetings along, relay information, etc. But I know now that I must do more. I must inspire others and educate my colleagues on culturally relevant lessons, literature, and practices. I must create advocates for biliteracy. I must mentor others to reach their fullest potential and reach as many kids as possible.

In an interview conducted a couple years after she graduated, Emma (who has always been exceptionally well organized) echoed the same distinction as she described how her mentoring changed pre- and post-Proyecto:

> I mentor, I've always mentored. But now it seems different. You know, before when I mentored I was more focused on getting new teachers started with organization or you know understanding the curriculum, and now I incorporate so much more what I learned as far as being culturally relevant in what I'm choosing to do and how I'm viewing parental involvement and how different aspects of it, not just the planning and the conferencing.

Emma described having integrated into her mentoring some of the core ideas at the heart of Proyecto: funds of knowledge for teaching (Moll *et al.*, 1992) and culturally relevant pedagogies (Ladson-Billings, 1995b). Beyond making sure new teachers could survive their first year, she now ensured that they learn from her some of these core principles that drive her teaching. The value of this for all the future teachers who work with her is undeniable.

For these Proyecto teachers, and indeed potentially for all bilingual education teachers, the need to expand their mentoring vision to embrace the development of critical awareness, assets-based orientations and culturally relevant pedagogies became clear because of their own experiences (or having borne witness to the experiences of colleagues, students or families) in often-subordinated positions within schools. Such expansive and critical missions are in fact crucial for *all* teachers as they mentor or are mentored; critical sociocultural awareness and centering children's identities in school support learning and success for students in our diverse world regardless of context.

Professional Development for Colleagues

Teachers were also engaged in teaching their peers in many other ways. Some, like Lupe above, were officially charged with supporting teachers with professional development, which became another route to developing and expanding professional networks and further illustrated the importance of this networking to supporting bilingual teachers' leadership identities.

Patricia (Cohort 4), for example, who began in an official role of dual language coach the year she did the master's program, two years later in an interview explained her role as a 'facilitator' of professional learning, supporting the teachers in her school to develop their reflective practices:

> You should be providing opportunities for teachers or for conversation, for learning, you know, and facilitating not so much giving it, just facilitating

it. Just making people or helping people become reflective because I know that for me it was a big change like for me it was one thing that Proyecto did for me. It just really made me be *reflective* and know that right now I'm thinking this but maybe later I'm going to be thinking something different because I'm going to see results or not. And so, I think that as a leader you have to do that.

She also lamented, however, that although teaching others has benefits, it does not adequately feed her own thirst for community and ongoing professional learning:

> ...it's the 'ok, we have these issues' or 'we see this' or 'let's read something and talk about it and how can we do this in the classroom'. How can we do this with teachers? Because a lot of what I am doing right now, I pretty much do, I mean, I do *classes* with them pretty much. We are doing a book study; we meet every month, every month after school, but then also we do half days where we do a more in depth, like they know, they know Ofelia García (2010). They know Kathy [Escamilla *et al.*, 2014], you know. They know the research. They've read it. We've talked about translanguaging. We've talked about best practices. So, I get that [professional stimulation], I have that with them and I think that's what keeps *them* going, right, but for *me* sometimes I'm like...
> DP: You need something to keep *you* going.
> R: Yes. Yes. Yeah.

In many cases, even if they were not in official coaching/mentoring/ professional development roles, teachers simply embraced identities not just as teachers of children, but as teachers of teachers. They carried this new identity into every professional experience, thinking about possibilities. An excellent example is Lucia (Cohort 4, fourth bilingual math/science), who learned in a class at UT with Literacy Professor Jim Hoffman (1992) about a particular approach to thematic instruction called the iChart. She saw it as a powerful pedagogical tool. Thus, she immediately began to consider how to better disseminate it among her fellow teachers, as she explained in her interview:

> And I thought, ok, they should organize this better so that people can actually do it, you know, and have a training. And that's kind of one of my goals. I mean, I foresee, I'm always thinking ahead, and I foresee, I would *love* to teach this iChart to the district, to teachers. I'd actually have a session and share this with teachers. You know, not just at NABE (national conference for bilingual educators) and TABE (state conference for bilingual educators), but the *district*.

It is intriguing that Lucia positioned the opportunity to present in state and national bilingual education conferences as 'just', while her own district – full of mainstream teachers, not 'just' bilingual teachers – became an aspirational space in which to share this innovative idea. This could be because, with Dr Hoffman's support, Lucia and her cohort colleague Emma did in fact bring a presentation about the iCharts to the NABE conference in 2017, and when Lucia spoke with me about it they had already put together their proposal, whereas she had not yet put together a presentation for the district. The idea of bringing presentations to state and national conferences had been new to most of the teachers when they began the Teacher Leadership course, as was the idea of developing and offering targeted professional learning opportunities to their colleagues at their own schools or districts. The course required them to try their hand at both these tasks, thus demystifying the process. Lucia and Emma, therefore, had no difficulties in developing a proposal for the NABE conference. Lucia explained:

> One project that we did with you [talking to me] of creating a proposal for a conference, I mean that was powerful. I mean, that was incredibly powerful! Because it was like, 'Oh, it's so easy! (laughs). Like, this is it? That's it?' You know. And it was funny because when I was doing the NABE proposal [recently], submitting it, and I had a busy summer and I had asked Emma to join me and it was the date before the deadline and she said, 'I don't think you're going to make it', and I was like, 'No, I know what to do. Remember? We did it with Dr. Palmer. It's easy'. And I did, you know. I think I might have submitted it a half hour before midnight, you know. And I got... my proposal was accepted.

Because their experience in my class had demystified the conference proposal process, these two teachers were regularly able to turn their insights and creativity into opportunities to share ideas with other teachers.

Yet, Lucia in describing potential venues for her ideas about using iCharts in bilingual classrooms still appeared to position the idea of presenting to teachers across her district as more intimidating, or perhaps more important, than at a national conference. This holds echoes of Mariana's and Lupe's (above) reflections about never having seen themselves as a potential mentor to *all* teachers, but only to other bilingual teachers. Bilingual teachers, given their capacity to bridge home and school communities for bilingual children and their extensive additional training in language acquisition, biliteracy development, etc., certainly have plenty of expertise to offer their mainstream colleagues; it is intriguing (to say the least) that they are not always perceived, or perceive themselves, to have this expertise.

Teaching teachers also became a medium in which bilingual teachers engaged in explicit advocacy. George (Cohort 5, first grade), for example, in an online post with cohort classmates, described a 'teachable moment' with his grade-level team at his school, when one of his colleagues brought up the topic of the new handwriting curriculum:

> This year we received a handwriting curriculum replete with cute workbooks and scripts to read as lessons are taught. My team thought the program looked great and have been conducting whole group handwriting lessons every day since school started. One day last week one of them complained about how difficult it was to fit handwriting into the schedule and that some of the kids really hated it. She then asked me how it was going in my classroom. (Like Lupe [Palmer *et al.*, 2006], my team and I often disagree and to be honest I didn't fight them when they 'agreed' to teach handwriting as a grade level. I just quietly decided I wasn't going to do it.) Now that I had been asked directly I thought I might actually be able to effect change by sharing my reflections about something as mundane as handwriting with this one individual. I explained to her that I didn't think it was appropriate to teach handwriting to students who already have 'good' penmanship, as some of the students do, and that I believed handwriting would develop as the students became real writers of real writing. That is, authors of their own stories and chroniclers of their own lives. She didn't really respond to what I said and mentioned something about alignment as she left. I think the challenge for me is to work harder to develop relationships with teachers like those on my team so that they don't see me as a rebel but as someone who actually puts a great deal of thought into my decisions. As of this moment we are not meeting Smith's standard of reflecting on and communicating our practice. But I'll keep trying.

George, by his admission, was only just beginning to speak up with his grade-level teammates about his own educational philosophies and pedagogical practices that may differ from theirs. He realized that he needed to further develop his skills in this arena if he wished for his advocacy to have greater impact.

Mireya (Cohort 4, dual language coach) described her work as a mainstream district language arts specialist:

> I think what I'm trying to do is just to educate them [mainstream teachers and administrators]. That there's a world out there that they don't know about. There are children in poverty that don't learn the same way that children at [an upper middle-class neighborhood school] learn. ... So, I am kind of just broadening the horizon, as to how their perspective needs to be wider.

Mireya's medium-sized suburban district had a history of marginalizing the needs of bilingual students, characterized by their expectation that bilingual teachers should just on-the-fly adapt English-only mainstream curriculum and professional development to their bilingual classrooms. When Mireya chose to take on this mainstream coordinator role, she first confirmed she would have allies among the other dual language coaches:

> ...before I took the position ... we had a group chat, all the DL coaches, 'Oh, Mireya, you should accept it', you know. I said, 'I'm going to accept it under one condition, yeah', I said, 'I need you to know that I'm here to advocate for you guys, but you guys need to know that I need you also... I need your help also in return, because you guys are going to have to provide the professional development. You guys are going to have to provide the knowledge out there... There's got to be a bridge...' I said. 'And I can be the bridge from here to the schools, but you guys have to help me out'.

Mireya acknowledged that 'at first [the position] was really hard', because she felt out of place and professionally alone serving in the district office as a general education language arts coordinator. But she articulated the need to take risks in order to accomplish real change:

> But then you know, I realized, if I never get out of that position where I'm just there in my comfort zone and I don't challenge myself and expose myself out there, and try to educate the people that we really want them to get it, then it's never going to happen. Because there will never be those opportunities for you to educate them because you belong to another group. But if you immerse yourself in that group, then you can make a difference.

Mireya's assertion that getting out of her 'comfort zone' and challenging herself is the only way to 'educate the people that we really want them to get it' holds echoes of Freire's dialogue. It is the responsibility of the oppressed to engage in dialogue directly with the oppressor, and this is the path to liberation. Only by moving into this less comfortable space and engaging people of privilege in authentic dialogue can Mireya move her district to a more open set of policies and practices for emergent bilingual learners.

Ensuring that she had allies, Mireya proceeded to position her fellow dual language coaches as mainstream professional development specialists – to deliberately sign them up for the district's specialized literacy trainings so they could offer presentations to *all* teachers about reading and writing. Then, she introduced what seemed to her district a revolutionary idea: that these now-trained dual language coaches could offer the literacy trainings in Spanish for bilingual teachers, with added components such as cultural relevance and assets orientations that were fundamental to bilingual instruction. The excitement in her voice and in her eyes was palpable as she described the unfolding of these events:

> And so, once those DL coaches, you know, kind of graduated [from their trainings], because we did a little celebration in February, I said ok, I told my partner, my coordinator, 'Ok, so now, the second part is, we need to add something in Spanish'. And she is like, 'Ok but I don't want you get too excited with all these things and then we can't handle things'. I said, 'no, I'm not going to do it. We already have these DL coaches who went through the whole course work, you know...I said, so now that they are more knowledgeable, they can spread their knowledge to everybody else, but in Spanish'. And she said, 'But how are we going to do it? We can't really'. I said, 'ok, let me tell you what my plan is (laughs)'.

Because she took these risks and carefully nurtured trust with her partner and supervisors, Mireya's 'plan', strategically put in place with the collaboration of the dual language coaches with whom she had developed strong professional relationships, moved her district toward authentic curriculum and professional development for their growing number of emergent bilingual students. She had indeed embraced the skills and dispositions of a powerful teacher leader.

Collaboration is a Core Element of Bilingual Teacher Leadership

There is no doubt that *all* teachers benefit from a collaborative orientation to their work. However, bilingual teachers *require* this collaborative orientation in order to be problem-posing, critical educators for social justice. Too often, bilingual educators find themselves in marginalizing spaces that diminish their professional agency and undermine their leadership identities. They *must* have allies, locate like-minded colleagues and pool/share ideas and resources, in order to continue to accomplish their work. Their work as teachers, as coaches or mentors to other professionals and as advocates for their students and families within oppressive systems literally becomes impossible without the dialogic relationships that are made possible with collaboration.

8 Conclusion: Bilingual Teacher Leaders are Advocates and Change Agents

...honestly, if I think about it, before Proyecto Maestría I wasn't really that passionate about social justice issues in the classroom, you know. I mean I was, you know, I mean, of course, you know, I am to a... but I think that the program, you know, bumped it up a thousand percent. (Lucia, Cohort 4, fourth bilingual math/science)

Deb: What's leadership to you?

George: Now I think it's the advocacy, I guess would be the word. You know, for me trying to make sense of things and trying to change them. See, trying to develop these theoretical perspectives on things and using that as knowledge that can inform how I place myself and try to make difference, I guess. (George, Cohort 5, first grade)

The experience of Proyecto teachers along the road to leadership, as the previous three chapters have attempted to illustrate, was an intermingling of growth along several connected dimensions.

The teachers developed critical consciousness through a deeper sense of connection to their own cultural and linguistic identities and increased respect for the value of their and their students' life experiences for learning. This came along with awareness of curricular tools, instructional materials and vocabulary – exposure to ideas such as 'culturally relevant literature', 'hegemony' and 'marginalization' that gave them the words to define their experience, both past and present, and to teach their students and engage their communities in these profoundly important conversations about self and world. They learned to read their own lives in order to help their students read 'the word and the world' (Freire, 2000).

Exposure to new curricular and instructional tools, and to new narratives for their students' school experiences, led many teachers directly toward a new and urgent reflexivity in their teaching and learning. Teachers embraced the new discourses and materials and the community in which they learned about them, and began to take a new kind of ownership of their work. Teaching became no longer just an act of 'following' but an act of 'leading'. For many teachers, teaching has so often required *following*... the districts rules and mandates, the curriculum, the instructions on their science kits, the directives of their principals, the lesson plans written by other members of their grade-level teams.... Even if they themselves were developing these directives – which was often the case with Proyecto teachers, since many of the teachers came to us with prior experiences as leaders in different capacities – many of the teachers spent years in their careers viewing teaching as an act of *following*. This changed for them as they absorbed radical new ideas in their graduate courses or other impactful professional development experiences. Teaching itself became a political act; teaching became leading others to change. This very local form of leadership, reflexive praxis, became integral to the professional identities of many of the teachers.

One of the central vehicles for embracing reflexive praxis was the cohort community. From the first day of class together, the teachers bonded; they realized they were not alone in desiring something more from their profession, not alone in feeling marginalized at times in their schools, in being Spanish/English bilinguals, in many cases in being Latinx in large mainstream institutions. They discovered others who shared a vision. Community, it is well documented, energizes people and helps them to sustain action, to organize for change. The cohort structure of Proyecto Maestría fed teachers' activism, and many teachers sought to maintain connections to professional communities after graduating. This activism became their leadership, and took form in different ways in their schools and communities.

Teachers felt a disconnect between the discourses and ideas they were discovering in their classes, and the realities they continued to experience in their schools. With the strength of confidence and pride in their own identities, the fortification of a like-minded community, the new knowledge of the tools and language of power and the skills to analyze and plan, teachers redefined their roles to be leaders and advocates. Each teacher began to take hold of the discourses of their schools – at least one small part of these – and lead instead of follow. Leadership took many forms; here are some of the directions the Proyecto teachers have gone:

- Engaging with their school parent-teacher association (PTA) or other parent groups – organizing in their communities (e.g. Raquel, Susana, Emilia).
- Putting their energies into creating new and exciting curriculum and finding and working with exciting new books and instructional delivery models; spreading these materials to other teachers via professional

conferences and networks (e.g. Lila, Aisha, Christine, Sofia, Emma, Lucia, Alondra, Gisela, Miguel, Natasha).
- Continuing connection to the university, by hosting student teachers (e.g. Raquel, Nicole) or collaborating with research projects (Alicia) or becoming university-based teacher educators (e.g. Leila, Patricia, Amanda) or doctoral students (e.g. Aisha, Lila, Ileana, George, Amanda).
- Moving into district curriculum development leadership positions (e.g. Lorena, Mireya, Julieta).
- Serving in leadership roles in local teacher's unions and professional organizations for bilingual educators (e.g. Susana, Emilia, Miguel, Sofia).
- Seeking administrative credentials and moving into official school leadership roles (e.g. Leti, Mariana, Alicia, Susana, Lupe, Lorena, Anabelle, Emma).

Defining Bilingual Teacher Leadership

How did the Proyecto teachers define teacher leadership as they neared the end of their graduate school experiences? The following are some reflections from teachers' online posts in response to the question posed at the end of the spring semester Teacher Leadership course: 'How do you define leadership now? (emphases mine)'

Leila (Cohort 1):

Our coursework has allowed us to **impact** our campuses by being superior mentors to our colleagues, impact our **teaching community** through webinars, and impact our **local community** through ¡Ahora Sí! How incredible is that. So looking at the big picture we are **making changes** already and it is amazing to me how it all happened in sequence. We learn with a **deeper understanding of ourselves and our profession** and we share the knowledge. This course has given me the **confidence** to move forward as a creditable [sic] teacher and colleague. ... having read and shared so much prior to taking this course, gave us all the confidence and understanding of where we stand as teacher leaders and mentors.

Raquel (Cohort 1):

I hope that by **supporting the teachers** in the implementation of their projects in the school, we will be **empowering** them as leaders in the classroom and school; at the same time, we will strengthen the bilingual team. I hope that by **empowering our families** in our school, we will also show the importance of empowering our students through their **culture and language in the classroom.** I hope this will result in the implementation of a strong bicultural bilingual program in our school.

Ileana (Cohort 4):

I have personally grown as a leader this year with the mentoring of Proyecto. I have always known that I was a leader, but felt I was not knowledgeable enough to luchar for ciertos temas como la instruccion de dual, la participacion de padres y como debemos enfocarnos en el aprendizaje de los estudiantes (y no en el STAAR). Tomar los cursos de Proyecto me ha dado la **confianza** que siempre ha estado ahi enterrado. Yo siempre he tenido la confianza pero vivia en el mundo 'de la maestra'. Pero en el momento que yo senti que era hora de ofrecer **mi voz**, me di cuenta que realmente **tenia el respeto de mi directora y de mis colegas**. Yo creo que es importante tener una colaboracion saludable y honesta. Aveces, la politica envuelve la humanidad en envueltos sin necesidad. Pero realmente, todos los maestros **estamos aqui para mejorar la educacion de todos los estudiantes**. *[I have personally grown as a leader this year with the mentoring of Proyecto. I have always known that I was a leader, but felt I was not knowledgeable enough to fight for certain themes like dual language instruction, parent participation and how we should focus on student learning (and not on the STAAR state test). Taking Proyecto courses has given me the confidence that has always been buried there. I have always had the confidence but I lived in the world 'of the teacher'. But the moment I felt that it was time to offer my voice, I noticed that I really did have the respect of my principal and my colleagues. I think it's important to have healthy and honest collaboration. Sometimes politics wraps humanity up in circles unnecessarily. But in reality, all teachers are here to improve the education of all students.]*

Consuelo (Cohort 4):

Mainly, I think it's **an attitude of collaboration and empowerment**; that teachers who see problems in the school or district have the **confidence, skills, and dedication** to make a plan to bring about improvements.

Patricia (Cohort 4):

Cuando tomé este trabajo de coach, mi intencion era el lograr este tipo de cambio, pero honestamente me sentia como un conductor sin mapa. Sabia a donde queria llegar pero no sabia que camino tomar. Esta clase me ha dado una nueva definicion de lo que es ser un entrenador. He visto **la asociación entre el poder y el liderazgo**. El poder no es exclusivo a un grupo elegido por la población dominante. Todos podemos lograr éxito, **todos podemos ser líderes ya sea en nuestro salon, en nuestra escuela o en nuestro distrito**. El poder no significa tener control sobre otros, ni el ser el dictador que toma las decisiones que afectan a todos los miembros de la comunidad. **El poder significa tener el conocimiento** necesario para poder implementar efectivamente las estrategias de ensenanza que lograrán el éxito de cada estudiante y cada maestro. Tambien aprendí que un líder no es la persona que lo sabe todo o que manda a los demás. El ser un líder es el poder **guiar a los demas a construir su propio conocimiento** basandose en las experiencias que cada persona experimenta en su vida profesional. *[When I took this position of coach, my intention was to achieve this type of change, but honestly I felt like a driver without a map. I knew where I wanted to go but I didn't know what path to take. This class has given me a new definition of what it is to be a trainer. I've seen the **association between power and leadership**. Power does not belong exclusively to a chosen group elected by the dominant population. All of us can achieve success, **all of us can be leaders whether in our classroom, in our school or in our district.** Power doesn't mean having control over others, nor being a dictator who makes the decisions that affect all members of the community. **Power means having the knowledge** necessary to be able to effectively implement the teaching strategies that will achieve success for every student and every teacher. I also learned that a leader is not a person who knows everything or who directs everyone else. Being a leader is the ability to **guide everyone else to construct their own knowledge** basing it in the experiences each person has in his/her professional life.]*

Maya (Cohort 5):

I see leadership as **taking a stand**, taking the time to be informed, voicing opinions and needs and **advocating** for the needs of the students and providing **tools for other teachers to grow** too.

Gisela (Cohort 5):

The way that I view my job, my profession, has evolved and grown. I used to have a very narrow view of what a teacher does (should do). My view involved little parent contact, and was mostly contained to what happened in my classroom and in my team planning. I don't think I ever thought of issues of social justice, even though they exist at my campus.
My role as a teacher is bigger, I now realize. A teacher can be a leader. A teacher leader goes beyond his/her classroom. A teacher leader can touch not only the lives of his/her students and their families, but the lives of others. A teacher leader **forms relationships with peers** that are beyond superficial, by creating mentor relationships with peers, learning from them, and helping them in their journey. A teacher leader **encourages his/her parents to become leaders,** and **advocates** for them, when they face adversity in their attempts to do so. A teacher leader is well informed about what is going on at his/her school. A teacher leader is a **learner**.

Natasha (Cohort 5):

To be a teacher leader is to be **active, to be informed, to care, to have willingness, to have a vision and to follow dreams**. I've learned that to be a leader you need to go against the convenience of staying in your classroom and wish for the best. Just like we want our students to have a voice and to take ownership in their learning, we as leaders need to **participate in** our school's, our district's, hey even in our state **decision making** concerning schools. For this we need to be informed. Proyecto Maestría has done a great job in educating us, we've learned about the history and theory of bilingual education. I feel that **I was blind and now I see**... I had lost the sensibility concerning the real needs of my **students and their families** and I had forgotten that ultimately their needs are my needs. What my job is and how I perform it is completely related to my students and my students don't come to my classroom alone, they bring their families, they bring their **culture,** they bring their **language**. This is something we all care about.

Julieta (Cohort 5):

My current definition of teacher leadership is teachers who are **student advocates** and at any level **share their knowledge wealth with other teachers** in good faith because they want to positively impact education for all students.

Alondra (Cohort 5):

I believe that there are people who are natural born leaders. They have this innate talent to influence others and make changes. On the other hand, the rest of us have the potential to become leaders; it is just a matter of **developing the awareness to transform** into one. John Quincy Adams once said, 'If your actions inspire others to dream more, learn more, do more and become more, you are a leader'. I find his words to be true, especially when you are a teacher. ... For many years, I have limited my role as a leader by only practicing my skills in my own classroom. To be honest, I was afraid to **step out of my comfort zone** and figured that by 'pretending' to agree with everything, my problems would go away. Through Proyecto Maestría I have learned thoroughly about the history behind bilingual education. Native Spanish speakers have been discriminated in the past; I was discriminated when I was growing up and my students still experience a level of blatant discrimination at school. Enough is enough. **If we do not stand up for our students, who will?**

I am learning how to **hold conversations with colleagues** in a way that actually leads to **positive change**. Before, I would remain silent, and allow them to make decisions that most of the time had nothing to do with my students. At the end of the day, I would go back to my classroom and make my own decisions about what my students needed. With this course, I feel more comfortable saying certain things that I would not before. ... At UT, I have been able to **collaborate** with other teachers in my courses to become better at creating Professional Developments that are helpful for other teachers. In fact, this was my first time ever presenting at NABE and at a Vertical Team District Staff Development. The first times were scary, but when I saw the impact I was making, I began to develop more **confidence** in myself. I also feel that I have grown significantly as a teacher. This year, I have tried different things I have learned in my courses that have improved the way I teach my students. As a result, I see that my students are more engaged in their learning. **Parents have also become more involved** in the classroom due to changes I have made to create better relationships with them. ... **Making changes at a bigger level** such as my campus is going to take a little bit more time, but I hope that I am able to deliver Professional Developments that educate others about bilingual education and the **importance of using the students' funds of knowledge**.

Common themes that cut across these definitions include:

- Continuous learning; seeing oneself as a learner and always open to new ideas and experiences.
- The importance of engaging in authentic dialogue with parents and connecting with students' cultural/linguistic funds of knowledge.
- The value and expertise that bilingual teachers bring to leadership, despite their being frequently undervalued or experiencing marginalization either as individuals or professionals.
- Defining empowerment, understanding one's role and purpose, as pushing back directly against discrimination and advocating vocally on behalf of bilingual children and families.
- Collaborating with other professionals, either as an ally, an outspoken peer or a mentor/coach supporting growth across the profession.

The teachers' definitions above merge with those offered in the literature; yet in every aspect, they articulate an additional layer of urgency and critical praxis.

Two divergent cases offer a comprehensive illustration of the interconnection of the various strands: reflexivity, cultural/linguistic identity, collaboration and community, and activism.

Two Cases

Emilia: An activist teacher leader going public

Emilia (Cohort 4, pre-K) had been an activist and teacher leader for many years prior to beginning Proyecto Maestría. She explained in an interview, when asked what influenced her to take on leadership activities, 'I think that I've always been an advocate of our children at different levels. I think seeing injustice really upsets me and it really makes me do something about it'. In January of her Proyecto year, Emilia responded online to the questions I posed, 'In what way are teachers powerful? How can teachers tap into their power? What makes you feel more empowered professionally?' with:

> Teachers are powerful when they work and advocate together. When they convey that their main purpose is the well-being of their students. When they have a unify [sic] message, constant communication and negotiation with their administration. When teachers feel motivated and believe in their power to advocate. Teachers can tap into their power if they organize and start making changes. I personally feel empower[ed] when I see the parents of my students speaking on behalf of their children. I feel empower[ed] when I am surrounded with teachers that are active participants of change and their main focus is the students.

Thus, Emilia had a clear vision of activism and had developed many of the tools to enact her vision. She pointed to particular experiences growing up that drove her passion for justice: her sudden departure from her native Mexico as a child with her sister and mother, her arrival to and transition into this country and the importance of a caring teacher:

> I moved to Austin 20 years ago and I only spoke Spanish and I started middle school, eighth grade, actually not knowing a word of English and learning the language and having a really great ESL teacher and she made the class fun and it was easy for me to transition to an all English class in ninth grade when I started high school and I graduated from high school and I always kept in touch with the teacher.

Her mother's dedication to education; her documentation status:

> I graduated in 1997 and I was undocumented and there was no way for me to attend college, so my mom has always been kind of always about education and really pushing my sister and I to become – to get a degree and to really do something out of our lives. So I decided to go back to Mexico and I went back to the university of Guanajato and I lived there for two years and I started my degree in pedagogy...

The support of others in her life:

> ...I was able to get a tourist visa and I came back to Austin with my family
> – my mom and my sister. And then my mom's boss was my sponsor to
> become an international student...

Emilia's activism began early. As an undergraduate education
student, Emilia worked with classmates to create a student organization,
still thriving today, that advocated for the rights of undocumented and
immigrant students. The first time I met her was when, during her first
year of teaching in 2005, we both spoke out at a meeting of the Texas State
Board of Education against an initiative they were considering to embrace
an English-only program for bilingual learners. When she was teaching in
a public pre-kindergarten center, she initiated a movement against budget
cuts, to keep the full-day pre-kindergarten program for bilingual children
funded by the state. In her interview, she offered the following example
briefly as one of the events that fueled her fire for activism:

> Then the state two years ago took money away from the Pre-K program
> so I was able to organize other teachers and the community, and other
> organizations and we were able to keep the full day pre-K program [in
> this district].

The experience of organizing the community to preserve full-day
pre-kindergarten seems to have been very impactful for Emilia. On my
invitation, she came to speak to my undergraduate class in November 2015
about a bilingual teacher's role to advocate for students. She described the
event to them as one experience, very early in her own teaching career, in
which she found she had to become an activist. She explained the issue to
my preservice bilingual teachers:

> Nosotros por mucho tiempo tuvimos – el estado pagaba el 100% del
> tiempo – tiempo completo para prekinder. Entonces un día ... los
> legisladores [del estado] dijeron, 'vamos a pasar un ley que solamente
> van a dar la mitád dinero para que las escuelas tengan mitád de tiempo
> de Pre-K'. ... [Yo me dije] 'Los niños que van más afectados van a ser
> English language learners y van a ser estudiantes inmigrantes y van a ser
> estudiantes que *se ven como yo* porque los papas no van a poder mandar
> a sus hijos por medio tiempo. Vamos a perder estudiantes número uno y
> nuestros estudiantes no van a tener prekinder...'. [We for a long time had
> – the state paid 100% of the time – full time prekindergarten. Then one
> day... the [state] legislators said 'we're going to pass a law that only gives
> half the money so that the school have half time Pre-K'. [I said to myself],
> 'The children who are going to be most affected are going to be English

language learners and they're going to be immigrant students and they're going to be students that look like me because the parents won't be able to send their children half time'.]

She explained how she worked with the union to organize against this change:

Entonces, eh empezamos a organizarnos y empezamos hablar con maestros eh maestras y maestros de prekinder y empezamos a organizarnos. O sea el número de gente que se puede organizar puede hacer un gran impacto. Entonces empezamos a tener un comité de prekinder, hablamos con todas las nueve personas de la mesa directiva, hablamos con la superintendente, empezamos hablar con profesores, organizaciones... Y el día que iba a decidir si iban a pagar por el prekinder por tiempo completo o si lo iba a cortar a medio tiempo, nos paramos todos en solidaridad y cada persona habló sobre por qué el prekinder era algo importante para nuestra comunidad y como invertir en un programa de early childhood y nos iba ayudar como comunidad. *[So, we began to organize ourselves and we began to talk to teachers of Prekinder and we began to organize ourselves. Which is to say, the number of people that can organize can make a big impact. So we began to have a prekinder committee, we spoke to all nine people on the School Board... and the day that they were going to decide if they were going to pay for full time prekinder or if they were going to cut to half time, we stood together in solidarity and each person spoke about why prekinder was something important for our community and how investing in early childhood programs would help us as a community.]*

She shared the outcome with tremendous pride in her voice:

Y al final de la junta, la superintendente y los de la mesa directiva dijeron no-no-no sí, vamos a tener el programa de prekinder por tiempo completo. Y ahora hasta la fecha eso fue hace como seis, siete años. Hasta la fecha el distrito pone ay, 12 millones – la otra mitád [que no pone el estado] para que tengamos un programa de tiempo completo. *[And at the end of the meeting, the superintendent and the board members said no, no, Yes, we are going to have the prekinder program full time. And now to this day this was like six, seven years ago. To this day the district puts ah 12 million – the other half (that the state doesn't put) so that we have a full-time program.]*

Emilia explained that this early success fueled her. Indeed, she seemed – still seems – to have an endless supply of the hope and energy required to stand up and be counted, to push back and hold fast, to change the world by organizing.

Emilia took a couple extra semesters to complete her master's degree, because in the spring of her program year, she was offered the opportunity to run for a leadership role in the local teacher's union. She decided to run, she won and she has embraced this leadership activist role ever since.

Meanwhile, Emilia was also an exceptional teacher. She was National Board Certified in Early Childhood Education. She took pride in the beautiful garden she and her very young students, together with parents to help, grew as a central focus of their science curriculum every year. She embraced – and presented to other teachers – new technologies in her classroom, demonstrating the range of uses her young emergent bilingual students had for iPads and computers as they developed their nascent literacy and numeracy skills in meaningful ways. She drew in the parents of her students as her closest allies in assuring quality education for her students. And she stayed in touch with her students. Even now, having been a union leader for almost five years, she occasionally posts photos to social media of former students she has run into at the store, or photos of herself with former students and their families at events such as graduations.

Emilia asserted in an interview that her experiences in Proyecto gave her the chance to reflect in a safe community about her leadership, which allowed her to say yes to the opportunity to lead the union:

> ...last spring, I was taking Dra. Palmer's leadership class and having a lot of conversations on what leadership is in the classroom and outside as an instructional coach, and having those conversations and really it was like a stepping stone.

She explained that the theory, the ideas, that she and her classmates grappled with supported her to become an even more impactful advocate:

> I could see by talking to teachers and seeing that sometimes we are *scared* of advocating or pushing for what is – what our rights are and how we can work in collaboration with others. I think those, I think that's something that really pushed me to the next level like, 'Ok as a teacher I can only do so much' and really having those conversations in the classroom and seeing different examples and reading *Pedagogy of the Oppressed* and how Paolo Freire (2000) talks about 'conscientizão' and all of these things, and the funds of knowledge and how all of these really helps our community and our children to have a successful learning outcome. And to me it was like, 'I can be that advocate', because I was undocumented – I have gone through the struggles, and I know what it feels, and I know that sometimes we need a voice whether as a teacher, as an undocumented immigrant.

Emilia's own background, her experiences firsthand of immigration and the challenges she faced as a young undocumented student in a US school added strength to her authoring herself as an advocate: 'I can be that advocate'. Her experiences in the cohort community taught her that risk-taking leads to growth and increased impact as a professional:

> Being quiet is not going to help anything. You have to be part of the process of advocating in different levels and I felt that that class really taught me ok this [teaching Pre-K] is my comfort zone, this is what I love, this is what I do but sometimes stepping out of that comfort zone is important.

Discomfort is an important part of growth; dissonance leads to learning and to change. Freire's dialogue requires tension, pushing past the comfortable and engaging opposites together. Similarly, Bakhtin's dialogic space is where words are in tension. As with Mireya, Emilia described moving outside her 'comfort zone', and like Mireya she asserted that it is 'important' to do so, if one's goal is indeed to make change – to liberate. Moments of discomfort are critical to authentic dialogue.

Emilia is an exceptional activist bilingual teacher, there is no doubt. Her experiences in Proyecto may have supported her decision to take on official leadership in the teacher's union, and participating in the master's program may have strengthened her skill set, but she was clearly a vocal and outgoing leader before beginning the program.

Emilia's definition of teacher leadership at the end of the spring semester put many of these elements together:

> 'Once social change begins, it cannot be reversed. You cannot uneducate the person who has learned to read. You cannot humiliate the person who feels pride. You cannot oppress the people who are not afraid anymore. We have seen the future, and the future is ours'. As I was reading this question [what is a teacher leader?], this quote from Cesar Chavez came to my mind. The last two semesters have been empowering in all the senses of the word. My definition of teacher leadership has become more defined. It has also empowered me to take a different role in education. I have decided to expand my role of grassroots organizer to be the voice of all teachers in AISD through the teacher's union. This decision was not easy because I love teaching and working with students. My role as a pre-K teacher has limited me to a certain exten[t] The attack on public education, emphasis on testing, charter schools and the implementation of the dual language program are just a few of the issues that I want to work on during my term with [the union]. A teacher leader is someone who leads and collaborates. A teacher leader advocates for her students, parents, colleagues and community. A teacher leader is strategic and courageous when advocating for her students. A teacher leader builds trust and inspires others. The research and theories

we have read and learned about have been useful when talking with other colleagues and administrators.

For Emilia, vocal activism was and always had been a central part of her identity as a Latina, a Mexican immigrant and a bilingual teacher. Mariana (Cohort 1), who had also been a teacher leader – a bilingual literacy coach – for several years prior to entering Proyecto, had a different path.

Mariana: Developing a voice and identity as a Latina bilingual teacher leader

> I dearly believe that in order to be a leader you have to believe in yourself and your capabilities. I remember my last California principal wanted me to be the team leader of 1st grade and I was [so] astonished that I had to hear it from someone else in order to believe it. Two years ago when I was offered the chance to be an Instructional Specialist, a position that had been held by white women since I started working at [my current school], it caught me by surprise. (Mariana, Cohort 1, online reflection)

Sometimes teachers willingly embrace new roles; sometimes they require the encouragement of a supervisor or colleague to take on new challenges. Emilia seemed born to leadership and activism, and embraced this identity from her earliest days as a teacher, driven by her experiences with marginalization as a Latina immigrant young woman. In Mariana's case, by contrast, a significant piece of her career-long reticence in taking on leadership responsibilities appears to have been related to grappling with oppression and subtle racism related to her identity as a Latina immigrant woman. The community of teacher leaders together with the rules that govern members' behaviors and identities within that community, seemed to Mariana for many years to be mainly white and mainstream, and thus she did not fit in. Graduate school gave Mariana an opportunity to critically examine these impressions, this aura of exclusion, and to embrace her developing identity and her own voice as a leader. Although, as she described above, supervisors encouraged Mariana to take on leadership roles long before she entered graduate school, and although she had done so with evident success, she articulated that she had taken on these roles with discomfort – like Emilia and Mireya, she found herself outside her comfort zone when taking on leadership. Her voice developed significantly in confidence and professional capacity as she read and explored materials for her graduate courses.

Before coming to her current school as a third-grade teacher several years prior to graduate school, Mariana spent four years as a teacher aide as she worked toward her teacher certification, and then taught in several schools in California. Like Emilia, she had immigrated to the United States in secondary school and experienced English as a second language (ESL) programs as she learned English.

Having completed her seventh year as a bilingual classroom teacher as she entered Proyecto Maestría, Mariana was an Instructional Specialist, which is an official teacher leadership position, at a large elementary school with over 800 students, 88% Latinx, with a nearly 30% mobility rate. The classrooms at Mariana's school were predominantly bilingual, and all teachers at the school except 'special areas' teachers (i.e. PE, art and music) were certified either bilingual or ESL teachers. Mariana had moved almost reluctantly into leadership positions since arriving at her current school. In the description of her school with which she opened her campus needs/strengths assessment and 'Vision Project', the final project for her fall semester class, Mariana wrote:

> Since I came into this campus in 2003 the teacher population has changed; the Hispanic teachers have increased and the White teachers have decreased. It is interesting to point out that having a Latina as a principal has made a difference in our school. It creates a different environment; she has made me feel more powerful. I firmly believe that without her, I would not be in the same position.

While she credited the principal for bringing her into these roles and instilling her with confidence, her principal – who served on Proyecto Maestría's advisory board and was a strong proponent of teacher leadership – spoke very highly of her as a coach, mentor and instructional leader. The discourses of teacher leadership may have felt a bit foreign to Mariana and she required some encouragement to embrace them, but she exhibited agency as she made that world her own, developing her own voice and leadership style.

In stark contrast with Emilia, Mariana was a quiet leader. Speaking out was not easy for her; she was more often an engaged and thoughtful listener. In her own words as she reflected upon herself as a leader in February of her graduate school year:

> I am the type of leader who likes to work in collaborate [sic] groups and guide the learning according to the needs. I am the type of leader who feels [it] is important for everyone to get along and listen to others. I am the type of leader who wants others to feel at ease, I was a new teacher once. I will never finish learning how to better support others and lead those new teachers into being leaders too. I am the type of leader who learns from making mistakes. My biggest barrier is making people do something my principal has asked me to tell them. I still feel like a teacher I guess. Dealing with adults is much harder than dealing with children. It's hard to make people happy.

One area in which Mariana felt she grew during graduate school was in confidence. In her March reflection on her experience designing and presenting a webinar to second-year teachers, and on learning to present in front of groups of adults in general, Mariana commented:

> I can now say with confidence that I am not afraid of talking in front of people. I have been so shy all of my life that now when I need to speak I feel ok about it. We need to do at least one presentation per class [in graduate school]; every one of them has provided me with the skills to do better next time.

As Mariana pointed out, Proyecto Maestría was intentionally designed to offer participants a safe space for developing skills for leadership, rehearsing leadership roles and ultimately embracing the twin identities as both knowledgeable professionals and bilingual adults.

Race and her own identity as a Latina emerge in Mariana's reflections about her university experiences. The University of Texas (UT) is a large research university with a predominantly white mainstream student body and faculty, and cohort members supported one another to enter and even at times to work to transform that world. Speaking on a panel with her cohort colleagues at the National Association of Bilingual Education (NABE) conference in February 2009, for example, Mariana commented on the impact her presence as a Latina appeared to be having on her university classes:

> I do reflect a different perspective to classes, like one of our professors… she keeps saying all through class like you know 'it's a different color that we have in classes' because most of the time it's just white teachers that are there.

Mariana's final spring semester online reflection on her hopes for her school in the coming year expressed a strong voice and a solid sense of herself as a leader and advocate for bilingual students; it offers insight into the kinds of work she envisioned herself carrying out as a leader. She drew on Spanish to make a direct appeal to voice ('que nos escuchen') and used all-caps to express urgency, or perhaps just plain loudness:

> I hope we can keep our teachers because they are extremely hard workers and if we start guiding them to become leaders, I can't wait to see what our school can do. It is time for the Bilingual teachers to take over y que nos escuchen [and for them to listen to us]. We have so much more to offer our Bilingual students. I hope this changes next year and our principal can really appreciate her Bilingual staff and what we have to say about OUR STUDENTS! I believe the only way we can accomplish this is by developing the staff's weaknesses into strengths. We need to EMPOWER all of the Bilingual teachers. I hope I can do this next year.

Mariana, who the reader will recall experienced mentoring a non-bilingual, white novice teacher for the first time during her Proyecto year, pointed out that even with a Latina bilingual principal, bilingual teachers' expertise at her school had been undervalued. Her voice got louder in all-caps as she asserted the expertise she and her bilingual colleagues had to offer: that they understood the bilingual students, who were the vast majority of the population at her school. Her emphasis was clear when she moved briefly into Spanish, addressing her bilingual colleagues – or perhaps addressing her English-only colleagues, but assertively doing so in Spanish, expressing that she felt bilingual teachers should feel confident to raise their voices so everyone would listen.

As she engaged in dialogue with classmates and texts and reflected on experiences, Mariana's dual identities as a bilingual/bicultural Latina and as a teacher leader moved from what seemed to be a place of tension toward a powerful fusion that she hoped would have the potential to create and sustain change on her school campus. No longer alone but now part of a community of bilingual leaders in education – primarily Latinx – she asserted that she had valuable contributions to make to all audiences, including white mainstream teachers and school leaders.

Although Mariana was developing a completely different style of leadership from Emilia, like Emilia she also expressed in her various reflections the importance of collaborating with other professionals (both for support and for sharing expertise), critical reflexive practice, tuning into her own and her students' (and colleagues') cultural/linguistic identities and a critical multicultural awareness to support bilingual students' school success. Like Emilia, Mariana articulated the ways in which these various elements gave her the courage to take risks, move into spaces that were not always comfortable and take strong advocacy stands.

Mariana served as an assistant principal for several years while also gaining her counseling certificate. Then, just a couple of years ago due to her husband's career, she and her family moved back to southern California, where she has returned temporarily to a teaching role as the Spanish-strand classroom teacher in a multilingual language immersion program. She tells me that although she is enjoying being back in the classroom, she will actively seek to return to leadership in the coming year as either a principal or a district bilingual/dual language director.

Conclusion

Personally, I see myself as an agent of change at this point, with the realization that my words have an impact on those within my surroundings. (Eustolia, Cohort 1, first-grade bilingual, final spring semester online reflection)

The Proyecto Maestría teachers came to graduate school with a sense of urgency and responsibility. Many of the teachers, in part because of the nature of the program that paid their tuition, pursued a graduate education not solely for themselves and their own career advancement but also for their students and their schools – for the families and communities they served. There is no doubt that the bilingual, immigrant communities where most bilingual teachers work, struggle within an oppressive system. With growing numbers of increasingly segregated Latinx bilingual students in many of our nation's schools and the increasing hostility of federal policies and rhetoric toward immigrants and Latinx, the urgency is real.

In fact, with growing numbers of emergent bilingual students nationally, study of program and instructional improvements that might support these students in any context is crucial. Teacher educators can take important lessons from the Proyecto Maestría teachers in terms of preparing *all* teachers to serve as leaders and advocates for emergent bilingual students and their families.

Bilingual teacher leaders play a unique role on their school campuses. Not only do they fulfill the expected teacher leadership roles such as offering support to novice teachers, helping administrators to plan and carry out professional development, etc., but they also provide a level of expertise about the education of bilingual children, and advocate for bilingual children and families. In addition, as adult bilinguals in a predominantly monolingual English-speaking society, they bring new voices to educational leadership with insight into the growing diversity in our schools.

Research on mainstream teacher leadership and professional development calls for the need to develop teachers' critical awareness of the structures of power in schooling. However, bilingual teachers – at least the teachers who worked with me in Proyecto – take this call much further. When bilingual teachers co-construct leadership identities, they build their skills for reflexive practice: i.e. for classroom-based action research for sociocultural transformation. They deepen their appreciation for the richness of the language and culture of bilingual/multicultural students and they form meaningful relationships with colleagues both for support and solidarity, and for professional teaching and learning. By these means, each teacher in this project developed their own unique voice, the confidence to speak up and the means to advocate for their students even in uncomfortable moments and spaces.

In order to support bilingual teacher leadership for equity and transformation, teacher preparation and teacher leadership programs should embrace these three core principles: develop praxis, engage cultural/linguistic identities and promote sustained professional communities and networks. These seem to be crucial building blocks as teachers co-construct identities as authentic leaders, advocates and change agents. Let me elaborate on these three core ideas (Figure 8.1):

• **Develop praxis.** *Center* critical perspectives and critical engagement with structural forces of inequity in schools and society. A program with critically oriented readings at the core will help teachers dive quickly and deeply into conversations that will push and deepen their own critical awareness. Critical readings must be in the beginning, the middle and the end of every conversation. The fields of cultural studies and educational anthropology continue to advance, with much to offer teachers of all backgrounds, in all contexts and with a wide range of personal/professional goals. Work that directly addresses the ongoing struggles for equity of Latinx and bilingual communities, work that encourages teachers to develop lessons and try out new pedagogical techniques in a reflective and connected context, work that embodies culturally relevant and sustaining pedagogies for classrooms and communities, can all contribute to developing reflexive, critically aware professional educators who have the theoretical tools to make empowering decisions and stand up for kids and families.

One aspect of engaging teachers in critical reflection is to support them to become action researchers, to engage Freire's praxis cycle in their professional life. Teachers must develop the tools to frame and answer their own questions of practice within their contexts; they must have a toolkit to be on-the-ground advocates for social justice in each moment and decision.

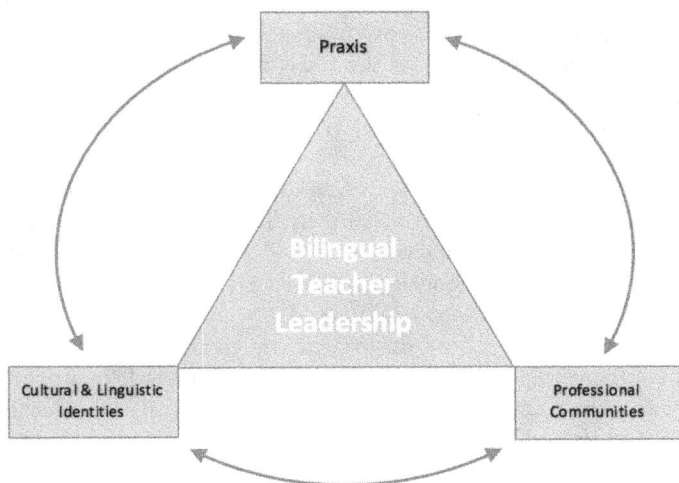

Figure 8.1 Bilingual Teacher Leadership for Social Change

- **Engage cultural/linguistic identities.** Engage teachers in projects and reflections that allow them to explore their own cultural/linguistic identities and those embedded and evolving in the families and communities they serve. This is supported not just by the reactions of the Proyecto teachers, but also the work of many others in the fields of teacher education and multicultural education (e.g. J. Nieto, 2006; S. Nieto, 2002; Villegas & Lucas, 2002). Teachers may not see the importance or relevance of interrogating their own cultural/linguistic identities... until they do so. As Myles Horton asserted, 'there is no such thing as neutrality. It's a code word for the existing system' (Horton *et al.*, 1990a: 102). A teacher who attempts to teach content without explicitly accounting for social context, even as a teacher of biology or physics, merely ratifies dominant sociocultural norms. Paolo Freire, in conversation with Horton, explained it this way:

  I cannot put history and social conditions in parenthesis and then teach biology exclusively... there is no such a thing named biology in itself... biology and all the disciplines are not isolated from the social life. (Horton *et al.*, 1990a: 108–109)

  It is essential that teachers acknowledge and center the histories and identities of the members of their classroom community – including themselves – to ensure the curriculum they are teaching is responsive to their students as learners and as individuals.

- **Promote sustained professional communities and networks.** Facilitate teachers to build sustained professional communities across schools and districts with shared mission and commitments. Explicitly expose teachers to the tools for engagement with national professional networks, particularly networks for bilingual teachers or critical reflexive activist teachers, such as NABE and its state and local affiliates, Teachers for Social Justice or the National Association of Multicultural Educators (NAME). The isolation of day-to-day teaching is counterproductive and draining and can lead quickly to burnout, especially for teachers of color and bilingual teachers. Allies help us maintain the energy and drive required to move systems to change. The Proyecto teachers drew energy from their cohort communities; all teachers deserve to be part of such communities. They also renewed their energies by contributing to larger professional networks through participation in conferences, publication and continued study. Teaching as a profession needs to embrace norms of collaboration that support such ongoing and energizing professional development.

This requires also an explicit emphasis on learning the tools for engaging colleagues in learning: how to create effective professional development sessions for adult learners, how to mentor/coach colleagues in respectful and effective ways, how to reach out proactively to parents and community partners to build networks of support for children in school. Graduate schools, or a leadership preparation program, are excellent spaces in which to explicitly learn these skills.

These three core principles will help teachers develop the tools to frame their work as activism or advocacy, and support teachers to develop the language and identity of change agents and leaders. Teachers need to be the leaders in our schools; they are the professionals in the midst of the most important work the school does: the dialogue with students that leads to learning. A critical pedagogy for bilingual teacher leadership – indeed, for all teacher leadership – necessarily supports professionalism, leadership and agency not just for teachers but for their students and the families in their school communities.

Epilogue

In the final stages of putting together this book, I checked in with the primary informants. I sent each of them an email and asked them to look over the passages in the book pertaining to their own lives and narratives. One response, from Lorena Pacheco (Cohort 2), took my breath away. Lorena's brief email aligned with my arguments and the many other narratives I have shared, but she took the argument a step further, linking the professional to the personal in a way I do not think I have done in the book. I choose to paste her words here, and to close the book with them:

Dra. Palmer,
I hope you had a wonderful Thanksgiving! I am just coming in from seeing my family and the ranchito *[little ranch]* that they live in and am finally catching up with e-mails :) Yes, I was able to review the information and it is correct…
Personally, my family is doing well. I am almost 2 years divorced now and I am in a good place. Although you may think that the classes and the experience of Proyecto may have only affected my professional life, they did not. The sense of self-worth, identity, and value for my culture, gender, language, heritage, and family that was a constant in the classes that we took helped shape us then, and still shape us now. I was able to recognize how strong I am as a Latina who is independent, secure in her identity, and grounded in her values as a person…all of this helped me through my divorce. I really know that I am a better and stronger person because of my experiences and learning in Proyecto.

Bueno...Espero el e-mail que dice 'ya esta publicado!' *[Well... I'm waiting for the email that says 'It's published!']*
Gracias, Dra. Palmer, por todo! *[thank you for everything]*
Bendiciones, *[blessings]*
Lorena

Appendix A Program of Work: Bilingual/Bicultural Education MA/MEd Degrees, 2009–2013

Plan A: MEd Coursework Only (36 hours)
Plan B: MEd + Report (33 hours)
Plan C: MA + Thesis (30 hours)

PREREQUISITES

- Admission to graduate school.
- 12 hours of upper-division education courses.
- Evidence of spoken and written proficiency in Spanish (see bilingual/bicultural education adviser for details).
- Student teaching (MEd only).

C&I DEPARTMENTAL REQUIREMENT

Plan A: 3 hours   **Plan B: 3 hours**   **Plan C: 6 hours**

_____ EDC 380R Educational Research and Design _____ (Plan C ONLY) One **additional** research methods course

SPECIALIZATION

(1) Major Area Bilingual Education

(a) Required coursework

Plan A: 18 hours   **Plan B: 15 hours**   **Plan C: 12 hours**
                             (any 5 of the following)   (any 3 of the following)

_____ EDC 390T Foundations of Bilingual & Dual Language Education

_____ EDC 385G Teacher Leadership for Bilingual/ESL

_____ EDC 382E Teaching Elementary School Subjects: Bilingual Education

_____ One course in teaching content-based English as a second language (e.g. EDC 382E [elementary] 382S [secondary])

_____ EDC 385G: Sociolinguistics **OR** Assessment and Evaluation in Language Education **OR** Second Language Acquisition

_____ EDC 385G: Language Policy in Education **OR** Biliteracy **OR** Biliteracy and New Literacy Studies

(b)   **Elective courses, the following or their equivalent** (to be chosen with adviser approval)

Plan A: 9 hours   **Plan B: 6 hours**   **Plan C: N/A**

_____ EDC 385G: Immigration Theory in Education

_____ EDC 385G: Classroom Discourse and Teacher Research

_____ EDC 385G: Multicultural Curriculum & Teaching

(2)   **Supporting coursework: 6 hours outside of C&I: Plans A, B, C**

_____ Course Dept. Number and Title _____

_____ Course Dept. Number and Title _____

Plan B ONLY (MEd + Report) 3 hours

_____ EDC 398R

Plan C ONLY (MA + Thesis) 6 hours

_____ EDC 698 A _____ EDC 698B

Appendix B Syllabus, EDC 385G Teacher Leadership for Bilingual/ESL: Mentoring, Coaching and Professional Development

Professor Deborah Palmer, Spring 2013

Course Description

This course will prepare experienced, practicing elementary bilingual educators for teacher leadership roles in their schools and districts. We will examine current definitions and expectations for teacher leadership in the educational leadership literature, analyzing the particular challenges posed to the bilingual teacher leader and the particular roles for teacher leaders in building and enhancing programs serving English language learners in schools. Students will develop skills and gain experience with coaching/mentoring novice teachers, classroom-based teacher inquiry/research, developing presentations for professional conferences and developing and presenting professional workshops in the context of their own school/district's needs.

Texts

Required

Fogarty, R. and Pete, B. (2006) *From Staff Room to Classroom: A Guide for Planning and Coaching Professional Development*. Thousand Oaks, CA: Corwin Press. ISBN 1-4129-26-4-1

Freeman, R. (2004) *Building on Community Bilingualism*. Philadelphia, PA: Caslon Publishing. ISBN 0-9727507-0-3

Katzenmeyer, M. and Moller, G. (2009) *Awakening the Sleeping Giant: Helping Teachers Develop as Leaders* (3rd edn). Thousand Oaks, CA: Corwin Press. ISBN 9781412960403

Lindsey, D., Martinez, R. and Lindsey, R. (2007) *Culturally Proficient Coaching*. Thousand Oaks, CA: Corwin Press. ISBN 978-1-4129-0972-3

Kegan, R. and Lahey, L. (2001) *How the Way We Talk Can Change the Way We Work*. San Francisco, CA: Jossey-Bass. ISBN 978-0787963781

Selected articles available as PDF on the course's Blackboard site.

Recommended

Allen, R. (2008) *TrainSmart: Effective Trainings Every Time* (2nd edn). Thousand Oaks, CA: Corwin Press. ISBN 978-1-4129-5578-2

Fogarty, R. and Pete, B. (2009) *From Staff Room to Classroom II: The One-Minute Professional Development Planner*. Thousand Oaks, CA: Corwin Press. ISBN 9781412974998

Lipton, L. and Wellman, B. (2003) *Mentoring Matters: A Practical Guide to Learning-Focused Relationships* (2nd edn). Sherman, CT: MiraVia. ISBN 0-9665022-2-1.

Requirements

Attend class, come prepared and be an active participant in all in-class discussions and activities. (10% of course grade)

Reading Reflections: Each week for at least *9 of the 12 weeks* with readings, upon completion of readings, please write up your reactions and post a reflection to the Blackboard discussion board. Reflections may be in English, Spanish or both. I will have some questions on the Blackboard discussion board to guide you, but you should not feel limited to them; feel free to expand in a different direction if your thoughts take you there. Do not summarize readings; rather offer your colleagues your reflections about the readings, connecting the ideas to your practice and personal development as an educator and teacher leader, to other readings (both in the class and outside) and to the larger field of education. Reflections should be at least a couple of meaty paragraphs in length, and incorporate all the readings in some way. You are also invited to incorporate discussion themes and reflections on your work in the class, readings from previous weeks or previous/other classes. The goal is to synthesize, react, connect, critique and/or reflect. A successful reflection will do at least some of the following:

- Refer to specific ideas, theories, stories or research described in the text.
- Pick out the most important concepts for your own work/research/ thinking/teaching.
- Include connections to your own experiences or to other things you've seen or read on the topic.
- Mention themes previously discussed in class.
- Relate different readings/authors to one another.
- Go into depth about one or two ideas that particularly strike you.

Please also read and respond to colleagues' postings. Strong participation will be rewarded in your grade.

Please note: There will be 12 opportunities to reflect with your colleagues; you are expected to *participate a minimum of 9* weeks; *first and last weeks are mandatory!* Beyond the 9-week minimum participation, additional reflections and responses and will count as extra credit. (10% of course grade)

Community Outreach Project: Column for ¡Ahora Sí!: Each class member will write one 400-word column *en español* for our 'Preguntale a la Maestra' weekly column in the local Spanish newspaper *¡Ahora Sí!.* We will brainstorm topics together, with the guidance of the editor, and each choose one. We will share drafts on 2/26 – please bring three paper copies to class. Second drafts are due electronically (as a word document) to your student editor 3/5 and final drafts to me by 3/19. (15% of course grade)

Teacher inquiry project: Classroom-based research

For students who took EDC 382E in fall 2012: Report of findings: Based on the research project proposal you developed in the fall semester, you will collect and analyze data and write up a brief report on your findings. Each individual's project will require a unique timeline, but your final report should be ready by the last week of class in order to share them in class.

For others: Proposal: You will develop a focused research question that emerges from your own classroom practice. You'll ground your question in a theoretical frame and develop a *proposal* for data collection and analysis that would begin to answer your question. There will not be time or support for actual data collection this semester.

More details will be provided. Approximately 5–10 pages, *due* 4/16. (15% of course grade)

Professional development project #1: Team conference presentation

Working in groups of three or four, you will choose a topic on which you have some expertise and that would be of interest to other professionals at a regional conference for bilingual/dual language educators. Drawing on what we are learning in class about adult learning and effective presentations, you write up an appropriate presentation proposal (due February 12) and then design your presentation (due March 5 or March 19). Though not required, you are *highly* encouraged to actually submit your presentation for consideration at the First Annual ¡Adelante! Conference, a new regional collaborative conference co-sponsored by Proyecto Maestría and AISD's BELL office. Conference will be Friday/Saturday March 21–22 at Thompson Conference Center on UT campus. In class, your group will have 40 minutes for your presentation on either 3/7 or 3/21. More details will be provided. (15% of course grade)

Professional development project #2: Campus workshop

If you are a teacher on a school campus: you will choose one specific topic of relevance to your campus' improvement of services to English language learner (ELL) students. Keeping in mind your own campus staff personalities and needs, you will design an appropriate professional development workshop. As part of the project, you will need to schedule at least one meeting with your principal/AP and/or other relevant colleagues at your school to check in. For class, you will prepare a PowerPoint that revisits your campus vision project from last semester and situates this workshop within the plan you had proposed, describes the topic/need you are addressing, the audience you are aiming to reach, the plan for the workshop as you have designed it, materials you've developed for it and any follow-up you think would go with it. Ideally, you will actually use this workshop on your campus (at some point!), so the aim is to make it as authentic and real (and detailed) as possible – to the point of creating materials and handouts as necessary for the workshop. More details will be provided.

If you are not a teacher on a school campus at this time: you may choose to work with another student to support their campus presentation, or to develop a workshop relevant to the context in which you work.

Presentations 4/23. (20% of course grade)

Mentoring project

Throughout the semester, you will work one-on-one with a colleague at your school, preferably a novice, first-year or second-year teacher. You should ask someone who might be interested in volunteering to go through this process with you. Using the cognitive coaching strategies we will be learning in class, you will develop a relationship with this colleague, working toward offering support in whatever areas they most need. You will document the experience with a final reflection paper due 5/7. More details will be provided. (20% of course grade)

Bibliography of PDF Articles/Chapters (Available on Canvas)

Anzaldúa, G. (1987) How to tame a wild tongue. In G. Anzaldúa (ed.) *Borderlands/la frontera: The New Mestiza* (pp. 53–64). San Francisco, CA: Aunt Lute Books.
Bernal, D.D. (2001) Learning and living pedagogies of the home: The mestiza consciousness of Chicana students. *International Journal of Qualitative Studies in Education* 14 (5), 623–639. https://doi.org/10.1080/09518390110059838
Diana Jr., T.J. (2011) Becoming a teacher leader through action research. *Kappa Delta Pi Record* 47 (4), 170–173. https://doi.org/10.1080/00228958.2011.10516586
Fitts, S., Winstead, L., Weisman, E.M., Flores, S.Y. and Valenciana, C. (2008) Coming to voice: Preparing bilingual-bicultural teachers for social justice. *Equity & Excellence in Education* 41 (3), 357–371. https://doi.org/10.1080/10665680802174916
Glickman, C., Gordon, S. and Ross-Gordon, J. (2005) *The Basic Guide to Supervision and Instructional Leadership* (Chapters 4, 6–10). Boston, MA: Pearson.
Gordon, S.P. (2004) Teacher leadership. In S.P. Gordon (ed.) *Professional Development for School Improvement: Empowering Learning Communities* (Chapter 5). Boston, MA: Pearson.
hooks, bell (2003) Talking race. In bell hooks (ed.) *Teaching Community: A Pedagogy of Hope* (pp. 25–41). New York: Routledge.

Krovetz, M.L. and Arriaza, G. (2006) The role of inquiry. In M.L. Krovetz and G. Arriaza (eds) *Collaborative Teacher Leadership: How Teachers can Foster Equitable Schools* (pp. 83–100). Thousand Oaks, CA: Sage.

Lieberman, A. and Miller, L. (2008) In A. Lieberman and J. McDonald (eds) *Teachers in Professional Communities: Improving Teaching and Learning* (Chapters 1–3). New York: Teachers College Press.

McCarty, T. (2005) The power within: Indigenous literacies and teacher empowerment. In T. McCarty (ed.) *Language, Literacy, and Power in Schooling* (pp. 47–66). Mahwah, NJ: Lawrence Erlbaum Associates.

References

Ackerman, R.H. and Mackenzie, S.V. (eds) (2007) *Uncovering Teacher Leadership: Essays and Voices From the Field*. Thousand Oaks, CA: Corwin Press.

Ada, A.F. and Zubizrreta, R. (2001) Parent narratives: The cultural bridge between Latino parents and their children. In M. de la Luz Reyes and J.J. Halcon (eds) *The Best for Our Children: Critical Perspectives on Literacy for Latino Students* (pp. 229–244). New York: Teachers College Press.

Adair, J.K., Tobin, J. and Arzubiaga, A.E. (2012) The dilemma of cultural responsiveness and professionalization. *Teachers College Record* 114 (12), 1–37. https://asu.pure.elsevier. com/en/publications/the-dilemma-of-cultural-responsiveness-and-professionalization-li

Alemán, A.M. (2006) Latino demographics, democratic individuality, and educational accountability: A pragmatist's view. *Educational Researcher* 35 (7), 25–31.

Altrichter, H., Feldman, A., Posch, P. and Somekh, B. (2013) *Teachers Investigate Their Work: An Introduction to Action Research across the Professions*. London: Routledge.

Anzaldúa, G. (1987) *Borderlands/la frontera: The new mestiza*. San Francisco, CA: Aunt Lute Books.

Ascenzi-Moreno, L., Hesson, S. and Menken, K. (2016) School leadership along the trajectory from monolingual to multilingual. *Language and Education* 30 (3), 197–218. https://doi.org/10.1080/09500782.2015.1093499

Athanases, S.Z. and Martin, K.J. (2006) Learning to advocate for educational equity in a teacher credential program. *Teaching and Teacher Education* 22 (6), 627–646. https://doi.org/10.1016/j.tate.2006.03.008

Baecher, L. (2012) Pathways to teacher leadership among English-as-a-second-language teachers: Professional development by and for emerging teacher leaders. *Professional Development in Education* 38 (2), 317–330.

Bakhtin, M.K. (1998) *The Dialogic Imagination*. Austin, TX: University of Texas Press.

Ball, A.F. and Freedman, S.W. (eds) (2004) *Bakhtinian Perspectives on Language, Literacy, and Learning*. Cambridge/New York: Cambridge University Press.

Barbian, E., Gonzales, G.C. and Mejía, P. (eds) (2017) *Rethinking Bilingual Education*. Milwaukee, WI: Rethinking Schools.

Barthes, R. (2007) The teacher leader. In R.H. Ackerman and S.V. Mackenzie (eds) *Uncovering Teacher Leadership: Essays and Voices from the Field* (pp. 9–36). Thousand Oaks, CA: Corwin Press.

Bartolomé, L. and Balderrama, M. (2001) The need for educators with political and ideological clarity: Providing our children with 'the best'. In M. Reyes, J. Halcón and C. Genishi (eds) *The Best for Our Children: Critical Perspectives on Literacy for Latino Students* (pp. 48–64). New York: Teachers College Press.

Bernhardt, P.E. (2012) Two teachers in dialogue: Understanding the commitment to teach. *The Qualitative Report* 17 (52), 1–15.

Blanton, C.K. (2005) *The Strange Career of Bilingual Education in Texas*. College Station, TX: Texas A&M University Press.

Bourdieu, P. (1991) *Language and Symbolic Power*. Cambridge, MA: Harvard University Press.

Bowles, S. and Gintis, H. (2002) Schooling in capitalist America revisited. *Sociology of Education* 75 (1), 1–18. https://doi.org/10.2307/3090251

Boylan, M. (2016) Deepening system leadership: Teachers leading from below. *Educational Management Administration & Leadership* 44 (1), 57–72. https://doi.org/10.1177/1741143213501314

Brooks, K., Adams, S.R. and Morita-Mullaney, T. (2010) Creating inclusive learning communities for ELL students: Transforming school principals' perspectives. *Theory Into Practice* 49 (2), 145–151. https://doi.org/10.1080/00405841003641501

Bunch, G.C. (2013) Pedagogical language knowledge: Preparing mainstream teachers for English learners in the new standards era. *Review of Research in Education* 37 (1), 298–341. https://doi.org/10.3102/0091732X12461772

Burke, C.J.F. and Adler, M. (2013) Personal consequences of compliance and resistance to mandated reforms for teachers in low-performing schools. *Journal of Urban Learning, Teaching, and Research* 9, 6–17.

Cahnmann, M. and Varghese, M.M. (2005) Critical advocacy and bilingual education in the United States. *Linguistics and Education* 16 (1), 59–73. https://doi.org/10.1016/j.linged.2005.10.002

Callahan, R. (2005) Tracking and high school English learners: Limiting opportunity to learn. *American Educational Research Journal* 42 (2), 305–328.

Campano, G. (2007) *Immigrant Students and Literacy: Reading, Writing, and Remembering*. New York: Teachers College Press.

Capitelli, S. (2015) Dilemmas in facilitating a teacher inquiry group focused on English language learners: Is there a place for an authoritative voice? *Studying Teacher Education* 11 (3), 246–254. http://www-tandfonline-com.colorado.idm.oclc.org/doi/abs/10.1080/17425964.2015.1073971

Carranza, T.M. (2010) Principals' ethical and social justice leadership in serving English language learners: English as a second language and bilingual teachers' perceptions. *ProQuest LLC*. See http://eric.ed.gov/?id=ED523372 accessed April 9, 2018

Casares, C. (2012, February 10) Five hundred years in the making: The Tejano Monument. *Texas Observer*. See https://www.texasobserver.org/five-hundred-years-in-the-making-the-tejano-monument/ (accessed 27 May 2017).

Cervantes-Soon, C., Dorner, L., Palmer, D., Heiman, D., Schwerdtfeger, R. and Choi, J. (2017) Combating inequalities in two-way language immersion programs: Toward critical consciousness in bilingual education spaces. *Review of Research in Education* 41 (1), 403–427.

Chestnut, C. (2015) 'But I'm a language teacher!' Dual immersion teacher identities in a complex policy context. *Mid-Western Educational Researcher* 27 (4), 339–362.

Cloud, N., Genesee, F. and Hamayan, E. (2000) *Dual Language Instruction: A Handbook for Enriched Education*. Boston, MA: Heinle & Heinle.

Cochran-Smith, M. and Lytle, S.L. (2015) *Inquiry as Stance: Practitioner Research for the Next Generation*. New York/London: Teachers College Press.

Collier, V.P. and Thomas, W.P. (2004) The astounding effectiveness of dual language education for all. *NABE Journal of Research and Practice* 2 (1), 1–20.

Craviotto, E., Heras, A.I. and Espindola, J. (1999) Cultures of the fourth-grade bilingual classroom. *Primary Voices K-6; Urbana* 7 (3), 25–36.

Crawford, J. (2004) *Educating English Learners: Language Diversity in the Classroom* (Vol. 5). Los Angeles, CA: Bilingual Education Services.

Crowther, F., Kaagan, S.S., Ferguson, F. and Hann, L. (2007) Teachers as leaders: Emergence of a new paradigm. In R.H. Ackerman and S.V. Mackenzie (eds) *Uncovering Teacher Leadership: Essays and Voices From the Field* (pp. 51–64). Thousand Oaks, CA: Sage Publications.

Dantas-Whitney, M. and Dugan Waldschmidt, E. (2009) Moving toward critical cultural consciousness in ESOL and bilingual teacher education. *Bilingual Research Journal* 32 (1), 60–76. https://doi.org/10.1080/15235880902965888

Dantley, M.E. and Tillman, L.C. (2006) Social justice and moral transformative leadership. In C. Marshall and M. Oliva (eds) *Leadership for Social Justice: Making Revolutions in Education* (pp. 16–30). Boston, MA: Pearson/Allyn and Bacon.

Darder, A., Baltodano, M. and Torres, R.D. (eds) (2003) *The Critical Pedagogy Reader.* New York: Routledge Falmer.

de Jong, E. (2011) *Foundations for Multilingualism in Education.* Philadelphia, PA: Caslon Publishing.

Delgado Bernal, D. (2000) Historical struggles for educational equity: Setting the context for Chicana/o schooling today. In C. Tejeda, C. Martinez and Z. Leonardo (eds) *Charting New Terrains of Chicana(o)/Latina(o) Education* (pp. 67–90). Creskill, NJ: Hampton Press.

Delgado Bernal, D. (2001) Learning and living pedagogies of the home: The mestiza consciousness of Chicana students. *International Journal of Qualitative Studies in Education* 14 (5), 623–639. https://doi.org/10.1080/09518390110059838

den Hartog King, C. and Peralta Nash, C. (2011) Bilingual teacher beliefs and practice: Do they line up? *Gist: Revista Colombiana De Educación Bilingüe,* 66–83.

Dewey, J. (1938) *Experience and Education.* New York: The Macmillan Company.

Dickinson, E. (1924) Hope is the thing with feathers. In M. Dickinson Bianchi (ed.) *The Complete Poems of Emily Dickinson.* Boston, MA: Little Brown and Company.

Division of Research and Analysis, Office of Academics (2016) *Enrollment in Texas Public Schools, 2015-16* (No. GE17 601 04). Austin, TX: Texas Education Agency.

Drago-Severson, E. (2007) Helping teachers learn: Principals as professional development leaders. *Teachers College Record* 109 (1), 70–125.

Dubetz, N.E. and de Jong, E.J. (2011) Teacher advocacy in bilingual programs. *Bilingual Research Journal* 34 (3), 248–262. https://doi.org/10.1080/15235882.2011.623603

Duncan-Andrade, J.M.R. and Morrell, E. (2008) *The Art of Critical Pedagogy: Possibilities for Moving from Theory to Practice in Urban Schools.* New York: Peter Lang.

Dunlap, K. and Hansen-Thomas, H. (2011) Taking the reins: Preservice teachers practicing leadership. *Educational Horizons* 90 (1), 21–24. https://doi.org/10.1177/0013175X1109000107

Echevarria, J., Vogt, M. and Short, D.J. (2008) *Making Content Comprehensible for English Learners: The SIOP Model* (3rd edn). Boston, MA: Pearson.

Ek, L.D., Sánchez, P. and Quijada Cerecer, P.D. (2013) Linguistic violence, insecurity, and work: Language ideologies of Latina/o bilingual teacher candidates in Texas. *International Multilingual Research Journal* 7 (3), 197–219. https://doi.org/10.1080/19313152.2013.768144

Ekiaka Nzai, V., Gómez, G.P., Reyna, R.C. and Kang-Fan Jen, J.K. (2012) Non-native English speaking elementary ELL teachers' culturally responsive leadership profile in an ESL context. *Colombian Applied Linguistics Journal* 14 (2), 88–108.

Ernst-Slavit, G. and Wenger, K.J. (2006) Teaching in the margins: The multifaceted work and struggles of bilingual paraeducators. *Anthropology & Education Quarterly* 37 (1), 62–82. https://doi.org/10.1525/aeq.2006.37.1.62

Escamilla, K., Hopewell, S., Butvilofsky, S., Sparrow, W., Soltero-González, L., Ruiz-Figueroa, O. and Escamilla, M. (2014) *Biliteracy from the Start: Literacy Squared in Action.* Philadelphia: Caslon Publishing.

Estrada, V.L. (1999) Living and teaching along the U.S./Mexico border: Midwestern student interns' cultural adaptation experiences in Texas schools. *Bilingual Research Journal; Philadelphia* 23 (2/3), 247–275.

Evans, A.E. (2013) Educational leaders as policy actors and equity advocates. In L.C. Tillman and J.J. Scheurich (eds) *Handbook of Research on Educational Leadership for Equity and Diversity* (pp. 459–475). New York: Routledge.

Faltis, C. and Valdés, G. (2016) Preparing teachers for teaching in and advocating for linguistically diverse classrooms: A vade mecum for teacher educators. In D.H. Gitomer and C.A. Bell (eds) *Handbook of Research on Teaching* (5th edn, pp. 529–592). Washingon, DC: American Educational Research Association.

Feger, M.-V. (2006) 'I want to read': How culturally relevant texts increase student engagement in reading. *Multicultural Education* 13 (3), 18–19.

Fillmore, L.W. and Snow, C.E. (2000) What teachers need to know about language. See http://eric.ed.gov/?id=ED444379 accessed April 9, 2018

Fitts, S. and Weisman, E.M. (2010) Exploring questions of social justice in bilingual/bicultural teacher education: Towards a parity of participation. *Urban Review: Issues and Ideas in Public Education* 42 (5), 373–393.

Fitzsimmons-Doolan, S., Palmer, D.K. and Henderson, K. (2015) Educator language ideologies and a top-down dual language program. *International Journal of Bilingual Education and Bilingualism* 20 (6), 704–721. https://doi.org/10.1080/13670050.2015.1071776

Flores, N. (2016) A tale of two visions: Hegemonic Whiteness and bilingual education. *Educational Policy* 30 (1), 13–38. https://doi.org/10.1177/0895904815616482

Forster, E.M. (1997) Teacher leadership: Professional right and responsibility. *Action in Teacher Education* 19 (3), 82–94. https://doi.org/10.1080/01626620.1997.10462881

Foucault, M. (1995) *Discipline and Punish: The Birth of the Prison* (2nd Vintage Books edn). New York: Vintage Books.

Fránquiz, M.E., Martínez-Roldán, C. and Mercado, C.I. (2011) Teaching Latina/o children's literature in multicultural contexts: Theoretical and pedagogical possibilities. In S. Wolf, K. Coats, P.A. Enciso and C. Jenkins (eds) *Handbook of Research on Children's and Young Adult Literature* (pp. 108–120). New York: Routledge.

Fránquiz, M., Avila, A. and Lewis, B. (2013) Engaging bilingual students in sustained literature study in Central Texas. *Journal of Latino/Latin American Studies* 5 (3), 142–155. https://doi.org/10.18085/llas.5.3.e13g5462g7341x05

Freeman, R. (2004) *Building on Community Bilingualism*. Philadelphia, PA: Caslon Publishing.

Freire, J.A. and Valdez, V.E. (2017) Dual language teachers' stated barriers to implementation of culturally relevant pedagogy. *Bilingual Research Journal* 40 (1), 55–69. https://doi.org/10.1080/15235882.2016.1272504

Freire, P. (2000) *Pedagogy of the Oppressed: 30th Anniversary Edition*. New York: Continuum Publishing.

Freire, P. and Freire, A.M.A. (1994) *Pedagogy of Hope: Reliving Pedagogy of the Oppressed*. New York: Continuum.

Galloway, M.K. and Ishimaru, A.M. (2015) Radical recentering equity in educational leadership standards. *Educational Administration Quarterly* 51 (3), 372–408. https://doi.org/10.1177/0013161X15590658

Garcia, L.-G. (2012) Making cultura count inside and out of the classroom: Public art & critical pedagogy in South Central Los Angeles. *Journal of Curriculum and Pedagogy* 9 (2), 104–114. https://doi.org/10.1080/15505170.2012.743446

García, O. (2010) *Educating Emergent Bilinguals: Policies, Programs, and Practices for English Language Learners*. New York: Teachers College Press.

García, O. and Wei, L. (2014) *Translanguaging: Language, Bilingualism and Education*. Basingstoke: Palgrave Macmillan.

Gay, G. (2010) *Culturally Responsive Teaching: Theory, Research, and Practice*. New York: Teachers College Press.

Giroux, H. (2003) Critical theory and educational practice. In A. Darder, M. Baltodano and R.D. Torres (eds) *The Critical Pedagogy Reader* (pp. 27–56). New York: Routledge Falmer.

Glaser, B.G. (1965) The constant comparative method of qualitative analysis. *Social Problems* 12 (4), 436–445. https://doi.org/10.2307/798843

Glickman, C., Gordon, S. and Ross-Gordon, J. (2005) *The Basic Guide to Supervision and Instructional Leadership.* Boston, MA: Pearson.

Gomez, L., Freeman, D. and Freeman, Y. (2005) Dual language education: A promising 50-50 model. *Bilingual Research Journal* 29 (1), 145–164.

Gomez, L. and Gomez, R. (1999) Dual Language Training Institute. See http://dlti.us/ accessed April 9, 2018

Gonzalez, N., Moll, L.C., Tenery, M.F., Rivera, A., Rendon, P., Gonzales, R. and Amanti, C. (1995) Funds of knowledge for teaching in Latino households. *Urban Education* 29 (4), 443–470. https://doi.org/10.1177/0042085995029004005

González, N., Moll, L.C. and Amanti, C. (eds) (2005) *Funds of Knowledge: Theorizing Practice in Households, Communities, and Classrooms.* Mahwah, NJ: L. Erlbaum Associates.

Gort, M. (2014) Transforming literacy learning and teaching through translanguaging and other typical practices associated with 'doing being bilingual'. *International Multilingual Research Journal* 9 (1), 1–6. https://doi.org/10.1080/19313152.2014. 988030

Greene, M. (1995) *Releasing the Imagination: Essays on Education, the Arts, and Social Change.* San Francisco, CA: Jossey-Bass Publishers.

Greenleaf, C. and Katz, M.-L. (2004) Ever newer ways to mean: Authoring pedagogical change in secondary subject-area classrooms. In A.F. Ball and S.W. Freedman (eds) *Bakhtinian Perspectives on Language, Literacy, and Learning* (pp. 172–202). Cambridge: Cambridge University Press.

Grinberg, J. and Saavedra, E.R. (2000) The constitution of bilingual/ESL education as a disciplinary practice: Genealogical explorations. *Review of Educational Research* 70 (4), 419–441.

Guajardo, M.A. (2009) Collective leadership: Practice, theory, and praxis. *Journal of Leadership Studies* 3 (2), 70–73. https://doi.org/10.1002/jls.20113

Guajardo, M.A. and Garcia Jr., S. (2016) Educational leadership for community development. *National Forum of Applied Educational Research Journal* 29 (1), 62–72.

Guerrero, M.D. and Guerrero, M.C. (2017) Competing discourses of academic Spanish in the Texas-Mexico borderlands. *Bilingual Research Journal* 40 (1), 5–19. https://doi.org /10.1080/15235882.2016.1273150

Hafner, M.M. (2006) Teaching strategies for developing leaders for social justice. In C. Marshall and M. Oliva (eds) *Leadership for Social Justice: Making Revolutions in Education* (pp. 167–193). Boston, MA: Pearson/Allyn and Bacon.

Henderson, K. and Palmer, D.K. (2015) Teacher and student language practices and ideologies in a third grade two-way dual language program implementation. *International Multilingual Research Journal* 9 (2), 75–92. https://doi.org/10.1080/ 19313152.2015.1016827

Hilty, E.B. (ed.) (2011) *Teacher Leadership: The 'New' Foundations of Teacher Education: A Reader.* New York: P. Lang.

Hoffman, J.V. (1992) Critical reading/thinking across the curriculum: Using I-charts to support learning. *Language Arts* 69, 121–127.

Hoffman, P., Dahlman, A. and Zierdt, G. (2009) Professional learning communities in partnership: A 3-year journey of action and advocacy to bridge the achievement gap. *School-University Partnerships* 3 (1), 28–42.

Holland, D., Lachicotte, W., Skinner, D. and Cain, C. (1998) *Identity and Agency in Cultural Worlds*. Cambridge, MA: Harvard University Press.

Holmes, M.A. and Herrera, S.G. (2009) Enhancing advocacy skills of teacher candidates. *Teaching Education* 20 (2), 203–213. https://doi.org/10.1080/10476210802538271

hooks, bell (2003) *Teaching Community: A Pedagogy of Hope*. New York: Routledge.

hooks, bell (2015) *Feminist Theory: From Margin to Center*. New York: Routledge.

Hornberger, N.H. (2003) *Continua of Biliteracy: An Ecological Framework for Educational Policy, Research, and Practice in Multilingual Settings*. Clevedon: Multilingual Matters.

Hornberger, N. and Johnson, D. (2007) Slicing the onion ethnographically: Layers and spaces in multilingual language education policy and practice. *TESOL Quarterly* 41 (3), 509–533.

Horton, M., Bell, B., Gaventa, J. and Peters, J.M. (1990a) *We Make the Road by Walking: Conversations on Education and Social Change*. Philadelphia, PA: Temple University Press.

Horton, M., Kohl, H. and Kohl, J. (1990b) *The Long Haul: An Autobiography*. New York: Doubleday.

Huerta, M.E.S. and Riojas-Cortez, M. (2011) Santo remedio: Latino parents & students foster literacy through a culturally relevant folk medicine event. *Part of a Special Issue: Linguistically Diverse Students and Their Families* 18 (2), 39–43.

Illich, I. (1971) *Deschooling Society* (1st edn). New York: Harper & Row.

Illich, I. (1992) *In the Mirror of the Past: Lectures and Addresses, 1978–1990*. New York: M. Boyars.

Jacobs, J., Beck, B. and Crowell, L. (2014) Teacher leaders as equity-centered change agents: Exploring the conditions that influence navigating change to promote educational equity. *Professional Development in Education* 40 (4), 576–596.

Jesse, D., Davis, A. and Pokorny, N. (2004) High-achieving middle schools for Latino students in poverty. *Journal of Education for Students Placed at Risk (JESPAR)* 9 (1), 23–45. https://doi.org/10.1207/S15327671ESPR0901_2

Jiménez, R.T. (1997) The strategic reading abilities and potential of five low-literacy Latina/o readers in middle school. *Reading Research Quarterly* 32 (3), 224–243. https://doi.org/10.1598/RRQ.32.3.1

Johnson, J. and Hynes, M.C. (1997) Teaching/learning/leading: Synonyms for change. *Action in Teacher Education* 19 (3), 107–119.

Johnson, J.F. and Willis, C. (2013) Culturally responsive teaching and high-performing schools that serve diverse populations. In L.C. Tillman and J.J. Scheurich (eds) *Handbook of Research on Educational Leadership for Equity and Diversity* (pp. 435–458). New York: Routledge.

Katzenmeyer, M. and Moller, G. (2009) *Awakening the Sleeping Giant: Helping Teachers Develop as Leaders* (Vol. 3). Thousand Oaks, CA: Corwin Press.

Katzenmeyer, M. and Moller, G. (2011) Understanding teacher leadership. In B. Hilty (ed.) *Teacher Leadership: The 'New' Foundations of Teacher Education: A Reader* (pp. 3–21). New York: Peter Lang Publishing.

Khalifa, M.A., Gooden, M.A. and Davis, J.E. (2016) Culturally responsive school leadership A synthesis of the literature. *Review of Educational Research*, 86, 12, 1272–1311. https://doi.org/10.3102/0034654316630383

Khalil, D. and Brown, E. (2015) Enacting a social justice leadership framework: The 3 C's of urban teacher quality. *Journal of Urban Learning, Teaching, and Research* 11, 77–90.

Kloss, H. (1998) *The American Bilingual Tradition*. Washington, DC/McHenry, IL: Center for Applied Linguistics/Delta Systems.

Kohl, H. (1994) *'I Won't Learn From You' and Other Thoughts on Creative Maladjustment*. New York: The New Press.

Kohl, H. (2003) *Stupidity and Tears: Teaching and Learning in Troubled Times*. New York: New Press.

Kohli, R. and Solórzano, D.G. (2012) Teachers, please learn our names!: Racial microaggressions and the K-12 classroom. *Race Ethnicity and Education* 15 (4), 441–462. https://doi.org/10.1080/13613324.2012.674026

Krovetz, M.L. and Arriaza, G. (2006) *Collaborative Teacher Leadership: How Teachers can Foster Equitable Schools*. Thousand Oaks, CA: Sage.

Labbo, L.D. and Field, S.L. (1999) Journey boxes: Telling the story of place, time, and culture with photographs, literature, and artifacts. *The Social Studies* 90 (4), 177–182. https://doi.org/10.1080/00377999909602411

Ladson-Billings, G. (1995a) But that's just good teaching! The case for culturally relevant pedagogy. *Theory Into Practice* 34 (3), 159–165. https://doi.org/10.1080/00405849509543675

Ladson-Billings, G. (1995b) Toward a theory of culturally relevant pedagogy. *American Educational Research Journal* 32 (3), 465–491. https://doi.org/10.3102/00028312032003465

Ladson-Billings, G. (2009) *The Dreamkeepers: Successful Teachers of African American Children* (2nd edn). San Francisco, CA: Jossey Bass.

Lambert, W.E. (1975) Culture and language as factors in learning and education. In A. Wolfgang (ed.) *Education of Immigrant Students: Issues and Answers* (pp. 55–83). Toronto: Ontario Institute for Studies in Education.

Lara, G. and Leija, M. (2014) Discussing gender roles and equality by reading Max: The Stubborn Little Wolf. *Social Studies and the Young Learner* 27 (2), 22–25.

Lemov, D. (2010) *Teach Like a Champion: 49 Techniques that Put Students on the Path to College* (1st edn). San Francisco, CA: Jossey-Bass.

Lerma, R., Linick, M., Warren-Grice, A. and Parker, L. (2013) The politics of education: Its development and what is needed for the future for advocacy leadership in post-racial America. In L.C. Tillman and J.J. Scheurich (eds) *Handbook of Research on Educational Leadership for Equity and Diversity* (pp. 22–42). New York: Routledge.

Levine, L.N. and McCloskey, M.L. (2012) *Teaching English Language and Content in Mainstream Classes: One Class, Many Paths* (2nd edn). Boston, MA: Pearson.

Lewis, C., Enciso, P. and Moje, E.B. (eds) (2009) *Reframing Sociocultural Research on Literacy: Identity, Agency, and Power*. New York: Routledge.

Lieberman, A. and Miller, L. (2008) *Teachers in Professional Communities: Improving Teaching and Learning*. New York: Teachers College Press.

Lindholm-Leary, K. (2001) *Dual Language Education*. Clevedon: Multilingual Matters.

Lindsey, D., Martinez, R. and Lindsey, R. (2007) *Culturally Proficient Coaching: Supporting Educators to Create Equitable Schools*. Thousand Oaks, CA: Corwin Press.

Lipton, L. and Wellman, B. (2003) *Mentoring Matters: A Practical Guide to Learning-Focused Relationships* (Vol. 2). Sherman, CT: MiraVia.

Lohfink, G. and Loya, J. (2010) The nature of Mexican American third graders' engagement with culturally relevant picture books. *Bilingual Research Journal* 33 (3), 346–363. https://doi.org/10.1080/15235882.2010.529346

López, N. (2008) Antiracist pedagogy and empowerment in a bilingual classroom in the U.S., circa 2006. *Theory Into Practice* 47 (1), 43–50. https://doi.org/10.1080/00405840701764755

Lucas, T. and Villegas, A.M. (2013) Preparing linguistically responsive teachers: Laying the foundation in preservice teacher education. *Theory Into Practice* 52 (2), 98–109. https://doi.org/10.1080/00405841.2013.770327

Lucero, A. (2010) Dora's program: A constructively marginalized paraeducator and her developmental biliteracy program. *Anthropology & Education Quarterly* 41 (2), 126–143.

Luz Reyes, M. de la and Halcon, J.J. (eds) (2001) *The Best for Our Children: Critical Perspectives on Literacy for Latino Students*. New York: Teachers College Press.

Macedo, D. (2000) Introduction. In P. Freire (ed.) *Pedagogy of the Oppressed, 30th Anniversary Edition* (pp. 11–27). New York: Continuum.

Mangin, M. and Stoelinga, S.R. (2008) *Effective Teacher Leadership: Using Research to Inform and Reform*. New York: Teachers College Press.

Marshall, C. and Oliva, M. (eds) (2006) *Leadership for Social Justice: Making Revolutions in Education*. Boston, MA: Pearson/Allyn and Bacon.

Martínez, R.A., Hikida, M. and Durán, L. (2015) Unpacking ideologies of linguistic purism: How dual language teachers make sense of everyday translanguaging. *International Multilingual Research Journal* 9 (1), 26–42. https://doi.org/10.1080/19313152.2014.977712

Martínez-Álvarez, P. and Bannan, B. (2014) An exploration of hybrid spaces for place-based geomorphology with Latino bilingual children. *Journal of Geoscience Education* 62 (1), 104–117.

McCarty, T. (2005) *Language, Literacy, and Power in Schooling*. Mahwah, NJ: Lawrence Erlbaum Associates.

McCollum, P. (1999) Learning to value English: Cultural capital in a two-way bilingual program. *Bilingual Research Journal* 23 (2 & 3), 113–133.

Menard-Warwick, J. (2014) *English Language Teachers on the Discursive Faultlines: Identities, Ideologies and Pedagogies*. Bristol: Multilingual Matters.

Menken, K. and García, O. (2010) *Negotiating Language Policies in Schools: Educators as Policymakers*. New York: Routledge.

Menken, K. and Solorza, C. (2015) Principals as linchpins in bilingual education: The need for prepared school leaders. *International Journal of Bilingual Education and Bilingualism* 18 (6), 676–697. https://doi.org/10.1080/13670050.2014.937390

Mertler, C.A. (2016) *Action Research: Improving Schools and Empowering Educators*. Thousand Oaks, CA: Sage Publications.

Moll, L., Amanti, C., Neff, D. and Gonzalez, N. (1992) Funds of knowledge for teaching: Using a qualitative approach to connect homes and classrooms. *Theory Into Practice* 31 (2), 132–141.

Montaño, T. and Burnstein, J. (2006) Maestras, mujeres y mas: Creating teacher networks for resistance and voice. *Journal of Latinos and Education* 5 (3), 169–188.

Moraes, M. (1996) *Bilingual Education: A Dialogue with the Bakhtin Circle*. Albany, NY: State University of New York Press.

Murakami, E., Valle, F. and Mendéz-Morse, S. (2013) Latino/a learners and academic success: ¡Sí se puede! In L.C. Tillman and J.J. Scheurich (eds) *Handbook of Research on Educational Leadership for Equity and Diversity* (pp. 134–199). New York: Routledge.

Nieto, J. (2006) The cultural plunge: Cultural immersion as a means of promoting self-awareness and cultural sensitivity among student teachers. *Teacher Education Quarterly* 33 (1), 75–84.

Nieto, S. (2002) *Language, Culture, and Teaching: Critical Perspectives for a New Century*. Mahwah, NJ: Lawrence Erlbaum Associates.

Nieto, S. (2003) Challenging current notions of 'highly qualified teachers' through work in a teachers' inquiry group. *Journal of Teacher Education* 54 (5), 386–398. https://doi.org/10.1177/0022487103257394

Nieto, S. (2013) *Finding Joy in Teaching Students of Diverse Backgrounds: Culturally Responsive and Socially Just Practices in U.S. Classrooms*. Portsmouth, NH: Heinemann.

Noddings, N. (1984) *Caring: A Feminine Approach to Ethics and Moral Education*. Berkeley, CA: University of California Press.

Noguera, N.P. (2003) *City Schools and the American Dream: Reclaiming the Promise of Public Education*. New York: Teachers College Press.

O'Hair, M.J. and Reitzug, U.C. (1997) Teacher leadership: In what ways? For what purpose? *Action in Teacher Education* 19 (3), 65–76. https://doi.org/10.1080/01626620.1997.10462879

Olsen, L. (1997) *Made in America*. New York: New Press.

Orfield, G. and Lee, C. (2005) *Why Segregation Matters: Poverty and Educational Inequity*. Cambridge, MA: Harvard Civil Rights Projects. See internal-pdf://Why_Segreg_Matters-2108525824/Why_Segreg_Matters.pdf

Ovando, M.N. and Casey, P. (2010) Instructional leadership to enhance alternatively certified novice bilingual teachers' capacity. *Scholar-Practitioner Quarterly* 4 (2), 144–168.

Ovando, C., Combs, M.C. and Collier, V. (2006) *Bilingual & ESL Classrooms: Teaching in Multicultural Contexts, 4th Edition* (Vol. 4). Boston, MA: McGraw-Hill.

Palkki, J. (2015) 'If it fits into their culture, then they will have a connection': Experiences of two Latina students in a select high school choir. *Research and Issues in Music Education* 12 (1). See https://eric.ed.gov/?id=EJ1100149

Palmer, D.K. (2009) Middle-class English speakers in a two-way immersion bilingual classroom: 'Everybody should be listening to Jonathan right now...'. *TESOL Quarterly* 43 (2), 177–202.

Palmer, D.K. (2011) The discourse of transition: Teachers' language ideologies within transitional bilingual education programs. *International Multilingual Research Journal* 5 (2), 103–122.

Palmer, D.K. and Ortiz, A.A. (2007–2013) *Proyecto Maestría: A Collaborative for Teacher Leadership in Bilingual/ESL Education (National Professional Development Grant, U.S. Department of Education, T195N070272)*. Austin, TX: University of Texas at Austin.

Palmer, D.K. and Snodgrass-Rangel, V. (2011) High stakes accountability and policy implementation: Teacher decision making in bilingual classrooms in Texas. *Education Policy* 25 (4), 614–647.

Palmer, D.K. and Martínez, R.A. (2013) Teacher agency in bilingual spaces: A fresh look at preparing teachers to educate Latina/o bilingual children. *Review of Research in Education* 37 (1), 269–297. https://doi.org/10.3102/0091732X12463556

Palmer, D.K., Chavez, G. and Cancino-Johnson, M. (2006) Supporting change in our schools and classrooms: Two teachers' journeys towards additive bilingual education. *TABE Journal* 9 (1), 66–81.

Palmer, D.K., Martínez, R.A., Mateus, S.G. and Henderson, K. (2014a) Reframing the debate on language separation: Toward a vision for translanguaging pedagogies in the dual language classroom. *The Modern Language Journal* 98 (3), 757–772. https://doi.org/10.1111/modl.12121

Palmer, D.K., Snodgrass Rangel, V., Gonzales, R.M. and Morales, V. (2014b) Activist teacher leadership: A case study of a programa CRIAR bilingual teacher cohort. *Journal of School Leadership* 24 (5), 949–978.

Palmer, D.K., Henderson, K., Wall, D., Zúñiga, C.E. and Berthelsen, S. (2015a) Team teaching among mixed messages: Implementing two-way dual language bilingual education at third grade in Texas. *Language Policy* 1–21. https://doi.org/10.1007/s10993-015-9361-3

Palmer, D.K., Henderson, K. and Zuñiga, C.E. (2015b) A dual language revolution in the United States? On the bumpy road from compensatory to enrichment bilingual education in Texas. In O. Garcia and W.E. Wright (eds) *The Handbook of Bilingual and Multilingual Education* (1st edn, pp. 449–460). Hoboken, NJ: John Wiley & Sons.

Paris, D. (2012) Culturally sustaining pedagogy: A needed change in stance, terminology, and practice. *Educational Researcher* 41 (3), 93–97. https://doi.org/10.3102/0013189X12441244

Paris, D. (2015) The right to culturally sustaining language education for the new American mainstream: An introduction. *International Multilingual Research Journal* 9 (4), 221–226. https://doi.org/10.1080/19313152.2015.1092849

Phelps, R., Fisher, K. and Ellis, A. (2007) Effective literature searching. In R. Phelps, K. Fisher and A. Ellis (eds) *Organizing and Managing Your Research* (pp. 128–149). London: Sage Publications Ltd. https://doi.org/10.4135/9781849209540

Pratt, M.L. (1999) Arts of the contact zone. In D. Bartholomae and A. Petrosky (eds) *Ways of Reading* (pp. 581–600). Bedford: St. Martin's.

Prieto, L. and Villenas, S.A. (2012) Pedagogies from Nepantla: Testimonio, Chicana/Latina feminisms and teacher education classrooms. *Equity & Excellence in Education* 45 (3), 411–429. https://doi.org/10.1080/10665684.2012.698197

Puzio, K., Keyes, C.S., Cole, M.W. and Jiménez, R.T. (2013) Language differentiation: Collaborative translation to support bilingual reading. *Bilingual Research Journal* 36 (3), 329–349. http://www-tandfonline-com.colorado.idm.oclc.org/doi/abs/10.1080/15235882.2013.845118

Reyes and Halcón (2001) The best for our children: Critical perspectives on literacy for Latino students. New York: Teachers College Press.

Rodríguez, C., Martinez, M.A. and Valle, F. (2016) Latino educational leadership across the pipeline for Latino communities and Latina/o leaders. *Journal of Hispanic Higher Education* 15 (2), 136–153. https://doi.org/10.1177/1538192715612914

Rolstad, K., Mahoney, K. and Glass, G.V. (2005) The big picture: A meta-analysis of program effectiveness research on English language learners. *Educational Policy* 19 (4), 572–594.

Rosado, L., Amaro-Jiménez, C. and Kieffer, I. (2015) Stories to our children: A program aimed at developing authentic and culturally relevant literature for Latina/o children. *School Community Journal* 25 (1), 73–93.

Ruiz, R. (1984) Orientations in language planning. *National Association for Bilingual Education Journal* 8 (2), 15–34.

Salinas, C. and Lozano, A. (2017) Mapping and recontextualizing the evolution of the term Latinx: An environmental scanning in higher education. *Journal of Latinos and Education* 1–14. https://doi.org/10.1080/15348431.2017.1390464

Salinas, C., Rodríguez, N.N. and Lewis, B.A. (2015) The Tejano history curriculum project: Creating a space for authoring Tejanas/os into the social studies curriculum. *Bilingual Research Journal* 38 (2), 172–189. https://doi.org/10.1080/15235882.2015.1066275

San Miguel, G. and Donato, R. (2010) Latino education in twentieth-century America: A brief history. In E.G. Murillo Jr., S.A. Villenas, R. Trinidad Galván, J. Sánchez Muñoz, C. Martínez and M. Machado-Casas (eds) *Handbook of Latinos in Education* (pp. 27–62). New York: Routledge.

Santamaría, L.J. (2014) Critical change for the greater good: Multicultural perceptions in educational leadership toward social justice and equity. *Educational Administration Quarterly* 50 (3), 347–391. https://doi.org/10.1177/0013161X13505287

Sayer, P. (2013) Translanguaging, TexMex, and bilingual pedagogy: Emergent bilinguals learning through the vernacular. *TESOL Quarterly* 47 (1), 63–88. https://doi.org/10.1002/tesq.53

Scanlan, M. and López, F.A. (2013) Leadership promoting equity and excellence for bilingual students. In L.C. Tillman and J.J. Scheurich (eds) *Handbook of Research on Educational Leadership for Equity and Diversity* (pp. 380–404). New York: Routledge.

Schmid, C. (2000) The politics of English only in the United States: Historical, social, and legal aspects. In R.D. Gonzalez and I. Melis (eds) *Language Ideologies: Critical Perspectives on the Official English Movement* (Vol. 1; pp. 64–86). Mahwah, NJ: Lawrence Erlbaum Associates.

Schroeder-Arce, R. (2014) Toward culturally responsive artistry: Implications for institutions, artists, educators and audiences. *International Journal of Education & the Arts* 15 (19/20), 1–24.

Sherrill, J.A. (1999) Preparing teachers for leadership roles in the 21st Century. *Theory Into Practice* 38 (1), 56–61.

Sherrill, J.A. (2011) Preparing teachers for leadership roles in the 21st century. In E.B. Hilty (ed.) *Teacher Leadership: The New Foundations of Teacher Education* (pp. 221–228). New York: Peter Lang.

Shields, C.M. (2004) Dialogic leadership for social justice: Overcoming pathologies of silence. *Educational Administration Quarterly* 40 (1), 109–132. https://doi.org/10.1177/0013161X03258963

Shields, C.M. (2010) Transformative leadership: Working for equity in diverse contexts. *Educational Administration Quarterly* 46 (4), 558–589. https://doi.org/10.1177/0013161X10375609

Simon, R. and Campano, G. (2013) Activist literacies: Teacher research as resistance to the 'normal curve'. *Journal of Language and Literacy Education* 9 (1), 21–39. http://jolle.coe.uga.edu/wp-content/uploads/2013/05/Teacher-Research.pdf

Slavin, R. and Cheung, A. (2005) A synthesis of research of reading instruction for English language learners. *Review of Educational Research* 75 (2), 247–284.

Souto-Manning, M. (2010) Teaching English learners: Building on cultural and linguistic strengths. *English Education; Urbana* 42 (3), 248–262.

Strauss, A. and Corbin, J.M. (1997) *Grounded Theory in Practice*. Thousand Oaks, CA: Sage.

Téllez, K. and Varghese, M. (2013) Teachers as intellectuals and advocates: Professional development for bilingual education teachers. *Theory Into Practice* 52 (2), 128–135. https://doi.org/10.1080/00405841.2013.770330

Texas Education Code (1995) See http://ritter.tea.state.tx.us/rules/tac/chapter089/ch089bb.html (accessed April 9, 2018).

Tillman, L.C. and Scheurich, J.J. (2013) *Handbook of Research on Educational Leadership for Equity and Diversity*. New York: Routledge.

Tonatiuh, D. (2013) *Pancho Rabbit and the Coyote: A Migrant's Tale*. New York: Abrams.

Umansky, I.M. and Reardon, S.F. (2014) Reclassification patterns among Latino English learner students in bilingual, dual immersion, and English immersion xlassrooms. *American Educational Research Journal* 51 (5), 879–912. https://doi.org/10.3102/0002831214545110

Urrieta, L. (2009) *Working from Within: Chicana and Chicano Activist Educators in Whitestream Schools*. Tucson, AZ: University of Arizona Press.

US Census Bureau (2015) Age by language spoken at home by ability to speak English for the population 5 years and over. See http://factfinder.census.gov/faces/tableservices/jsf/pages/productview.xhtml?src=bkmk

Valdés, G. (2004) Between support and marginalisation: The development of academic language in linguistic minority children. *International Journal of Bilingual Education and Bilingualism* 7 (2&3), 102–132.

Valdés, G. (2011) *Latino Children Learning English: Steps in the Journey*. New York: Teachers College Press.

Valdiviezo, L. (2009) Bilingual intercultural education in indigenous schools: An ethnography of teacher interpretations of government policy. *International Journal of Bilingual Education and Bilingualism* 12 (1), 61–79. https://doi.org/10.1080/13670050802149515

Valenzuela, A. (1999) *Subtractive Schooling: US-Mexican Youth and the Politics of Caring*. Albany, NY: SUNY Press.

Valenzuela, A. (2005) *Leaving Children Behind: How 'Texas-Style' Accountability Fails Latino Youth*. Albany, NY: SUNY Press.

Valenzuela, A. (ed.) (2016) *Growing Critically Conscious Teachers: A Social Justice Curriculum for Educators of Latino/a Youth*. New York: Teachers College Press, Columbia University.

Valenzuela, A., Zamora, E. and Rubio, B. (2015) Academia Cuauhtli and the Eagle: Danza Mexica and the epistemology of the circle | voices in urban education. *Voices in Urban Education* 41, 46–56. http://vue.annenberginstitute.org/issues/41/academia-cuauhtli-and-eagle-danza-mexica-and-epistemology-circle

Varghese, M.M. and Stritikus, T. (2005) 'Nadie me dijó (nobody told me)': Language policy negotiation and implications for teacher education. *Journal of Teacher Education* 56 (1), 73–87.

Villegas, A.M. and Lucas, T. (2002) Preparing culturally responsive teachers: Rethinking the curriculum. *Journal of Teacher Education* 53 (1), 20–32.

Villegas, A.M. and Lucas, T. (2007) The culturally responsive teacher. *Educational Leadership* 64 (6), 28–33.

Villenas, S. (2001) Latina mothers and small-town racisms: Creating narratives of dignity and moral education in North Carolina. *Anthropology and Education Quarterly* 32 (1), 3–28.

Vitanova, G. (2010) *Authoring the Dialogic Self: Gender, Agency and Language Practices*. Amsterdam: John Benjamins.

Wall, D.J. (2016) Power and caring embodied through bilingual preservice teachers' choice of participant structures. Unpublished doctoral dissertation, University of Texas.

Weaver, R. (2003) *Meeting the Challenges of Recruitment and Retention: A Guidebook on Promising Strategies to Recruit and Retain Qualified and Diverse Teachers*. Washington, DC: National Education Association.

Wiemelt, J. and Welton, A. (2015) Challenging the dominant narrative: Critical bilingual leadership (liderazgo) for emergent bilingual Latin@ students. *International Journal of Multicultural Education* 17 (1), 82–101.

Wiese, A.-M. and Garcia, E.E. (1998) The Bilingual Education Act: Language minority students and equal educational opportunity. *Bilingual Research Journal* 22 (1), 1–18.

Wilson, D.M. (2011) Dual language programs on the rise. *Harvard Education Letter* 27 (2), 1–2. See http://hepg.org/hel-home/issues/27_2/helarticle/dual-language-programs-on-the-rise (accessed 7 December 2017).

Wong, J.W., Athanases, S.Z. and Banes, L.C. (2017) Developing as an agentive bilingual teacher: Self-reflexive and student-learning inquiry as teacher education resources. *International Journal of Bilingual Education and Bilingualism* 1–17. https://doi.org/10.1080/13670050.2017.1345850

Wortham, S. and Contreras, M. (2002) Struggling toward culturally relevant pedagogy in the Latino diaspora. *Journal of Latinos and Education* 1 (2), 133–144. https://doi.org/10.1207/S1532771XJLE0102_5

York-Barr, J. and Duke, K. (2004) What do we know about teacher leadership? Findings from two decades of scholarship. *Review of Educational Research* 74 (3), 255–316.

Yosso, T. (2005) Whose culture has capital? A critical race theory discussion of community cultural wealth. *Race, Ethnicity and Education* 8 (1), 69–91.

Yosso, T., Smith, W., Ceja, M. and Solórzano, D. (2009) Critical race theory, racial microaggressions, and campus racial climate for Latina/o undergraduates. *Harvard Educational Review* 79 (4), 659–691. https://doi.org/10.17763/haer.79.4.m6867014157m7071

Zeichner, K. (2006) Reflections of a university-based teacher educator on the future of college- and university-based teacher education. *Journal of Teacher Education* 57 (3), 326–340. https://doi.org/10.1177/0022487105285893

Zeichner, K. (2016) Independent teacher education programs: Apocryphal claims, illusory evidence. *National Education Policy Center*. See http://nepc.colorado.edu/publication/teacher-education (accessed April 9, 2018).

Zimpher, N. (1988) A design for the professional development of teacher leaders. *Journal of Teacher Education* 39 (1), 53–60.

Index

For Product Safety Concerns and Information please contact our EU Authorised
Representative:

Easy Access System Europe

Mustamäe tee 50

10621 Tallinn

Estonia

gpsr.requests@easproject.com